History in Depth

Collections of documents come in all shapes and sizes. Many attempt to cover a very broad period; in consequence they rely heavily on illustrative material which is thought to be typical. In practice, this means a patchwork of often isolated snippets, with material torn out of context. Single documents or even fragments of documents have to bear the whole weight of a period, a problem, a theme. Students derive from such collections a mistaken impression of the nature of history, of the character of historical research, and very often, a false impression of the subject of study.

History in Depth is based on the belief that historical perception demands immediacy and depth. Working to the principle that true breadth of history can be achieved only by examining a concrete problem in depth, each volume in the series is devoted to either a particular event or crisis of considerable significance, such as the Peasants' Revolt of 1381; or to a trend or movement running through a coherent period of time, such as West African Nationalism from the middle of the nineteenth century; or to a particular area of experience, such as Elizabethan Puritanism.

No artificial uniformity is imposed on the format of the volumes; each is shaped by the dictates of its subject. But there are certain basic elements common to all. The core of each book is a major collection of original material, translated into English where necessary, with editorial decisions on modernised punctuation and spelling governed by the nature of the subject. Each editor provides an introduction geared to the particular demands of his volume; each volume carries a full working bibliography, interpretative notes and an index.

This is a new approach to the teaching of history which has been evolved in response to a demand from practising teachers. The general editor has selected the subjects and the volume editors with care, so that each book stands in its own right and has something of the quality of a monograph.

History in Depth

GENERAL EDITOR: G. A. Williams

Henry S. Wilson: Origins of West African Nationalism
R. B. Dobson: The Peasants' Revolt of 1381
J. R. Pole: The Revolution in America, 1754–1788
D. S. Chambers: Patrons and Artists in the Italian Renaissance
H. C. Porter: Puritanism in Tudor England
Dorothy Thompson: The Early Chartists
W. N. Hargreaves-Mawdsley:
Spain under the Bourbons, 1700–1833
Edward Royle: The Infidel Tradition from Paine to Bradlaugh
Roger Mettam: Government and Society in Louis XIV's France
Jane Rendall: The Origins of the Scottish Enlightenment

THE ORIGINS
OF THE SCOTTISH
ENLIGHTENMENT

Jane Rendall

First published 1978 by
THE MACMILLAN PRESS LTD
London and Basingstoke
Associated companies in Delhi
Dublin Hong Kong Johannesburg Lagos
Melbourne New York Singapore Tokyo

Printed in Great Britain by
Unwin Brothers Ltd.
The Gresham Press
Old Woking
Surrey

British Library Cataloguing in Publication Data

Rendall, Jane
   The origins of Scottish enlightenment.–
   (History in depth).
   1. Teacher centres – Great Britain
   2. Scotland – Intellectual life
   3. Scotland – History – 18th Century
   I. Title   II. Series
   941.107   DA812

   ISBN 0-333-24688-8

Contents

Acknowledgements

I am indebted to the following for permission to use manuscript or copyright material:

To Sir John Clerk of Penicuik for the MS letter from Colin Maclaurin on pp. 64–5, on deposit in the Scottish Record Office; to Edinburgh District Council for the extracts from Edinburgh Town Council minutes on pp. 48–50, 52–3 and 54–5; to Edinburgh University Library for the MSS on pp. 51–2 and 57; to Mr J. T. T. Fletcher of Saltoun for the MSS letters to Lord Milton on pp. 58–9, on deposit in the National Library of Scotland; to the Court of the University of Glasgow for the MSS on pp. 59–62, from the Glasgow University Archives; to Glasgow University Library for the MSS material on pp. 55–6 and 141–3; to the Historical Society of Pennsylvania for the extracts from George Logan's MSS diary on pp. 226–9; to the Trustees of the National Library of Scotland for the extracts from the MSS Select Society Minutes on pp. 224–6; to the Council of the Scottish Text Society for the extract from *The Works of Allan Ramsay*, Vol. V, Fourth series, no. 7 (Edinburgh and London, 1972) on pp. 62–3.

I should like to thank Professor Gwyn Williams for his help in initiating this volume, Professor Norman Hampson for reading the typescript and for his most helpful comments, and Adam Middleton for his constant encouragement.

JANE RENDALL
April, 1978

Introduction:
The Origins of the
Scottish Enlightenment

During the eighteenth century, and particularly from 1740 on, Scottish writers won international recognition for the range of their learning, for the originality and penetration of their writings on philosophy, history, law and science, and for their centres of enlightened civilisation in Edinburgh and Glasgow. The achievement was a considerable one, especially in view of the problems of poverty, disunity and disorder which Scotland had faced at the beginning of the century. It was an achievement which was not rivalled in England, where there were no similar centres of intellectual activity, where the universities failed to respond to the challenge of new ways of thinking. David Hume and Adam Smith were not isolated figures, chance sparks of genius; they were surrounded by men of lesser but still substantial quality, by Francis Hutcheson, Adam Ferguson, Lord Kames, Thomas Reid, William Robertson, and John Millar. (See the Biographical Notes, for brief summaries of the careers of these men, and others indicated in the text.) The interest of Hume and Smith in the study of all aspects of man and society was shared by these men. These writers were united, too, by a common commitment to teaching and education, and to the creation of a social community of scholars, in which constant contact and friendship coexisted with often fierce critical discussion and debate. It was a congenial world which fostered the achievements of Hume and Smith; and only by an examination of this world as a whole, by looking at its intellectual and social roots, its institutions, its ideas, is it possible to illuminate the Enlightenment in eighteenth century Scotland. There is a danger, of course, of distorting and drastically oversimplifying the work of individuals by brief and inadequate treatment; but the risk does not outweigh the need to assess the nature of thinking about man and

society in eighteenth century Scotland. The view of the Enlightenment taken here is in many ways narrow and incomplete; I have
concentrated on some of the most distinctive intellectual features of
such writing. A fuller study would look at the world of science, at
chemistry, medicine, geology, at the arts, especially the work of the
Adam brothers, and at the whole range of eighteenth century
Scottish literature. What I have done in this collection of documents
and extracts is to look at the culture which created the 'modern
Athenian', or in another version, the 'Scotch feelosofer' so easily
caricatured by the early nineteenth century. This introduction will
sketch briefly the ways in which the changing social and political
background of Scotland contributed to the growth of learning, and
the changing nature of the intellectual climate of the early part of
the century.

The social and political life of Scotland from 1700 to 1730 or so
might seem an unlikely backcloth for such developments. The
major factor conditioning Scotland's political life in this period was
her relationship with England; and by 1700 it was clear that this
relationship had to be reassessed. After the revolution of 1689 the
Scottish Parliament was no longer the largely formal institution of
the seventeenth century, but an active and independent assembly,
anxious to promote Scottish interests, as it had done in sponsoring
the Company of Scotland and its scheme to found a new colony at
Darien, in Panama, in 1696, against the wishes of the English
government. The failure of this scheme, and the poverty of the
Scottish economy, especially its lack of access to English markets,
steadily drove the Assembly towards some closer form of union with
England. The English government, on the other hand, could see no
answer, within the existing system, to the rivalries of powerful
Scottish magnates; to govern smoothly, as English ministers saw it,
what was needed was the establishment of a single 'interest' in
Scotland, supporting the Crown, providing orderly government
through the judicious exercise of patronage. The question of the
union was also related to the dynastic problem, to the need to secure
the Hanoverian succession to both kingdoms after the death of
Queen Anne; this offered the assembly a useful bargaining weapon,
one of the few they had. The debates within the Scottish assembly
did revive claims for Scottish independence, made by members of
the 'country party', Lord Belhaven (1656–1708) and Andrew
Fletcher of Saltoun (1653–1716). Pragmatic considerations, both
economic and political, suggested, however, that Scotland had little

alternative but to acquiesce in the English proposals[1].

The Union of 1707 was not a popular measure; but its terms dictated the conditions of Scottish political life throughout the following century. The Scottish agencies of government were reduced almost to nothing; the Scottish Privy Council was abolished as well as the Scottish Parliament. New administrative departments were set up, following English models, including Scottish Boards of Revenue in 1707 and a Scottish Exchequer in 1708. Politically the Union succeeded in achieving over the next twenty years the aims of its English architects, in reducing the disruption of government by the greater Scottish magnates, and in assimilating Scottish representation at Westminster into the English political structure. Scottish peers were given 16 seats in the House of Lords, and 45 seats were allowed in the House of Commons. The elections of 16 representative peers were usually managed by the British government; the electoral system in Scotland rested on an even narrower representative base than that of eighteenth century England. Scottish representatives were seen at Westminster as safe government voters and court followers. The organisation of the Scottish 'interest' was undertaken, by the time of Walpole, by two leading Scottish noblemen, the second Duke of Argyll (1678 – 1743), and his brother, the Earl of Islay, later third Duke of Argyll (1682 – 1761); for most of the first half of the century these men provided the channel through which Scotland was governed, generally with the assistance of a man of business drawn from the Scottish legal profession, first by Duncan Forbes of Culloden (1685 – 1747), and later by Andrew Fletcher of Milton, later Lord Milton, (1692 – 1766). The energies of the great magnates were absorbed into the Westminster system; but the minor nobility and the gentry, the traditional local rulers, were less able to turn their interests from Edinburgh to Westminster, and were left with few political opportunities.

Especially relevant to a discussion of the Scottish Enlightenment are those Scottish institutions which survived the Act of Union: the Church of Scotland, the legal system, and the educational system. In 1690 the episcopal structure imposed on the Church of Scotland after the Restoration was abolished, and Presbyterianism confirmed as the official doctrine of the Church of Scotland. The Church had an elaborate system of government, an institutional hierarchy in which both laymen and ministers played a part. The parish was governed by the local kirk session, including the minister and lay elders; a group of kirk sessions made up the presbytery, a group of presbyteries the regional synod. The General Assembly was the supreme authority within the Church, meeting once a year in Edinburgh, with 364 members, of whom 202 were clergy and the rest laymen[2]. This structure, combined with strict Calvinist doctrine, made possible rigid ecclesiastical discipline, and wide ranging supervision of the country's religious and social life by the Church. In 1696 a young student, Thomas Aikenhead, was tried and executed for blasphemy, for allegedly denying the divinity of Christ; and in many aspects of social life the clergy made clear their intention of preserving the old and traditional Calvinist values. Such a climate could hardly be sympathetic to the emergence of new ideas or to wide ranging speculation. But there were signs by the beginning of the century that it would not be possible for the Church of Scotland to carry out its self-imposed role. First, the Toleration Act of 1712 permitted episcopalians to meet for worship, and to use the English prayer-book; the established Church now had to tolerate rivals. The implication of this was that Presbyterian discipline could bind only those who were prepared to accept it; though that was certainly not always the case in practice, church discipline was slowly loosening its hold.

Secondly, the laity were coming to play an increased part in the government of the Church. Under the Restoration the right of lay patrons to appoint the local minister had been affirmed; after 1690, however, the freedom of the individual congregation to elect or 'call' its own minister was asserted. The Patronage Act of 1712 found for the rights of lay patrons, reversing the situation once more. The General Assembly protested against the provisions of this Act, but their protests, and resistance throughout the country, were not sufficient to prevent the appointment of ministers by lay patrons. Some congregations defied the Act; and it was controversy over patronage, not theology, which brought about the most important secessions within the Church of Scotland, of Ebenezer Erskine (1680–1754) and his followers, later to form the Associate Presbytery, in 1733, and of Thomas Gillespie (1708–74), later leader of the Presbytery of Relief, in 1752. Lay patrons were more inclined to appoint ministers whose backgrounds were more similar to their own than to their congregations; and the strictest Calvinists and evangelicals, upholding the rights of the congregation, were more likely to join the various seceded bodies than to remain within the official Church. However, the association between the landed classes and the Church, and the scope for lay involvement in Church government at all levels, meant that the General Assembly became an important arena for discussion and debate, for both clergy and laity.

The Scottish legal system was also left more or less intact by the Act of Union. The supreme civil court of Scotland, the Court of Session, together with the Court of Justiciary, dealing with criminal law, and that of the Admiralty, remained in operation in Edinburgh; the first two were open only to members of the Scottish bar. The lawyers, including advocates (barristers) and writers to the signet (roughly the equivalent of solicitors, who practised in the Court of Session) were trained in Edinburgh, and might hope to become one of the fifteen Lords of Session, who together made up the Court of Session. Lawyers dominated Edinburgh society, closely linked to the country gentry of the Lothians, forming a closeknit and powerful community, united in their professional associations, the Faculty of Advocates, and the Society of Writers to the Signet. Leading lawyers were often politically well placed, as agents for important landowners or noblemen, and played a significant role in the development of Edinburgh cultural life. The distinctive nature of the Scottish legal system remained more or less untouched, in spite of a decision of 1710 which made the House of Lords the supreme court of appeal in civil cases. The legal systems of Scotland and England had in fact little in common. Scottish law was based mainly on an inheritance of Roman law and canon law; young Scottish lawyers went abroad, especially to Holland, to Leyden, Groningen, and Utrecht, to complete their legal education. In 1681 the principles of Scottish private law were clarified and codified, in the authoritative work by Lord Stair (1619–95), Lord President of the Court of Session, *The Institutions of the Law of Scotland*; and in 1684 his contemporary Sir George Mackenzie of Rosehaugh (1636–91) had published *The Laws and Customs of Scotland in Matters Criminal* which did the same for the criminal law in Scotland. The principles of Scottish law, drawn from a variety of sources, were in line with European concepts of 'natural', 'universal' law, based partly on a common inheritance of Roman law. In contrast with English common law, Scottish law had more in common with legal teaching and practice in Europe, was less dependent on customary law and precedent, and was set out in modern systematic treatises, of which the best were in English[3]. This responsiveness to changing legal developments, combined with a cosmopolitan European outlook, was of importance; as will be seen, it was essential to the appearance of a new historical and social context for the study of law.

The educational institutions of Scotland survived the Union; and the strength of the Scottish Enlightenment is often attributed to the national tradition of education at all levels of society. There are important qualifications to be made to this; nevertheless in the Lowlands it was true that in the first half of the eighteenth century the great majority of children would receive some form of education. The statute of 1696, passed by the Scottish Parliament, had provided that every parish should take the responsibility of erecting a school, and by around 1760 this ideal was virtually achieved in the Lowlands. In the Highlands the situation was entirely different. The barrier of language, since most Highlanders spoke Gaelic, the size of the parishes, the continuing poverty, meant that the efforts of evangelical Lowlanders, or of the Scottish Society for the Propagation of Christian Knowledge, had relatively little effect. Within the towns, the obligation to provide schooling fell on the town council; although councils did not always provide elementary education for the children of the poor, they were able, generally, to offer schools which provided secondary education for the sons of the middle classes, education which might be flexible in its approach to the classics, and ready to adapt to the needs of a commercial career. The secondary schools, or burgh schools, would normally provide a sufficient grounding in classics (or, more probably, Latin) for the student at 14 or 15 to go on to his local university. The universities of Scotland were, at the beginning of the century, facing serious difficulties; political and religious changes, and the burden of poverty, had left them in a state of disorder and indecision. Yet from the first decade of the century, a programme of development and expansion, bringing new fields of study, and new approaches to learning, began to place the universities at the centre of intellectual developments in Scotland. The stability provided after the Union, and the forceful influence of Principal William Carstares (see Biographical Notes) at Edinburgh University from 1703 to 1715, were essential to this expansion, which was led by the Universities of Edinburgh and Glasgow; the Colleges of Aberdeen and St Andrews followed some way behind. It was these universities which provided the jobs for the writers of the Enlightenment, the important link with the landed classes through the exercise of political influence, and the education of their sons, and the constant stimulus of teaching. The part of the universities in generating the atmosphere of the Scottish Enlightenment is considered in more details in Chapters 1 and 7.

The Union did provide a stable political and social background for the cultural achievement of eighteenth century Scotland; the ordered way of life of the landed classes of the Lowlands was essential to the glittering life of Edinburgh. Yet the Union was not universally accepted, and opponents of the Union should not be ignored, for the part that they played, in stimulating Scottish patriotism, and in opening up the country to European influences, was not negligible. It has been argued that, after the dramatic political and religious changes of the second half of the seventeenth century, those who first brought a cosmopolitan outlook to a country which, in the 1690s was still dominated by a Calvinist orthodoxy, were not loyal Presbyterians, but Jacobites, and often Episcopalians[4]. The Episcopalian Church, although disestablished, remained in some strength, especially in the north-east of Scotland; and there were early signs that the educated laity of the north-east were actively interested in new ideas circulating in Europe. Professor Trevor-Roper quotes the interest taken in the work of Pietro Giannone, translated into English by the Scot, James Ogilvie, and published as *The Civil History of the Kingdom of Naples*, in 1729; the work was one of the earliest examples of a kind of historical writing later to be popularised by Enlightenment writers – and the subscription list reveals that many orders for it came from the nobility and gentry of the north-east, including one from Marischal College, Aberdeen[5].

A number of Scots of distinction and achievement at the beginning of the century counted themselves as opponents of the established regime; for that reason they were more likely to travel and study abroad, and to bring their experience back to Scotland. Sir Archibald Pitcairne (1652 – 1713), one of the founders of the Royal College of Physicians at Edinburgh, and Professor of Physic for a year at Leyden from 1692, was an Episcopalian (and also a rumoured deist) and a Jacobite, whose satirical poems on the Scottish kirk were not welcomed by the General Assembly. Pitcairne's awareness of scientific advances, gained in his studies in France, Holland and Italy, and his interest in mechanical interpretations of medical phenomena, made him an outstanding scientist of the period, at the centre of intellectual developments in Edinburgh. And in Edinburgh too, a group of men associated with printing and publishing responded to the Union by a commitment to revive what was seen as the Scottish heritage from the past. There was a linguistic problem; the old Scottish literary language was no longer a living one and contemporaries regarded Lowland Scots as an uncouth dialect. James Watson (1664? – 1722) and Robert Freebairn (?–1747) two keen Jacobites, owned the only serious printing presses in Edinburgh at the time of the Union, and published patriotic pamphlets, older and contemporary Scottish poetry, and historical studies. Freebairn especially was responsible for new editions of important Scottish literary works, including a new edition of the sixteenth century poet, Gavin Douglas' translation of the *Aeneid* into Scots verse, made in 1512–3, which was published in 1710. This was produced partly at the initiative of Pitcairne, and in association with Thomas Ruddiman (1674–1757), Underkeeper of the Advocates Library, a Jacobite and an outstanding Latin scholar. Allan Ramsay (1684–1758) poet and Jacobite, was more interested in the revival of the Scottish vernacular tradition, in ballads, broadsides, and songs; he published several collections, as well as reviving the work of some of the earlier Scottish writers of the fifteenth and sixteenth centuries. There was, therefore, a movement, roughly in the first forty years of the eighteenth century, for the assertion of a genuinely Scottish culture, inspired by hostility towards the Union; yet such a movement was losing its impetus, and by mid-century was less and less apparent[6]. Allan Ramsay and the Jacobite publishers and scholars of this group did help to create the polite Edinburgh world of the eighteenth century; and this is discussed further in Chapter 1. But their patriotism should be distinguished from the ambivalent response of 'enlightened' writers to the consequences of the Union; among later writers there was a much more finely tuned sense of both the advantages and the disadvantages of a closer relationship with England. Though some Jacobites and some Episcopalians, like Sir Archibald Pitcairne, were in certain respects fore-runners of the Enlightenment, the interesting careers of these individual Jacobites should not mask the continuity of institutional contacts between Scotland and the Continent, especially Holland, in medicine, in law and in religion. The slow, steady influx of liberal ideas, in these three fields, laid the groundwork, undramatically, but securely, for the later achievements of the Enlightenment.

It should also be remembered that the establishment of political stability throughout Scotland was continuing through this period. The major problem was, of course, the appeal of Jacobitism, an appeal with effect mainly in the Highlands. The contrast between Highland and Lowland society was stark; the still primitive, archaic and tribal Highland society had little in common with the Lowlands. The brief attempts of 1708 and 1719, and the risings of 1715 and 1745, showed how little the Highlands were committed to the British Crown, and also how greatly the power of the clan Campbell, headed by the Duke of Argyll, was distrusted as the 'civilising' agent of the British Government. Lawlessness and political disaffection was finally reduced after 1745; but the contrast between the patriarchal, economically impoverished Highlands, and the rapidly changing agricultural and commercial world of the Lowlands, persisted.

The clan organisation still dominated the Highlands; the re-sponsibilities of the clan chief to his followers, the existence of private courts, the obligation to do military service, were still a reality in the early eighteenth century. Chiefs leased land often to tacksmen, their own kin, perhaps minor gentry; but those who farmed the land were the tenants and subtenants, relying on pastoral agriculture and the export of cattle. Clearly the nature of the clan made a large number of tenants and followers desirable to the chieftain; such a policy could certainly impede agricultural improve-ment. The military rationale still outweighed the economic in this pastoral society. But there were signs of change; the Dukes of Argyll introduced new farming methods, and imposed certain conditions of efficiency on their tenants—the old established tenants could no longer compete[7]. After 1745, political defeat, and the example of economic change in the Lowlands, began to transform Highland life. The power of the clan chieftains had been broken; but there was still an important role for the Highland landowner to play. The demand for Highland produce, for wool and for cattle, made a new and prosperous era appear a possibility. Highland landowners saw their task as the organisation of the transition from the older, wasteful forms of peasant cooperative agriculture, to a new, more efficient farming, oriented towards sheep, in which displaced tenants would be resettled in new villages devoted to fishing, to the linen industry, and to the gathering of kelp (seaweed). By the late eighteenth century, this movement was well developed, though it had not achieved much success. Highland landowners had taken their cue from the Lowlands; there some members of the landed classes were preoccupied with the responsibilities of their own social and economic leadership, with the deliberate 'improvement' of society along the lines suggested by the English example.

The earliest 'improvers' in Scotland were Lowland landowners; they had the capital and the energy, and above all the admiration for English progress, and the desire to rival it. Men like John Cockburn of Ormiston (1679–1758), a gentleman farmer and an M.P., enclosed their lands, laid down strict regulations for tenants in their leases, instructed them in the best agricultural practice, and rebuilt the local village, as Cockburn did the town of Ormiston, with the provision of suitable industries. Cockburn was an Anglophile, deeply interested in English achievements; yet his own concern was as much cultural as economic, and consequently his investment was not particularly profitable. Cockburn was bankrupt by 1747. But his work was similar to that of a number of other landowners, including such leading gentry 'improvers' as Archibald Grant of Monymusk (1696–1778), and members of the aristocracy, such as the Dukes of Argyll, who rebuilt the town of Inverary, and the Duke of Perth, who founded the town of Callander. 'Planned villages' became a part of the eighteenth century Scottish scene; again, on the model of the English village, they were intended to provide both markets for industrial produce, and a basis for domestic industry and the inculcation of solid habits of work, thrift, and enterprise[8].

Some of the leading Scottish lawyers were actively involved in agricultural innovation; Lord Kames (see Biographical Notes), for instance, worked for the improvement of the Scottish economy in a variety of ways. On his family estate in Berwickshire, he introduced the rotation of crops, turnip and potato cultivation, scientific manuring, enclosures, and other improvements; and he continued this work when his wife brought him the large estate of Blair Drummond in Perthshire in 1766. His book, *The Gentleman Farmer, Being an attempt to improve Agriculture, by subjecting it to the Test of Rational Principles*, published in 1776, testified to his own belief in a philosophy of improvement, and to the experience acquired after thirty years' practice of it. Kames had been involved not only privately but publicly with the campaign for improvement. From the mid-1750s he was a leading member of the Board of Trustees for Fisheries, Manufactures and Improvements in Scotland (set up in 1726) and of the Commission for Forfeited Estates, established after 1745. In 1766 Kames published a short book on *The Progress of Flax-Husbandry in Scotland*, drawn from his own experience at the Board of Trustees, in which he had helped to direct the aid given to the linen industry by providing instructors and equipment in different villages and by the encouragement of technical research. The work of the Commissioners had an even wider scope; for them economic improvement was only a part of the work of rescuing the Highlands from its archaic backwardness. Their brief was for:

> civilising the Highlands by instructing and training up their youth in the early knowledge and practice of the several branches of husbandry, manufactures and other necessary arts[9].

The work of improvers was often backed by membership of societies, such as the Honourable Society of Improvers in the knowledge of Agriculture in Scotland, founded in Edinburgh in 1723, with an extensive and aristocratic membership, which was responsible for the plan, submitted to the government in 1726, for the establishment of a Board of Trustees for Fisheries, Manufactures and Improvements. Allan Ramsay was an admirer of the Society, and dedicated his poem on 'The Pleasures of Improvement in Agriculture' to it, as the Honourable and Ingenious Fraternity for Improvement in Agriculture, Planting, Gardening, etc; the poem ends:

> Continue, best of clubs, long to improve
> Your native plains and gain your nation's love.
> Rouse every lazy laird of each wide field
> That unmanured not half their product yield.
> Show them the proper season, soils, and art,
> How they may plenty to their lands impart,
> Triple their rents, increase the farmer's store,
> Without the purchase of one acre more[10].

And there were other, less aristocratic societies, like the Gordon Mills Farming Club of Aberdeen, founded in 1758. The experiments of these years were frequently unsuccessful economically; these 'gentleman farmers' had no overriding economic incentive. They were drawn largely from classes who had most contact with 'enlightened' and 'improving' ideas, the lawyers and the larger and middling landowners. Yet their example was to be taken up by their tenants, and by practically minded farmers; after 1780 or so the initiative tended to pass to those who farmed the land directly. But in the period which is of interest here, the inspiration came from the

outstanding Anglophile, from the practical energies of the cultivated gentleman.

There was concern not only for Scottish agriculture, but also for
the improvement of her industrial output. The decades immediately following the Union saw no appreciable change; but
there had been a commitment by the British government to devote a
part of the revenue earned by the Union to the improvement of the
Scottish economy. The Board of Commissioners set up in 1726 was
intended specifically to encourage the Scottish linen industry and
Scottish fisheries. There were slow signs of growth in the most
important areas, in the linen industry, the tobacco trade and the
cattle trade; only from the 1740s onwards were these trends clearly
visible. The output of linen rose three-fold in volume and four-fold
in value between the years 1736–40 and 1768–72. The Navigation
Acts had offered Glasgow the opportunity, which was rapidly taken,
to become the entrepôt tobacco port for Europe, importing from the
American colonies to Britain and the rest of Europe. The Scottish
share of the tobacco trade in Britain rose from 10% in 1738 to 52% in
1769; though economic historians doubt whether this trade gave
much stimulus to other sectors of the economy. There were a few
major concerns founded within this period, which point ahead to
industrialisation at the end of the eighteenth century: the Pres-
tonpans Vitriol Works, for example, founded in 1749, and the great
Carron Iron Works, set up in 1759. A variety of small industries
were expanding, connected with paper, soap, dye, glass, distilling
and brewing; but apart from the linen textile trade there was little
dramatic growth within the Scottish economy in this period[11].

The inadequacy of Scottish financial machinery to cope even
with this degree of development, however, was increasingly being
demonstrated; new banks followed the lead of the Bank of Scotland,
founded in 1695, as the Royal Bank of Scotland, established in 1727,
and the British Linen Company, from 1746, responded to the
growing demand for banking services. From the 1760s a number of
unchartered banks grew up to meet local needs, and to offer a more
adventurous credit policy. Shortage of capital, and an imbalance of
trade with England still continued to create serious difficulties and
even disaster; the Ayr Bank crashed resoundingly in 1772, partly as
a result of its own generosity with credit. But this expansion
certainly created a sense of change within Lowland Scottish society,
as a smart and fashionable city was created in Glasgow.

What was there in these historical circumstances which helped to

produce such a massive constellation of talent? One primary factor
which has been stressed is the complexity of the relationship
between England and Scotland in this period. Even before the
Union, the influence of William III and his advisers, especially
William Carstares, had brought to Scottish affairs an awareness of
new intellectual currents, coming especially from Holland. Within
the Church, a more liberal Presbyterianism was encouraged; and
within the universities, Carstares pressed for reform of the old
curriculum. After the Union, Scotland became in political terms, an
outlying province of the United Kingdom, without political
institutions, but with the remains of a national identity: an identity
to be expressed through the institutions that survived, the Church,
the law and the universities. But the changes already set in motion
before the Union continued, intensified, if anything, by closer
contact with England. There was clearly a tension here, between
the 'progressive' example of England, and the need to preserve the
remnants of Scottish national identity. The patriotic Jacobitism of
the early eighteenth century has been contrasted with the ambivalent admiration felt for civilised, commercial English society, by
'enlightened' writers. The backwardness of Scotland was accepted
by such writers; so, too, was the obligation to raise her to the level of
her neighbour—though not without some reservations about the
benefits that were being offered. A commitment to rational social
improvement, at a steady pace, and largely on terms defined by
England, was shared by landed improvers, and by the majority of
writers discussed in this book; it was typical, too, of representatives
of the Moderate party within the Church of Scotland, of legal
improvers, and of university professors. The leaders of Scottish institutions were, for the most part, looking also to the English model,
determined to prove Scottish ability to emulate what was best in the
English example. A concrete instance of this may be found over the
agitation for a Scottish militia in the 1750s and 1760s; after the
revival of the English militia in 1757, Scots were eager to see it
established in Scotland, and affronted that the government should
consider their loyalty not sufficiently proven. The Poker Club,
founded in 1762 to 'stir up' the campaign for a Scots militia,
included:

> all the literati of Edinburgh and its neighbourhood, most of
> whom had been members of the Select Society, except very few
> indeed who adhered to the enemies of militia, together with a

great many country gentlemen, who, though not always resident in town yet were zealous friends to a Scotch militia, and warm in their resentment on its being refused to us, and an invidious line drawn between Scotland and England[12].

Such a specific example of Scottish patriotism among the ruling groups within society is rare by the middle of the century. Yet among the 'literati', the sense of Scottish economic backwardness was matched by an awareness of cultural backwardness. David Hume (see Biographical Notes) had a deliberate, if rather mis-directed, policy of encouraging Scottish writers. Hume and his friends were not interested in the vernacular Scottish literature, either of the past or of the present; they took no notice, for instance, of the poetry of Robert Fergusson (1750–74), who wrote of Edinburgh life in the 1770s. English was for them the language of literature; and Hume patronised the English-language poets that he knew, Thomas Blacklock (1721–91), the blind prodigy and poet, and William Wilkie (1721–72), the farmer whose epic poem, the *Epiconiad* was recommended by Hume to the London literary world—their work is now remembered only by Hume's recom-mendations. The concern of the 'literati' was to improve the standard of English spoken and written in Scotland; so the Select Society of Edinburgh introduced lectures in English elocution, because:

gentlemen educated in Scotland have long been sensible of the disadvantages under which they labour, from their imperfect knowledge of the ENGLISH TONGUE, and the impropriety with which they speak it[13].

Hume and Robertson worked hard to purge 'Scotticisms' from their prose style. The drive to emulate England, economically, socially, culturally, was an important part of the Scottish Enlightenment, though the relationship between province and metropolis was by no means a straightforward one. The same contrast which existed between England and Scotland was present, to an ever greater degree, between the Highlands and Lowlands of Scotland. These contrasts perhaps were also important, in encouraging Scottish writers to explore the nature of different societies, and the relationships between social forms and economic change.

Yet none of the 'literati', with the exception of Adam Ferguson, came from the Highlands; the Enlightenment was very much a Lowland phenomenon. Eighteenth century Scotland was ruled at a local level by the landed classes; yet the direct participation of the landed nobility and gentry was small. David Hume, the younger son of a small Border landed family, is an exception; but the rest of the writers represented in this book came from the learned professions and th middle classes. Adam Ferguson, John Millar and Thomas Reid were the sons of Church of Scotland ministers, Francis Hutcheson of an Ulster Presbyterian minister. Kames and Monboddo both came from minor gentry families, but made their own fortunes at the Bar. Yet these men depended for their advancement on their association with the landed classes; the patronage offered was invaluable. Adam Smith left his Chair at Glasgow in 1764 to be tutor to the young Duke of Buccleuch; Adam Ferguson took a year's leave of absence from the University of Edinburgh without permission, to go abroad with the young Earl of Chesterfield. A pension, often a substantial one, would be offered, and, as important, the right kind of influence exerted when a desirable government or university post became vacant. There was little divergence between the interest of these writers and those of the open-minded Scottish landowner; and this is one factor which perhaps explains the lack of political radicalism displayed in these writings, with the exception of those of John Millar. The influence of the government could be solicited and used, to assist individual careers; the influence of the Dukes of Argyll, for instance, could be decisive in an appointment to a University Chair (see Chapter 1 for examples of this). Government influence was never more favourable to the 'literati' than when Lord Bute (1713–92) held a position of power, from 1761–3. In this short period, William Leechman (1706–85), and William Robertson, both pillars of the Moderate party in the Church, became Principals of the Universities of Glasgow and Edinburgh respectively; Robertson in addition, on the strength of his popular *History of Scotland* (1759) received the valuable sinecure of Historiographer Royal for Scotland. John Home, (see Biographical Notes) minister turned dramatist, whose play *Douglas* greatly upset the General Assembly, was also well rewarded, with a sinecure worth £300 a year in 1763[14]. The Enlightenment was closely dependent on this relationship with the rulers of Scotland; such patronage, though indirect, was essential to the security and stability of these writers.

Yet the Enlightenment itself was an urban movement, largely

professional in character. The social contrasts existing between Scottish cities help to differentiate their cultural worlds. Aberdeen, small, remote, with its own intellectual traditions and colleges, offered few opportunities for the professional middle classes outside the colleges and the Church. The most notable society there, the Aberdeen Philosophical Society, founded in 1758, was clearly dominated by the professional concerns of local professors and ministers. There was little interest in the teaching of law, medicine, or science; the achievements of the men of letters in Aberdeen were above all in moral philosophy, where Thomas Reid formulated, and James Beattie (see Biographical Notes) popularised, the 'common sense' arguments that were later to dominate Scottish philosophy. This central concern with moral philosophy also informed the literary criticism of Alexander Gerard (1728–95), whose essays, *On Taste* (1759) and *On Genius* (1774), were first read at the Aberdeen Philosophical Society, and the work of George Campbell (1719–96) on the philosophy of language. Another interest was political economy; the *Essays on the History of Mankind* (1780) by James Dunbar (?–1798) and the *Essay on the Right of Property in Land* (1781) by William Ogilvie (1736–1819) both show an awareness of contemporary discussion in this field. There was, too, in Aberdeen some commitment to the philosophy of practical improvement, seen in the foundation of the Gordon's Mill Farming Club, which has already been mentioned, in which the local gentry were active. Aberdeen, then, was a strongly regional centre; intellectual life there focussed closely on the concerns of the classroom and the ministry[15].

Glasgow, on the other hand, was expanding rapidly throughout this period. Its population grew from about 13,000 at the time of Union to 40,000 in 1780. By mid-century the character of this developing city was entirely different from that of Edinburgh; its society was dominated by an oligarchy of businessmen, merchants and manufacturers whose fortunes were, for the most part, dependent on the spectacular success of the tobacco trade which had transformed the city. Glasgow still had an appreciable professional class, but one that was less than half the size of that of Edinburgh, in proportion to the population of the two cities. Even so, the role played by merchants in the local clubs and societies was relatively small. The Hodge-Podge Club in Glasgow, founded in 1752, started as a serious intellectual concern, but ended as a drinking club; of thirty one members admitted from 1752 to 1783, twenty were merchants. The Glasgow Literary Society, however, had a majority of university members. The Political Economy Club in Glasgow, which existed from around 1743 to sometime after 1762, was more successful in uniting the interests of merchants and academic economists; it stimulated the reprinting of some economic classics, and included among its members Adam Smith, and the lesser known Sir James Steuart (1712–80), an economist of some achievement. The concerns of teachers at the university of Glasgow were noticeably more biassed towards scientific and technical advances than at the other Scottish universities. A number of the most distinguished scientists of eighteenth century Scotland began their careers at Glasgow; Joseph Black (1728–99) taught medicine and chemistry there, and was consulted on a range of technical matters, from the Edinburgh drinking water to new textile dyes, before he went to Edinburgh in 1766. William Cullen (see Biographical Notes) began his career in the Glasgow medical school, where his interests included bleaching and agriculture as well as medicine and chemistry. Alexander Wilson (1714–86) was both the operator of the type-foundry for the Foulis Press of Glasgow, which specialised in fine editions of the classics, and the first Professor of Astronomy in Scotland. And Black's patronage of James Watt (1736–1819), whom he befriended and brought to Glasgow to help with his research, had far-reaching effects, stimulating Watt in the early stages of his career. The practical and commercial bias of these areas of study, and of the outstanding teaching at Glasgow University, is evident; even so, it appears the University provided the leaders of debate and discussion in Glasgow.

In Edinburgh, circumstances were rather different. The place of the Church and of the legal establishment in Edinburgh meant that the University was rivalled by other institutions, and by the position of Edinburgh as a provincial social centre for the governing classes. By mid-century the population of the Old Town of Edinburgh was reckoned to be around 36,000; it was a town which had, on the one hand, a reputation for squalor and violence, and, on the other hand, a growing polite social life. In spite of the loss of the Scottish Parliament, the minor nobility and the substantial gentry still focussed their lives on the social world of Edinburgh; London was too distant and too expensive. The aristocratic world of the landowners, linked to the legal establishment, with patronage to offer the intelligentsia, dominated the life of the city: perhaps around 400 families, closely knit by kinship and marriage, united professional and landowning interests. The growth of clubs and societies, not only the Rankenian Club, from 1716, and the Philosophical Society, from 1737, but also such meeting places as the Musical Society, founded in 1728, together with the growth of new journals and new lending libraries, were beginning to offer entertainment of a fashionable kind; it was a small and coherent world, one which provided the encouragement and the security necessary for the writers of the Enlightenment. Yet it was not this elite which carried the day to day responsibility for the government of Edinburgh or of its University. The Town Council of Edinburgh, a self-perpetuating, oligarchic body, drawing its membership from the Merchant Company and the incorporated trades, was both aware of and stimulated by the mood of improvement. From the beginning of the century, it was conscious of the potential of the University as a stimulant to Edinburgh's prosperity, and especially of the possibilities of developing the vocational faculties of law and medicine. The University owed much to the career of George Drummond (see Biographical Notes) six times Lord Provost of Edinburgh in this period, who took an active interest in the University. Beyond this interest in the University lay the whole ambitious new project for the redevelopment of Edinburgh itself, for the building of a New Town. In 1752, a pamphlet was published in Edinburgh, the *Proposals for carrying on certain Public Works in the City of Edinburgh* written by Sir Gilbert Elliot, but probably owing much to the inspiration of George Drummond. The *Proposals* opened with a statement of underlying aims:

> Among the several causes to which the prosperity of a nation may be ascribed, the situation, conveniency, and beauty of its capital, are surely not the least considerable. A capital where these circumstances happen fortunately to concur, should naturally become the centre of trade and commerce, of learning and the arts, of politeness and refinement of every kind. No sooner will the advantages which these necessarily produce, be felt and experienced in the chief city, than they will diffuse themselves through the nation, and universally promote the same spirit of industry and improvement[16].

It sketched a programme for the improvement of Edinburgh and the creation of a new town from motives which were partly economic—the revival of Edinburgh's prosperity—and partly patriotic—that Edinburgh should begin to rival London as a centre for society and for learning. To an extraordinary degree the proposals put forward here were to approach fulfilment, as by the end of the eighteenth century the New Town and the University did indeed appear as centres of 'politeness and refinement of every kind'. The building of the New Town, begun in 1767, was the most obvious expression of the drive towards improvement in Edinburgh, supported by all the leading groups of Edinburgh society.

Though the writers of the Enlightenment were drawn mainly from the professional classes, the closeness of these writers to the landed classes has been stressed. In Edinburgh particularly, the closeness of these ties was evident; in the clubs and societies, and in the University, the intellectual force of the 'literati' attracted the gentry and nobility, who made up the majority of the membership of the societies, and who were the patrons and readers of their published works. They shared a common belief in deliberate and conscious action, a belief that the cultural, social and economic backwardness of Scotland could be remedied, that Edinburgh could become a rival capital to London. Yet, on the other hand, the content of the works which form the main part of the selection here suggest the message could be ambivalent (see Chapter 6 for a discussion of this): that the problems with which Hutcheson, Hume, Smith and the others were concerned were related to the situation of Scottish society—but that the answers were by no means as straightforward as might at first appear.

The intellectual inheritance of the early eighteenth century was a complex one; the context of 'enlightened' thinking included several strands, of which the most significant were the impact and reception of Newtonian ideas, the developing debate on epistemology sparked off by John Locke, and the nature of the Scottish legal tradition. These themes were taken up, first in some depth in the writings of Francis Hutcheson, and later, to a greater or less degree, by all the writers represented in this collection.

It was constantly repeated by these writers, and most notably by David Hume, that their aim was to introduce the methods pioneered by Isaac Newton into the worlds of moral and political philosophy. Newton appeared as the patron of empirical method, a method which was infinitely adaptable to other worlds beside that of natural philosophy. Of course, the legacy of Newton was by no means as simple as it was often made to appear, as, for example, it was represented by George Turnbull (1698–1748), in his *Principles of Moral Philosophy* (1740):

> . . . I was led long ago, to apply myself to the study of the human mind in the same way as to that of the human body, or to any other part of *Natural Philosophy*: that is to try whether due enquiry into moral nature would not soon enable us to account for moral, as the best of *Philosophers* (i.e. Newton) teaches us to explain natural phenomena[17].

Newton's approach itself owed much to his seventeenth century predecessors; and it offered by no means a single coherent line of enquiry. The mathematics of his greatest work, the *Principia* (1687) were read and understood by few, though those few included some of the leading teachers at Scottish universities. The *Opticks* (1701), more speculative, more general, more popular, was better understood, and perhaps more widely read. It was the message spelt out so clearly in the *Opticks* which was to influence so profoundly the moral philosophers and social scientists of the Scottish Enlightenment:

> As in mathematics, so in natural philosophy, the investigation of difficult things by the method of analysis, ought ever to precede the method of composition. This analysis consists in making experiments and observations, and in drawing general conclusions from them by induction, and admitting of no objections against the conclusions, but such as are taken from experiments, or other certain truths. For hypotheses are not to be regarded in experimental philosophy. And although the arguing from experiments and observations by induction be no demonstration of general conclusions; yet it is the best way of arguing which the nature of things admits of, and may be looked upon as so much the stronger, by how much the induction is more general[18].

Newton here contrasted what he regarded as purely speculative hypotheses, with conclusions that were based on sound experimental work and observation. Many relied, rather than read Newton himself, on popular accounts of Newton's ideas; and among the transmitters of Newton's thought, several Scottish university teachers were prominent. David Gregory (1661–1708) became Professor of Mathematics at Edinburgh University in 1684 and was the first university teacher in Britain to teach the *Principia* to his students; he was, however, driven out by the Church of Scotland, as an Episcopalian, and became Savilian Professor of Astronomy at Oxford in 1692. The most outstanding expounder of Newton in the early eighteenth century was, however, Colin Maclaurin (1698–1746), a brilliant young mathematician, a member of the Royal Society, acquainted with Newton himself, and a member of the Rankenian Society in Edinburgh. He had become a Professor at Aberdeen in 1717 at the age of 19, and in 1725, backed by Newton's own letter of recommendation he became Professor of Mathematics there. His two top classes were again taught from the *Principia*, and were highly subscribed. On the death of Newton in 1728, Maclaurin composed a draft which was later to become his *Account of Sir Isaac Newton's Philosophical Discoveries*, published in 1748[19]. George Turnbull, also at Edinburgh, and perhaps Gershom Carmichael (1672–1729) (at least in his later years), were also teaching Newtonian principles[20]. Another source of Newtonian thinking lay in its indirect transmission through medical teachers; Hermann Boerhaave (1669–1738), the leading teacher of medicine in Europe, teaching at Leyden from 1709 to 1738, with a high proportion of his students from Britain, laid great stress on the experimental method and its British pioneers. And the Edinburgh medical school was to be modelled for the most part on Boerhaave's example. There is therefore much evidence to suggest that within the universities, by the late 1720s, Newtonian ideas were circulating freely; and that when Hume announced his *Treatise of Human Nature*, published in 1739, to be 'an attempt to introduce the experimental method of reasoning into moral subjects', he was using a generally accepted view of the 'Newtonian method'.

Besides this new emphasis on the Newtonian method, there was, too, a rising tide of interest in epistemology, in the problem of knowledge, in the debate initiated by John Locke (1632–1704) in his *Essay Concerning Human Understanding* (1690). Locke suggested in the *Essay* that the mind was a 'tabula rasa', a blank sheet, on which ideas could be imprinted either through sensations of external objects, or through introspective reflection, only. The basic elements of knowledge, simple ideas, were reflections of the outside world perceived through the senses; complex ideas were built up by piecing together these components. One theme which critics rapidly picked up was Locke's failure to define clearly what he meant by 'ideas' in this context: he seemed to suggest that men can be directly aware only of the ideas in their own minds, and have no direct awareness of the external material world. To Bishop Berkeley (1685–1753), such a doctrine was, in many respects, fundamentally dangerous. In his *Principles of Human Knowledge* (1710), Berkeley attacked Locke: he believed that Locke's arguments contravened the common sense of ordinary men, and that they could lead to religious scepticism. Berkeley's solution to the problem posed by Locke was to deny the existence of matter:

> The existence of matter, or bodies unperceived, has not only been the main support of atheists and fatalists, but on the same principle doth idolatry likewise in all its various forms depend. Did men but consider that the sun, moon and stars, and every other object of the senses, are *only* so many sensations in their minds, which have no other existence but barely being perceived, doubtless they would never fall down and worship their own *ideas*—but rather address their homage to that Eternal, Invisible Mind which produces and sustains all things[21].

Where Locke had accepted the mechanical, the materialist world, governed by discoverable laws, for Berkeley that world was inspired, created and sustained by the very being of God, whose spirit communicated directly with the human spirit. The argument, of course, ranged widely over a variety of fields; its richness pointed to the importance of the issues raised.

There is much evidence to suggest that Berkeley's work was discussed more actively in Scotland than in England in the early eighteenth century[22]. George Turnbull, in his *Principles of Moral Philosophy*, took a favourable view of Berkleian arguments; though his work was not published until 1740, it may well have expressed his own interest as a student at Edinburgh from 1717 to 1721, and then as regent at Marischal College Aberdeen until 1727. Colin Maclaurin's *Account* reveals a detailed knowledge of Berkeley, and some acute criticism. Both these men belonged to the Rankenian Club, founded in Edinburgh around 1716 or 1717; little is known about the Club, but its membership suggests that it attracted some of those who were to be prominent in the stages of the Scottish Enlightenment: Maclaurin, Turnbull, and also Robert Wallace (1697–1771), a young liberal minister, later an original political economist, William Wishart secundus (?–1753) son of the Principal of Edinburgh University, later himself Principal, John Stevenson

(1695–1755) later Professor of Logic at Edinburgh University, and others. It is suggested in Wallace's reminiscences that this Club carried on a correspondence with Bishop Berkeley before his departure to America in 1729:

> To their letters his Lordship transmitted polite and regular returns, endeavouring to avoid the consequences drawn from his doctrines: he was greatly pleased, too, with the extraordinary acuteness and peculiar ingenuity displayed in them, and has been heard to say, that no persons understood his system better than this set of young gentlemen in North Britain. Hence he offered to adopt them into his famous design of erecting a college at Bermudas for the benefit of the new world. But the club, thinking the project aerial, and having other agreeable prospects, mostly declined to accept his Lordship's invitation[23].

Turnbull's enthusiasm for Berkeley may, it has been suggested, reflect early interest among the Rankenians, while Maclaurin's criticisms may indicate later disillusion among the Edinburgh literati, after Turnbull's own departure for Aberdeen. Certainly Edinburgh students of the 1730s were set by John Stevenson to criticise Berkeley's work; their essays reflected the high standard of debate and awareness of these issues in Edinburgh at the time. These students also leant on the work of another Scottish writer, Andrew Baxter (1680–1750), whose work *An Inquiry into the Human Soul* (which went through three editions, in 1733, 1737 and 1745), was one of the first extensive examinations of Berkeley's ideas[24].

By the 1720s and 1730s certain philosophical questions had been posed at the highest levels; not only were the Scots concerned with these epistemological issues in themselves, but also with their bearing on the wider questions of moral philosophy. The empirical investigation of human nature was to yield a secure foundation upon which were to be founded moral laws; the first essential was, as Francis Hutcheson wrote, that:

> We must . . . search accurately into the constitution of our nature, to see what sort of creatures we are . . .[25].

The study of Locke and Berkeley had indicated the overriding importance of the observation of man, of the need to chart human beliefs, passions, understanding; the Scottish writers were to turn away from a naïve acceptance of man's rationality, and towards a clearer understanding of sensations, sentiment, passions. Their aim was, first, simply, to describe the operations of the human mind, and then, perhaps, to suggest its organising principles.

There was a distinctively Scottish element in the intellectual atmosphere of the early eighteenth century: and this is to be found especially in the Scottish legal tradition. Two aspects of this may be considered: first of all the close interest shown in the development of natural law theory in Europe, and, secondly, the use made of this in Scotland. As has already been pointed out, Scottish lawyers were strongly influenced by legal teaching abroad, especially by that of the Dutch universities; not only did they learn the traditional features of Roman law, but also the work of natural law theorists, like Hugo Grotius (1583–1645), author of *De Jure Belli ac Pacis* (1625) (*Of the Law of War and Peace*) and Samuel von Pufendorf (1632–94), the German author of *De Jure Naturae et Gentium* (1672) (*Of the Law of Nature and Nations*), and *De officio hominis et civis* (1673) (*The Whole Duty of Man*)[26]. These writers built a system of law upon what were seen as evident and obvious facts of nature; for those who could understand such things, the principles of natural law were 'the dictates of right reason', but for most people they were learnt by common language and use. Both Grotius and Pufendorf shared the view that man was by his very nature a social animal; from this assumption, they moved on to chart the rights and duties of mankind, to sketch the network of submission and authority, of mutual duties and obligations, that made up the social world. For Pufendorf, the most obvious way to discover the law of nature was 'the accurate contemplation of our natural condition and propensions'; the law sprang from human nature itself. The rights of property, the law of contracts and promises, the nature of government and its authority, are seen as human constructs designed to meet the needs of human nature. Here then was a framework on which to build a general and systematic view of the social world; the laws of nature could be discovered and described. It was not a purely secular creed; the assumption lay clearly in the background that the laws of nature were essentially God-given. Other, later, writers followed the lead given by Grotius and Pufendorf. In Scotland Gershom Carmichael translated and annotated Pufendorf's *De officio hominis et civis*, published in Glasgow in 1724; George Turnbull published in 1763 a translation of one of the standard later textbooks, Heineccius *A Methodical System of Universal*

Law, first published in 1738 as *Elementa Juris Naturae et Gentium*.

In Scotland, such works were used perhaps as much in the teaching of arts students as in the teaching of law. There is every reason to suppose that Carmichael, as a regent at Glasgow, employed Pufendorf's works as his textbooks. In 1707 a Chair of the Law of Nature and Nations was founded at Edinburgh, recalling the title of Pufendorf's own chair at Heidelberg; though it was only intermittently filled. But the Advocates Library in Edinburgh acquired a copy of Pufendorf's *De officio hominis et civis* only during the curatorship of Lord Kames, from 1737 to 1742[27]. Scots law had its own systematic codes, those of Lord Stair and Sir George Mackenzie. And Stair's assumptions differed from those of the natural lawyers; his Presbyterianism led him to ascribe a more direct role to the will of God: law was founded primarily on the will of God, to which man's reason was in all things secondary. And Stair, being also a practising lawyer, was inclined to ascribe rather more importance to precedent than would Pufendorf. Nevertheless Stair and the European writers had much in common. Stair described a system in which the principles of law were evident to man's reason, in which the contractual obligations were sacred, and in which the public interest could restrain the individual and his property, for the benefit of all[28].

Such a common framework of ideas, which had no parallel in England, and which offered some common ground to philosophers and lawyers, was to be of great importance as a basis for the development of speculation about man and society in the eighteenth century. The foundations of this speculation have been traced. Armed with what was seen as an infallible tool, the 'Newtonian' method, ready to begin their study with man himself, ready to expand the framework offered to them in the universities, the Scottish 'literati' began a programme of speculative discussion and debate about the role of men in society. And if in the pursuit of their objectives, the way seems a little dusty, a little dry, it should not altogether conceal the radicalism and the originality of the questions which were being asked.

NOTES

1. On the making of the Union, see P. W. J. Riley, 'The Structure of Scottish Politics and the Union of 1707', in T. I. Rae (ed.) *The Union of 1707. Its Impact on*

Scotland (Edinburgh, 1974); T. C. Smout and R. Campbell, 'The Anglo-Scottish Union of 1707', *Economic History Review*, 16 (1963–4).

2. For a general discussion of the Church of Scotland in this period, see Andrew L. Drummond and James Bulloch, *The Scottish Church, 1688–1843* (Edinburgh, 1973); for an account of its structure see Dugald Stewart, 'Account of the Life and Writings of William Robertson, D. D.', in *The Works of William Robertson D. D.*, 12 vols (London, 1817) I, pp. 109–116.

3. See T. B. Smith, *British Justice, The Scottish Contribution* (Edinburgh, 1961) Chapters 1 and 2; the Stair Society, *An Introduction to Scottish Legal History* (Edinburgh, 1958).

4. H. Trevor-Roper, 'The Scottish Enlightenment', in *Studies in Voltaire and the Eighteenth Century*, 58, 1967, 1635–58.

5. *Ibid*, 1652–3; 'A list of the name of subscribers', Pietro Giannone, *The Civil History of the Kingdom of Naples*, 2 vols, translated into English by James Ogilvie (London, 1729).

6. Ian Ross and Stephen Scobie, 'Patriotic Publishing as a Response to the Union', in Rae (ed.), *The Union of 1707*.

7. Eric Cregeen, 'The Changing Role of the House of Argyll in the Scottish Highlands', in *Scotland in the Age of Improvement, Essays in Scottish History in the Eighteenth Century*, edited by N. T. Phillipson and R. Mitchison (Edinburgh, 1970).

8. T. C. Smout, 'The Landowner and the Planned Village in Scotland, 1730–1830', in *Scotland in the Age of Improvement*, ed. Phillipson and Mitchison.

9. Quoted in Ian S. Ross, *Lord Kames and the Scotland of his Day* (Oxford, 1972) p. 317.

10. *The Works of Allan Ramsay*, III, edited by Alexander M. Kinghorn and Alexander Law. The Scottish Text Society, Series 3, 29 (1961) pp. 171–2.

11. Generally, see H. Hamilton, *An Economic History of Scotland in the Eighteenth Century* (Oxford, 1963) and for a recent assessment of the economic importance of the Union, R. Campbell, 'The Union and Economic Growth', in Rae (ed.), *The Union of 1707 (op. cit.)*.

12. Alexander Carlyle, *Anecdotes and Characters of the Times*, edited with an introduction by James Kinsley (London, 1973) pp. 213–4.

13. *Scots Magazine*, XXIII, (1761) pp. 440–1.

14. See J. Cater 'The making of Principal Robertson in 1762', *Scottish Historical Review*, 49 (1970) pp. 60–84.

15. See for a discussion of the contrasting milieux of different 'enlightened' cities, Roger Emerson,' The Enlightenment and Social Structures', in P. Fritz and D. Williams, *City and Society in the Eighteenth Century* (Toronto, 1973).

16. Quoted in A. J. Youngson, *The Making of Classical Edinburgh* (Edinburgh, 1966) p. 4.

17. George Turnbull, *The Principles of Moral Philosophy. An Enquiry into the wise and good government of the moral world* (London, 1740) iii.

18. Sir Isaac Newton, *Opticks, or a Treatise of the Reflections, Refractions, Inflections, and Colours of Light*, with a foreword by Albert Einstein, an introduction by Sir Edmund Whitaker, a preface by I. Bernard Cohen (Dover Publications, 1952) p. 404.

19. 'An Account of the life and writings of the Author', prefixed to Colin Maclaurin, *An Account of Sir Isaac Newton's Philosophical Discoveries*, in four books, 2nd edition (1750).

20. J. McCosh, *The Scottish Philosophy, biographical, expository, critical, from Hutcheson*

to Hamilton (London, 1875) reprint Hildesheim (1966) pp. 36–42, 95–106.

21. G. Berkeley, *The Principles of Human Knowledge* (Fontana edition, edited and introduced by G. J. Warnock, 1962) p. 112.

22. G. E. Davie 'Berkeley's Impact on Scottish Philosophers', *Philosophy*, 40 (1965) pp. 222–34.

23. *Scots Magazine*, 33 (July, 1771) p. 341.

24. Davie, *op. cit.* p. 228.

25. Francis Hutcheson, *A Short Introduction to Moral Philosophy in three books, containing the elements of ethicks and the law of nature.* Translated from the Latin (Glasgow, 1747) p. 2.

26. There is no authoritative discussion in English of the work of these men. See L. Krieger, *The Politics of Discretion* (Chicago, 1965) on Pufendorf, and the discussion in D. Forbes, *Hume's Philosophical Politics* (Cambridge, 1975) Chapters 1 and 2; and as an introduction, A. P. D'Entrèves, *Natural Law* (London, 1951).

27. Ross, *Lord Kames and the Scotland of his Day*, p. 29.

28. P. Stein, 'Law and Society in Eighteenth Century Scottish Thought', in *Scotland in the Age of Improvement*, edited by Phillipson and Mitchison, pp. 148–52.

Biographical Notes

The following notes are intended as a guide to the careers of the major figures represented in this volume; other biographical information is given where needed.

JAMES BEATTIE (1735–1803)

Born Laurencekirk, Kincardine, where his father was a shopkeeper and farmer. In 1749 he entered Marischal College Aberdeen, and in 1753 became schoolmaster at Fardoun near Laurencekirk. Attracting the patronage of Lord Gardenstoun and Lord Monboddo, he became a master in Aberdeen grammar school in 1758, and in 1760 Professor of Moral Philosophy and Logic at Marischal College, where he joined the Philosophical Society founded by Thomas Reid. He published poetry from 1761, and in 1770 his *Essay on Truth*, a crude attack on David Hume. His best known poem *The Minstrel* appeared in two volumes in 1770 and 1774. After a visit to London in 1773 he was awarded a pension of £200 a year by the Crown. His only other philosophical work was the *Elements of Moral Science*, 2 vols (1790 and 1793), largely based on his own lectures.

HUGH BLAIR (1718–1800)

Son of an Edinburgh merchant, he was educated at the University of Edinburgh from 1730–9, and in 1742 became minister of Colessie, Fife; in 1743 he moved to second charge of the Canongate Church in Edinburgh, and from there in 1754 to Lady Yester's Church, and in 1758 to the High Church. His preaching won him a considerable reputation; his sermons were simple, unimpassioned, and inclined to deal with moral and ethical problems rather than doctrinal issues. He was associated with the Moderate group in the General Assembly and with the literary circle that founded the Select

Society in 1754, of which he was a member. His lectures on rhetoric in Edinburgh from 1759 were so successful that the Town Council created him Professor of Rhetoric (unpaid) at the University; in 1762 a Regius Chair was created for him. His publications included: *Lectures on Rhetoric and Belles Lettres*, 2 vols (London, 1783) and his *Sermons*, 5 volumes of which appeared from 1777 to 1801.

JAMES BURNETT, LORD MONBODDO (1714–99)

Son of James Burnett of Monboddo, and heir to the family estate in Kincardineshire. Graduated MA at Aberdeen and read law at Edinburgh and Groningen. Admitted as advocate in 1737 and after a very successful career became Lord of Session in 1767. He was a member of the Select Society. His interests, in metaphysics and the origins of language, did not accord with those of his contemporaries; and his lengthy volumes did not attract a great readership. He was best known, and most ridiculed, for his attempts to relate human and animal behaviour. His main publications were: *Of the Origin and Progress of Language*, 6 vols (Edinburgh, 1773–92) and *Antient Metaphysics, or, the Science of Universals*, 6 vols (Edinburgh, 1779–99).

ALEXANDER CARLYLE (1722–1805)

Son of a minister at Annandale, he was educated at the University of Edinburgh from 1735 to 1743, studied at Glasgow under Hutcheson, and spent a year at Leyden. In 1748 he became minister of Inveresk, near Edinburgh, and soon moved into Moderate and literary circles in Edinburgh. In 1754 he was a founding member of the Select Society, and in 1756 he was at the centre of the controversy over *Douglas* (See Chapter 7); he was also a founder member of the Poker Club. He left extensive memoirs of the period in MSS, published most recently as *Anecdotes and Characters of the Times*, (ed.) J. Kinsley (London, 1973).

WILLIAM CARSTARES (1649–1715)

The son of a Presbyterian minister of Cathcart, who was deprived of his living after the Restoration, and after 1666 lived in Holland.

William Carstares, educated at Glasgow High School and Edinburgh University, then joined his father in Holland, and after studying at Utrecht, entered the service of the Prince of Orange. He came to England and Scotland on various missions for the Prince, and was imprisoned twice, from 1675–9, and from 1683–4. In 1688 he accompanied William III to England, and there was his principal adviser on Scottish ecclesiastical affairs, bearing much of the responsibility for the re-establishment of Presbyterianism, and the subsequent tolerant compromise with episcopalianism. His experiences in Holland led him to advocate reform and modernisation of the Scottish universities. Carstares was Principal of Edinburgh University from 1703–15, and Moderator of the General Assembly four times.

WILLIAM CULLEN (1710–90)

Born in Lanarkshire, where his father was factor to the Duke of Hamilton, he was educated at the University of Glasgow, and apprenticed to a Glasgow doctor. In 1729 he sailed as surgeon on a merchant ship to the West Indies; after returning he spent the years 1734–6 at Edinburgh medical school, and in 1736 became a surgeon in Hamilton, supported by the interest of the Duke and Duchess of Hamilton. In 1744 he moved to Glasgow where he began to lecture on medicine and botany. In 1749 he was introduced to the Earl of Islay by Lord Kames; the 'Argyll interest' helped his career considerably. In 1751 he became Professor of Medicine at Glasgow; he moved to Edinburgh in 1755, first as joint, and in 1756 as sole, Professor of Chemistry. He also lectured very successfully on the practice of medicine. In 1761 he took the Chair of the Theory of Medicine, and in 1773 his preferred position, the Chair of the Practice of Medicine. His publications included: *First Lines of the Practice of Physic*, 4 vols (Edinburgh, 1776–84), an outstanding textbook. He did a great deal to build up Edinburgh's reputation as the leading medical school in the country; as a teacher he was extremely successful, and his influence widespread.

GEORGE DRUMMOND (1687–1766)

Six times Lord Provost of Edinburgh, and the outstanding Edinburgh politician of the period. From 1707 he served as Accountant General of the Excise, and from 1717 as Commissioner of the Board of Customs. He first sat on the Town Council in 1715; in 1717 he was elected Treasurer, and in 1725 Lord Provost for the first time. His policy was that of the improvement and expansion of the city in general and especially that of the University. He was responsible for the building of the Royal Infirmary, completed in 1741; he was a member of the committee which was largely responsible for the 'Proposals' for the New Town in 1752, and initiated the building of the Royal Exchange. In his last term of office in 1762–4, the expansion of Edinburgh to the north was begun, as the North Loch was drained, and the North Bridge built. Drummond played a considerable part in the Town Council's policy of increasing the reputation of the University through the appointment of able men; though he acted in concert with the political managers of Scotland, political interest was not allowed to override academic excellence, and a number of outstanding appointments were made.

ADAM FERGUSON (1723–1816)

Son of a minister of Logierait, Perthshire, educated at grammar school and St Andrews University, he continued his studies at Edinburgh University from 1742, where he became friendly with William Robertson and John Home. From 1747 to 1754 he acted as chaplain to the Black Watch regiment, a post made easier by his being a Gaelic speaker. In 1757 he succeeded David Hume as Keeper of the Advocates Library. He was already a member of the leading group of Moderate clergymen, and had written a pamphlet in defence of John Home's *Douglas: The Morality of Stage Plays seriously considered* (Edinburgh, 1757). He was a founding member of the Select Society and the Poker Club. In 1759 he became Professor of Natural Philosophy at Edinburgh; although not really qualified for this, he lectured until 1764 when he took the Chair of Moral Philosophy. In 1774–5 he travelled abroad with Charles, 3rd Earl of Chesterfield; in 1778 he visited Philadelphia, as a member of the commission charged to negotiate a settlement with the American colonists. In 1767 he published his best known work, the *Essay on the History of Civil Society*. His later works, based mainly on his own lectures, included the *Institutes of Moral Philosophy* (Edinburgh, 1772), and the *Principles of Moral and Political Science*, 2 vols

(Edinburgh, 1792). In 1783 he also published the *History of the Progress and Termination of the Roman Republic* (Edinburgh, 1783).

JOHN HOME (1722–1808)

Son of the town clerk of Leith, educated at Leith and at Edinburgh University, minister of Athelstaneford, East Lothian, from 1747, he was associated with the Moderate group in the Church of Scotland. In 1749 his play, the tragedy *Agis*, was rejected by David Garrick for performance in London; Home continued to write, and when his play *Douglas* was also rejected in London, it was put on in Edinburgh in 1756 with considerable success, though causing great outrage to the General Assembly (see Chapter 7). Home resigned his parish and moved to London, where the play was also performed in 1757. He became personal secretary to Lord Bute, and a tutor to the young Prince of Wales. In 1760 he was given a pension of £300 a year, and in 1763 the sinecure of conservator of the Scottish privileges at Campvere in Holland, also worth £300 a year. His plays continued to be performed in London, though none with such success as *Douglas*.

DAVID HUME (1711–77)

One of the outstanding figures of the European Enlightenment. Son of Joseph Home of Ninewells, advocate and laird of Ninewells, a small Berwickshire estate. Educated at Edinburgh University from 1722 to 1725/6. From 1726 to 1734 he studied privately, leaving for France in 1734, where he stayed until 1737, by which time his first work was almost complete. The *Treatise of Human Nature* was published in 1739; though greatly disappointed at its reception, he was determined to continue the life of a man of letters, and published during the 1740s a series of essays on philosophical, political and literary topics. Financial reasons forced him to look for other sources of income. He failed to secure the Chair of Moral Philosophy at Edinburgh in 1744 because of opposition based on his reputation for scepticism. He temporarily acted as tutor to the insane young Marquess of Annandale in 1745, and also took a position as secretary to General St Clair, on a naval expedition to Canada in 1746 (though the expedition ended by attacking the

French coast). In 1751 he published *The Enquiry concerning the Principles of Morals*; but it was his essays, especially the *Political Discourses*, published in 1752, that won him most public reputation (see p.   for a list of these publications). In 1751 he had settled in Edinburgh, and in 1752 became Keeper of the Advocates Library; he was a leading figure among the Edinburgh 'literati' and one of the initiators of the Select Society of 1754. He was friendly with a number of Moderate clergymen who defended him from the General Assembly's attack in 1755. His *History of England* appeared in six volumes from 1754 to 1762, secured his success, and helped to win him international recognition. In 1763 he visited Paris as Lord Hertford's secretary to the British Embassy and was made much of there in the literary salons; he remained there until 1767, partly as chargé d'affaires. In 1767 he returned to London when he was appointed Under Secretary of State to the Northern Department. In 1769 he returned to Edinburgh where he remained for the rest of his life. His later works included the essay 'On the Natural History of Religion', first published in 1757, and his *Dialogues concerning Natural Religion*, unpublished till after his death, in 1779, because of its sceptical arguments.

FRANCIS HUTCHESON (1694–1746)

Son of a Presbyterian minister of Armagh, Northern Ireland, he was educated at a Presbyterian academy in Co. Down, and from 1711 at Glasgow University. After leaving Glasgow he acted for two years as tutor to the Earl of Kilmarnock; on returning to Ireland he entered the ministry, but before taking charge of a parish was called to Dublin by a group of Presbyterian clergy to establish an academy there. He taught in Dublin from 1721 to 1730. His early interests lay in aesthetic theory; in 1725 he published *An Inquiry into the Original of our Ideas of Beauty and Virtue*, and in 1728 the *Essay on the Nature and Conduct of the Passions and Affections*. In 1730 on the death of Gershom Carmichael, Hutcheson's name was proposed and actively supported by a number of younger faculty members for the Chair of Moral Philosophy at Glasgow. On being elected he became a highly successful and influential teacher there, and emerged as leader of a group representing the liberal thinkers within the Church of Scotland. His later works, though continuing some of the earlier themes, gave more prominence to legal and political philosophy.

While teaching at Glasgow he wrote, between 1734 and 1737 his *System of Moral Philosophy*, published later, in two volumes, in 1755. In 1742 he published two short works in Latin, *Metaphysicae Synopsis*, and the *Philosophiae Moralis Institutio Compendiaria*; the latter was addressed specifically to students, and was translated into English as a *Short Introduction to Moral Philosophy*, in 1747.

LORD KAMES, HENRY HOME (1696–1782)

Son of George Home of Kames in Berwickshire, he was heir to a small landed estate. He was educated privately, apprenticed to a Writer to the Signet in 1712, and admitted as advocate in 1723; he became a Lord of Session in 1752, and Lord of Justiciary in 1763. In 1766 he succeeded through his wife to the estate of Blair Drummond. He was possibly a member of the early Rankenian Society, a member of the Philosophical Society, and one of the founders of the Select Society. He was prominent among the Edinburgh literati, an important patron of younger men like Adam Smith and John Millar. His interests were varied, and his publications wide-ranging. His legal and historical work included: *Essays upon several subjects in law* (Edinburgh, 1732); *Essays upon several subjects concerning British antiquities* (Edinburgh, 1747); *Historical Law Tracts* (Edinburgh, 1758); *Principles of Equity* (Edinburgh, 1760); *Sketches of the History of Man* (Edinburgh, 1774). His other works ranged from the literary and philosophical to the agricultural: *Essays upon the Principles of Morality and Natural Religion* (Edinburgh, 1751); *Elements of Criticism* (Edinburgh, 1762); *Progress of Flax-Husbandry* in Scotland (Edinburgh, 1766); *The Gentleman Farmer* (Edinburgh, 1776).

JOHN MILLAR (1735–1801)

Son of a minister of Hamilton, he was also heir to the small estate of Milheugh, Kirk of Shotts, Lanarkshire. Educated at Hamilton grammar school and the University of Glasgow from 1746, where he spent six years, possibly longer, he attended the first lectures of Adam Smith in Glasgow. At some time in the late 1750s he became tutor to Lord Kames' son and spent two years in his household. In 1760 he was admitted to the bar, and in 1761 elected to the Chair of Civil Law at Glasgow. His appointment greatly improved

Glasgow's law school, and he attracted a considerable number of students, including many from England. He took part in the activities of the Glasgow Literary Society. His works included the *Observations concerning the Distinction of Ranks in Society*, first published 1771, revised under the title of *The Origin of the Distinction of Ranks* in 1779. In 1787 he published the *Historical View of the English Government from the Settlement of the Saxons in Britain to the Accession of the House of Stewart* in two volumes. He also wrote a number of pamphlets and articles, most notably the *Letters of Crito* (1796) and the *Letters of Sidney on Inequality of Property* (1796). Both strongly attacked Pitt's war policy and maintained what Millar saw as the essential principles of the French Revolution; he had been a member of the Society of the Friends of the People in 1792. He was more committed to political activity and radical ideas than any other of the writers considered here.

THOMAS REID (1710–96)

Son of a minister of Strachan, Kincardineshire, he was educated at Marischal College Aberdeen, from 1722 to 1726. He entered the ministry in 1731 and was made librarian of Marischal College in 1733. In 1737 he took up the living of New Macher, near Aberdeen. In 1751 he became a regent at Kings College Aberdeen; he founded the Philosophical Society there in 1758. Discussions there, centring on the provocation offered by David Hume, led to the publication in 1764 of Reid's *Inquiry into the Human Mind*. In 1764 he was elected Professor of Moral Philosophy at Glasgow, where he remained until his retirement in 1780, after which he prepared his two later publications, the *Essays on the Intellectual Powers of Man* (1785) and *Essays upon the Active Powers of Man* (1788).

WILLIAM ROBERTSON (1721–93)

Son of a minister from Dalkeith, he was educated at Dalkeith grammar school and Edinburgh University. In 1743 he became minister of Gladsmuir, East Lothian, and in 1756 moved to become minister of Lady Yester's Church, Edinburgh and in 1761 minister of Old Greyfriars Church. By 1751 he had clearly emerged as leader of the Moderates within the Church, notably in his defence of lay patronage; he also actively defended John Home in the *Douglas* affair in 1756. His *History of Scotland* (1759) won him much interest, and the patronage of Lord Bute, through whose intervention he became Principal of Edinburgh University from 1762 to 1793, one of the royal chaplains in 1761, and Historiographer Royal for Scotland in 1763. As Principal he presided over an outstanding period in the history of the University, guiding its teaching, improvement and expansion. He was also a founding member of the Select Society, a leading figure in Edinburgh literary circles for many years. He continued his historical writing, and published: *The History of the Reign of the Emperor Charles V*, 3 vols (London, 1769); *History of America*, 2 vols (London, 1777); *Historical Disquisition concerning the knowledge which the ancients had of India* (London, 1791).

ADAM SMITH (1723–90)

Born at Kirkcaldy, son of the comptroller of customs there, he was educated at Kirkcaldy grammar school, and at Glasgow University, from 1737–40. From 1740 he went to Balliol College, Oxford, where he stayed for seven years. In 1748 he went to Edinburgh, where he gave lectures on jurisprudence and on rhetoric, under the patronage of Lord Kames. In 1751 he won the Chair of Logic at Glasgow, and in 1755 moved to the Chair of Moral Philosophy. In 1759 he published a work based largely on his lectures, *The Theory of Moral Sentiments*. In spite of his teaching in Glasgow, he spent much time in Edinburgh, where, with Hume, he founded the Select Society, and also helped to write the first *Edinburgh Review*, in 1755, and later joined the Poker Club. In 1764 he left his University position and became tutor to the young Duke of Buccleuch, with whom he visited France, meeting some of the leading 'philosophes' there, Quesnay, D'Alembert, Turgot, and Necker. In 1766 he settled in Kirkcaldy on a pension from Buccleuch, and devoted himself to the writing of the *Wealth of Nations*, finally published in 1776. After a lengthy visit to London, in 1778 he accepted an appointment as one of the Commissioners of Customs for Scotland and returned to Edinburgh. Throughout his life his intellectual interests were wide – ranging. Student notes on his lectures on jurisprudence and history, and also rhetoric, have survived and have been reprinted. He also wrote essays on the evolution of language and on the history of astronomy; these were posthumously published in the *Philosophical Essays* (London, 1795).

1 Signs of Change

In the early part of the eighteenth century, there were clear indications that urban life and urban institutions in Scotland were beginning to face the challenge of the Union. This selection of documents attempts to illustrate some aspects of these changes: the successful drive towards the improvement and expansion of the universities, the increasing refinement of a social life in which books, theatres, clubs, were to play a greater part, and the growth of more moderate, less inflexible theology within the Church of Scotland. Inevitably such developments were piecemeal and slow, proceeding at different speeds in different parts of the country.

The clearest example of a deliberate drive towards improvement is to be found within the universities: the drive was the combined responsibility of the government, the professions, and the Universities themselves. Edinburgh and Glasgow were in the lead, sharing in the general expansion of those towns; the two colleges of Aberdeen, Marischal and Kings, continued to play an important regional role. The colleges of St Andrews hardly shared in this eighteenth century expansion and will not be considered here. The revolution of 1688 was an important event in the history of the Scottish universities; a Parliamentary Commission was set up in 1690 to visit and examine the Universities and to ensure their commitment to the Presbyterian Church, now again the Church of Scotland (Document 1). The Universities were in future to be dominated by a Whiggish Presbyterianism; William III's closest adviser on these matters, William Carstares, who admired many aspects of the Dutch university system, was to provide the initial force behind change. The problems were both financial and academic; all the universities were poorly endowed and struggling by the end of the seventeenth century. Carstares, with his brother-in-law, William Dunlop (?–1700), Principal of Glasgow University from 1690 to 1700, persuaded the new government to give some financial assistance; in 1693 a grant of £1200 a year was made to be shared between the four Scottish universities, and other individual grants followed. When Carstares was made Principal of Edinburgh in 1703, his interest and efforts increased; Document 4 illustrates his own attempts to appeal to potential students and their parents. At Edinburgh the patronage of the Town Council was also significant; the Town Council had inherited the right of appointing Professors of the University. They came to see the expansion of the University as a means of improving the status and prosperity of the city[1].

The government's financial assistance helped to tide the universities over a difficult period; but the major problems which interested reformers were academic ones. The curriculum taught in all Scottish universities remained the old mediaeval arts curriculum; boys, entering the university between the ages of 14 and 16, and sometimes earlier, continued to follow a course which differed little in outline from that of the fifteenth and sixteenth centuries, and was strongly biassed towards the works of Aristotle. The basic subjects included the advanced study of Latin, elementary and more advanced Greek, rhetoric, arithmetic, geometry, logic, and moral and natural philosophy. Each class was allotted its own regent, who taught all these subjects over the four year course; though even before the beginning of the eighteenth century there were a few attempts to create specialised Chairs. Teaching methods too often consisted merely of the dictation of set texts, and examination upon them, and teaching was intended to be conducted in Latin, though this was not always the case in practice. Since the Reformation, Divinity faculties had been added to the universities, though standards were not high, and many students went to Dutch universities to improve their theological education. Not all of this was to change during the eighteenth century. The first reform to be undertaken seemed clearly to be the abolition of the regenting system, and the introduction of more specialised teaching. This was pressed by the Parliamentary Commissions of 1690 and 1695 which proposed a standard philosophy course for all four universities, to which each would contribute a section. This proposal came to nothing; but after long pressure Edinburgh abolished regenting in 1708 (Document 2), Glasgow in 1727 (Document 3), followed by St Andrews in 1747, Marischal College in 1755, and Kings College in 1798. The regent, in each of these universities, was transformed into a specialist Professor; in 1727 in Glasgow, for instance, Gershom Carmichael, the longest serving regent, became Professor of Moral Philosophy. Together with this development went a movement towards the endowment of new chairs. In 1709 Glasgow used a part of a grant from Queen Anne to found a Chair of Oriental Languages, and in 1716 founded a Chair of Ecclesiastical History[2]; in Edinburgh, a new chair of Universal Civil History was created in 1719, and in 1760 the lectures on rhetoric and belles lettres already being given by Dr Hugh Blair (see Biographical Notes) were recognised by the creation of a Chair of Rhetoric and Belles Lettres (Document 6). But pressure for the expansion of teaching came especially from the two professions of medicine and law; it was in these areas that growth was especially spectacular.

Medical teaching in Edinburgh had been undertaken for some time by members of the Surgeons' Incorporation and the College of Physicians. The combined efforts of these teachers, of John Monro, father of Alexander Monro primus, (1697–1767), first effective Professor of Anatomy at Edinburgh, and of George Drummond, led to the appointments, in 1726, of four new Professors (Document 5)[3]. The building of the Royal Infirmary from 1729 was to give the school unrivalled clinical facilities. In Glasgow cooperation with the Faculty of Physicians and Surgeons was less easy. A Chair of Medicine was founded in 1713, and one of anatomy in 1720; but the Faculty maintained its monopoly of clinical teaching until much later in the century[4]. Similarly, in Edinburgh the work of the legal profession was linked with the University. In 1710 James Craig, already regularly lecturing on behalf of the Faculty of Advocates, was given the title of Professor of Civil Law, though he remained unpaid until 1717. By 1722 two further legal Chairs, of Universal Civil History, and Scots Law, had been set up, and a Faculty of Law, in which the right of appointment lay with the Faculty of Advocates, had been established. In Glasgow the Faculty of Procurators kept a closer hold on the teaching of law, but the Chair of Law endowed by Queen Anne in 1713 allowed the University to build up some reputation in this field.

After the death of Carstares, the growth within the universities continued steadily, though it was haphazard and piecemeal, hardly to be attributed to any single individual. The advancement of any scholar depended a good deal on patronage, and the influence of leading magnates could be critical. The influence of the 3rd Duke of Argyll was much sought after, often through the mediation of Lord Milton (Documents 9–10); and during his brief period of power, Lord Bute took an active interest in University affairs (Document 10). Often scholars had first served their time as tutors to Scottish aristocrats, or accompanied them on the continental tour. William Leechman, later Principal of Glasgow, had tutored in the house of William Mure of Caldwell (1718–76), a local landowner and politician, and John Millar in the household of Lord Kames. In Glasgow appointments were made by the Faculty, in Edinburgh by the Town Council. The choice of a Professor depended on several factors: the influence exerted, family relationships, the candidates' religious views, and, not always most important, the reputation of the scholar in his field. In spite of a developing tendency towards specialisation, scholars could be expected to teach in other disciplines. Nepotism certainly flourished. Alexander Dunlop (1684–1747), son of the Principal of Glasgow, was appointed as Professor of Greek there in 1702, and secured his own son the post of Professor of Oriental Languages in 1744 (Document 8)[5]. There were even more famous examples: the Chair of Anatomy at Edinburgh was held by three generations of Monros, all named Alexander, from 1720 to 1846. Many appointments were, however, clearly made on grounds of academic excellence. Francis Hutcheson was brought to Glasgow in 1730 for that reason. Joseph Black was lured from Glasgow to Edinburgh in 1766, like William Cullen before him, for the contribution he could make to the thriving medical school. Other areas of the curriculum might not do quite as well. Adam Ferguson was initially appointed, partly because of his own popularity among the leading literati of Edinburgh, to the only available Chair in 1759, that of Natural Philosophy, on which he conscientiously lectured, though claiming no great knowledge of the subject, for five years before moving with relief to the Chair of Moral Philosophy. Others were even less responsible. William Cross was appointed Professor of Civil Law in Glasgow in 1745; hoping to treat the post as a complete sinecure, he gave no lectures for four years, and was finally persuaded to resign. Though there was much that was corrupt and unreformed in the eighteenth century university system, nevertheless such behaviour was increasingly unacceptable. Professors' salaries were not large; more important than the fixed stipends paid to them were the fees paid directly to Professors by students attending their classes. Professors in arts subjects and in medicine could secure a good income from fees—the financial incentives for lecturers to attract students were considerable. Professors might also increase their income by writing, or by taking in as boarders their own students, often the sons of the aristocracy (Document 6).

The numbers of students admitted grew fast during the eighteenth century, especially in the arts and medical faculties. The universities still remained based largely on their own regions; but Edinburgh and Glasgow also attracted new kinds of students, including dissenters from England, barred from Oxford and Cambridge, students from the American colonies, a small international contingent and even some sons of the English gentry and aristocracy, who found that education in Scotland had certain advantages. But in the first half of the century these developments were just beginning. In the late seventeenth century Edinburgh had around 400 students; by 1789 the number was almost 1100[6]. Glasgow had 400 students in 1702, rising to 1240 by 1824[7]. The reform of the curriculum, although not altering the central philosophical areas of the Arts degree, allowed room for specialisation and choice both by teacher and student, and for the gradual transformation of the content of teaching; this transformation will be traced in later chapters.

Within the Church of Scotland, too, there were signs of change; the Church of Scotland was not untouched by the appearance of new ideas, and the revival of old ones. There was much fear of deism; as Thomas Halyburton (1674–1712), Professor of Divinity at St Andrews, wrote, in a work published in 1714:

The infection spreads, and many are daily carried off by it both in England and Scotland. Though it must be owned that Scotland, as yet, is less tainted with the poison[8].

These were years of theological nervousness, in which the questions that were eroding English Presbyterianism were also troubling the Church of Scotland. Doctrinal differences turned on the difficult question of redemption and election—had Christ died for all, or only for the elect? On the one hand, there was the Arminian view, that salvation was open to all believers leading a Christian life, since Christ had died for all; and on the other hand there were the perils of antinomianism, the belief that the elect were by grace set free from observing the moral law. The Church was determined to preserve its orthodoxy against these two extremes. In 1714 John Simson (1668?–1740), Professor of Divinity at Glasgow, was accused of spreading Arminian doctrines; after the case had been postponed he was finally acquitted in 1717. He was not to be so lucky when accused again of heresy in 1726; on this occasion there were suspicions of his teaching on the doctrine of the Trinity. He had been reading the English writer, Dr Samuel Clarke's *Scripture Doctrine of the Trinity* (1712) and seemed to be tending towards Arianism, the heresy which denied the divinity of Christ (Document 15). He was suspended in 1729 by the General Assembly (though left his salary). The pursuit of Simson was partly due to his influential position, and to the effect which he was undoubtedly having on his own students; though it is also clear that Simson was not the only source of student interest in the new thinking. Doctrinal debates continued through the 1720s but by 1730 there were clear signs of a shift away from the strictness of Calvinist theology. A few ministers with some sympathy for a liberal, rational Christianity, which laid more stress on ethical teaching and practical morality than on theological debate, were emerging into prominence in the Church; these men included William Leechman, later Professor of Divinity and Principal at Glasgow, William Wishart secundus, later Principal of Edinburgh, and Robert Wallace, later minister of the Tron Church, Edinburgh. And in the 1730s and 1740s conflicts over both patronage and theology tended to divide the ministry of the Church into evangelicals, supporting the rights of congregations to appoint ministers, maintaining orthodox Calvinist views, with much popular support, and those who were to become the Moderate party, and defended lay patronage, and a more 'enlightened' theology. It was in this context that Francis Hutcheson was to offer a more effective formulation of such a theology, which had considerable appeal to this Moderate group. Their role in the Church of Scotland by mid-century is considered further in Chapter 7.

As the educated men of the universities, the Church, and the professions embarked upon new courses, so the social and cultural world expanded for them. Books, magazines, societies, theatres—these signs of a polite culture came slowly to Scotland. Printing and publishing in Edinburgh and Glasgow lagged some way behind London in the early part of the eighteenth century. At the beginning of the century there were only four printing houses in Edinburgh, none of very high quality[9]. But the Copyright Act of 1709 was to make change possible; it laid down that copyright should be limited, and no longer the permanent property of the original publisher: works already published were given twenty-one years copyright, and those to be published after 1707 fourteen years, with a possible extension of another fourteen. The first three quarters of the

century, especially from 1731 onwards, saw a lengthy battle, in the
courts and in the bookshops, between London publishers and
booksellers, and provincial, especially Scottish and Irish competitors. The need for easier access to publishers and cheaper books
was certainly felt in Scotland during these years; in 1713, a student,
Thomas Harvie of Glasgow had put up a proposal to the Senate for
a University Printer, as necessary to any 'Seminary of learning'
(Document 11). This need, together with the new openings at a
national level, was to stimulate much Scottish activity; but it was
slow to get off the ground. The work of James Watson and Robert
Fairbairn, which has already been mentioned, was mainly directed
towards the revival of Scottish vernacular literature, and Scottish
history. Thomas Ruddiman had also developed a printing press, at
first jointly with Fairbairn, and Ruddiman, with James Davidson,
was appointed University Printer in 1728. But the Ruddiman press
was unadventurous in scope, with little interest in the reprinting of
European works; Ruddiman concentrated on Latin grammars and
the Latin classics, in the old humanist tradition, together with some
historical and legal works. However, as University Printer he did
offer some services to Edinburgh scholars, mainly in the mathematical and medical fields. It was Ruddiman who printed the complex
texts of Colin Maclaurin's mathematical works.

One commentator has suggested that the difference between
Ruddiman's work and that of the Foulis brothers of Glasgow,
strongly indicates the differences between 'the old culture of
humanist Scotland and the new Enlightenment'[10]. Certainly the
work of Robert Foulis (1707–76), and his brother Andrew (1712–
75) was a major contribution to the culture of the Scottish
Enlightenment. The Foulis brothers, both old students of Francis
Hutcheson, advertised for the first time, 'a variety of scarce and
valuable editions of the classics and books proper for the Grammar
School and University'[11]. Much of their stock was imported from
France; from 1741 they also began printing their own works and in
1743 the firm was designated University Printer. Their work was of
an extremely high technical and aesthetic standard, surpassing both
English and Scottish competitors; they printed works by Glasgow
scholars, including Francis Hutcheson's later works, new editions of
the classics, often in collaboration with Glasgow Professors, and
numerous reprints of English and Scottish literature, together with
a number of European works. Another rival, the Glasgow printer
Robert Urie (?–1771), maintained a similarly high standard. In

1744 the Edinburgh and Glasgow printers argued in the Court of Session that:

> The art of printing is daily improving in Scotland, at least in Edinburgh and Glasgow[12].

and from the 1740s it is clear that printing and publishing were beginning to expand beyond the narrower horizons of the Ruddiman press.

Such a development was necessary to the expansion of social life. These years saw also the beginnings of the newspaper and periodical press in Edinburgh and Glasgow. In Edinburgh Ruddiman published the *Caledonian Mercury* from 1720, the other Edinburgh newspaper being the *Edinburgh Evening Courant*, from 1718. Glasgow had the *Glasgow Journal*. These leant heavily on London news; and there were many demands too for reprints and imitations of the literary magazines of London, the *Spectator* and the *Tatler*, and similar works. In the *Northern Tatler* in 1717, the editor 'Duncan Tatler' announced his intention 'to instruct, rectify, and reform the North Country'[13]. Only in 1739 did a substantial literary journal, the *Scots Magazine* appear 'That the Caledonian muse might not be restricted by want of a public echo to her song'[14]. The first circulating library in the country appeared in Edinburgh, under the patronage of Allan Ramsay, in 1728. Other public libraries followed, not all in the major towns; that of Innerpeffray, near Crieff, operated as a lending library, used by all conditions of people, from 1747[15]. At a scholarly level, the Copyright Act of 1709 transformed a specialised legal library, the Advocates Library, into a major reference library, entitled to a copy of every work published in the country. Ruddiman was first appointed librarian there in 1722; during his career there, until 1752, the number of books grew fourfold and the catalogue he produced in 1742 was urgently needed. Ruddiman's notion of the library was a traditional one, seeing it as serving the learned purpose of lawyers, historians, and antiquaries; David Hume, his successor, found it sadly lacking in modern literature.

Edinburgh in the first decades of the eighteenth century saw a number of clubs and societies founded, ranging from the purely social, to literary, scientific, and agricultural groups. The Easy Club, founded by Allan Ramsay, intended 'that by a mutual improvement in conversation they may become more adapted for fellowship with the politer part of mankind' (Document 12). The Rankenian Club, founded in 1716 or 1717, has already been mentioned, as has the Honourable the Society of Improvers in the Knowledge of Agriculture in Scotland, established on the proposal of the Duke of Atholl in 1723. The Medical Society of 1731 was initiated by Alexander Monro primus, and published its own *Medical Essays and Observations, revised and published by a Society in Edinburgh*, 6 vols (Edinburgh, 1731–38); Colin Maclaurin suggested that its range should be widened to include other scientific fields (Document 14). It became the Philosophical Society, drawing in gentry and professional men, and lasting until 1783 as the forerunner of the Royal Society of Edinburgh. The students too had their own Medical Society from 1737, where they met weekly to read and discuss papers; student societies of all kinds were to grow in strength. The growth of these clubs was simply an expression of the physical and cultural growth of Edinburgh. In Glasgow there were no similar developments until a little later, in the 1740s, with the founding of the Political Economy Club, by Provost Andrew Cochrane (1693–1777), who was interested primarily in economic matters; there were, however, clearly active student clubs (Document 13). In Edinburgh there were many opportunities for social contacts: dancing, at the Assembly Rooms founded in 1710, or concerts, at the Musical Society of Edinburgh, from 1728. But there were still prejudices to be fought. In 1736 an attempt by Allan Ramsay to obtain a licence for a theatre in Edinburgh met with strong opposition from the magistrates, the Town Council, and the University of Edinburgh, although travelling companies continued to play there by tacit agreement; only in 1746 was a theatre firmly established in Edinburgh. Much business, discussion and conversation, still took place as always in the taverns; drinking clubs remained a feature of Edinburgh life throughout the eighteenth century.

Edinburgh in the first four decades of the eighteenth century was slowly developing the elements of that polite culture which was to come to fruition from the 1750s. Ideas of modernisation blended with a new intellectual approach, though commitment to the Scottish past, and to traditional patterns of Scottish scholarship was still strong, and indeed was in the future to coexist with the Enlightenment. The teaching of Colin Maclaurin and George Turnbull (Documents 17–18) indicates the changes in the atmosphere by the 1720s, before Francis Hutcheson began his career in Scotland.

NOTES

1. On Edinburgh University in these years, see D. B. Horn, *A Short History of the University of Edinburgh, 1556–1889* (Edinburgh, 1967) and A. Grant, *Story of the University of Edinburgh*, 2 vols (London, 1884); on the role of the Town Council, J. B. Morrell, 'The Edinburgh Town Council and its University, 1717–1766', in *The Early Years of the Edinburgh Medical School*, edited by R. G. W. Anderson and A. D. C. Simpson (Edinburgh, 1976).

2. J. D. Mackie, *The University of Glasgow, 1451–1951. A Short History* (Glasgow, 1954) p. 163.

3. J. Christie, 'The Origins and development of the Scottish scientific community, 1680–1760', *History of Science*, xii (1974) pp. 122–41.

4. Mackie, *op. cit.* pp. 224–6.

5. *Ibid*, p. 187.

6. Grant, *op. cit.* II, p. 200.

7. A. Chitnis, *The Scottish Enlightenment. A Social History* (London, 1976) p. 134.

8. Thomas Halyburton, *Natural Religion Insufficient and Revealed Necessary to Man's Happiness in his present state* (Edinburgh, 1714) quoted in Stewart Mechie, 'The theological climate in early eighteenth century Scotland' in Duncan Shaw (ed.) *Reformation and Revolution* . . . (Edinburgh, 1967).

9. Hugo Arnot, *The History of Edinburgh* (Edinburgh and London, 1779) p. 438.

10. D. Duncan, *Thomas Ruddiman. A study in Scottish scholarship of the early eighteenth century* (Edinburgh and London, 1965) p. 85.

11. David Murray, *Robert and Andrew Foulis and the Glasgow Press, with some account of the Glasgow Academy of Fine Arts* (Glasgow, 1913) p. 7.

12. *Ibid*, p. 42.

13. *The Mercury, or, The Northern Tatler*, 1 January, 1717, quoted in W. J. Couper, *The Edinburgh Periodical Press*, 2 vols (Stirling, 1908) II, p. 17.

14. *Scots Magazine*, 1 (1739) p. ii.

15. Chitnis, *The Scottish Enlightenment*, p. 19.

Signs of Change: Documents

THE MODERNISATION OF THE UNIVERSITIES

1. The impact of the revolution of 1688 on Scottish universities

Edinburgh, July 4th 1690. Act for visitation of Universities, colleges and schools. *Acts of the Parliaments of Scotland*, IX, pp. 163–4.

Our sovereign lord and lady the King and Queens Majesties and the three estates of Parliament considering how necessary it is for the advancement of Religion and learning and for the good of the Church and peace of the kingdom that the universities colleges and schools be provided and served with pious able and qualified professors principals regents masters and others bearing office therein well affected to their Majesties and the established government of Church and State therefore their Majesties with advice of the said three estates of Parliament do statute ordain and enact that from this time forth, no professors principals regents masters or others bearing office in any university college or school within this kingdom be either admitted or allowed to continue in the exercise of their said functions but such as do acknowledge and profess and shall subscribe to the confession of faith ratified and approved by this present Parliament and also swear and subscribe the oath of allegiance to their Majesties; and withall shall be found to be of a pious loyal and peaceable conversation and of good and sufficient literature and abilities for their respective employments and submitting to the government of the Church now settled by law and albeit it be their Majesties undoubted right and prerogative to name visitors and cause visit the said universities and schools, yet at this time their Majesties are pleased to nominate and appoint with advice and consent forsaid the persons under named, viz. (c. 72

names) . . . to be visitors to the effect under written viz. with full power and commission to them or major part of them hereby declared to be their quorum, to meet and visit all universities, colleges and schools within this kingdom, and to take trial of the present professors, principals, regents, masters and others bearing office therein according to the qualifications and rules above mentioned, and such as shall be found to be erroneous scandalous negligent insufficient or disaffected to their Majesty's government, or who shall not subscribe the Confession of Faith, swear and subscribe the oath of allegiance and submit to the government of the Church now settled by law to purge out and remove, as also to consider the foundations of the said universities colleges and schools, and the professors and manner of teaching therein and all things else relating thereto as they shall think most meet and convenient according to the foundations thereof and consistent with the present establishment of Church and State. And to the effect that these presents[1] may be more surely executed, their Majesties with advice foresaid, do further empower the foresaid persons visitors or their quorum to appoint committees of such numbers of their own members as they shall think fit to visit the several universities and colleges within this kingdom with the schools within the bounds to be designed to them, and that according to such instructions and injunctions as they shall think fit to give them; And to the effect that upon report made by the said committee to the aforesaid visitors or their quorum they may proceed and conclude thereupon as they shall see cause; And their Majesties appoint the foresaid visitors to meet at Edinburgh upon the twenty third day of July instant for the first date of their meeting with power to them to adjourn and appoint their own meetings to such days and places as for thereafter they shall judge convenient; And this Commission to endure ay and while their Majesties recall and discharge the same.

[1] 'these presents'—these words, these orders (legal usage).

2. The abolition of regenting in Edinburgh

Minute of the Town Council, 16 June, 1708. MSS Minutes, Edinburgh City Archives, Vol. 39, p. 105. Published in A. Morgan (ed.) *The University of Edinburgh, Charters Statutes, and Acts of the Town Council and the Senatus, 1583–1858* (Edinburgh and London, 1937) pp. 164–5.

The same day the Council, taking to their consideration what may be the most proper methods for advancing of learning in their own College of Edinburgh, have agreed upon the following articles as a Rule of Teaching in the said College:

Primo- That all the parts of Philosophy be taught in two years, as they are in the most famous Universities abroad.

Secundo- That as a consequence of this article there be but two Philosophy Classes in the College, to be taught by two of the four present Professors of Philosophy.

Tertio- That in the first of these Classes the students be taught Logic and Metaphysics, and in the last a compend of Ethics and Natural Philosophy.

Quarto- Because there are many useful things belonging to the Pneumatics [1] and Moral Philosophy which the two Professors in the present method of teaching classes cannot overtake, Therefore it is proposed that one of the two remaining Professors shall be appointed to teach these two parts of Philosophy more fully at such times as the students are not obliged to be in their classes, and because he has not the charge of a class he may have public lessons of Philosophy in the common hall, where all the students may be present at such times as shall be most convenient.

Quinto- That there shall be a fixed Professor of Greek, but so that neither he nor his successors shall upon any pretence whatsoever endeavour to hinder the admission of students into the Philosophy classes in the usual manner, although they have not been taught Greek by him [2].

Sexto- And in regard the present Professors have given proof of their qualifications in all the parts both of Philosophy and Greek, Therefore when any of these four Professors places becomes vacant the remaining Professors of these now in places allenarly [3] shall have the offer of the vacancy according to their standing, and when one chooses it the rest shall in the like manner be allowed to succeed him.

[1] 'Pneumatics'—defined in 1734 by the Senatus of the University as the study of 'the being and perfections of the one true God, the nature of Angels and the soul of man, and the duties of natural religion'. Grant, *op. cit.* II, p. 336. The word is increasingly used, by midcentury, to mean the science of the nature and function of the human mind.

[2] Students might still begin their course by Humanity (Latin) in the first year, and Greek in the second year; but students who had already reached a satisfactory standard in these subjects might enter one of the Philosophy classes immediately.

[3] Scots—sole, only.

3. The abolition of regenting in Glasgow

'Act regulating the University of Glasgow', 19 September, 1727. *Munimenta Alme Universitatis Glasguensis. Records of the University of Glasgow from its foundation till 1727*, 4 vols (Glasgow: Maitland Club, 1854) III, pp. 578–9.

. . . . That neither the professors of Philosophy nor Greek shall, after the 20th day of October, and during the session of the College, teach any other thing than their own proper business . . .

And the commissioners having recommended to the masters of the said three Philosophy classes, to make their election which of the classes they were severally to take, and they having agreed among themselves, and Mr Gershom Carmichael having made a choice of the Ethic class, Mr John Loudon[1] of the Logic class, and the teaching of the Physic class falling to Mr Robert Dick[2],—

The Commissioners statute and ordain, that the said persons respective have in time coming the teaching of the said several classes by them chosen, and that Mr Robert Dick teach the class falling to him, and that they remain so fixed to the said classes; and that all other and subsequent professors of Philosophy coming into the said University be still fixed to one class, and the teaching of the foresaid particular parts of Philosophy allotted to the class in which he shall be fixed.

That the professors of Divinity, Law, Medicine, Oriental Languages, Mathematics, and History, shall yearly teach the business of their respective professions whenever five or more scholars shall apply to them, and that they give not under four lessons every week.

That in case the said number of five scholars do not apply to the said professors betwixt the sitting down of the College and the first day of December thereafter, that such professors shall, after the first day of December aforesaid, prelect publicly once every week at such hour and upon such day of the week as the Faculty shall appoint.

[1] John Loudon—Regent at the University of Glasgow since 1699, he remained Professor Logic until his death in 1750.
[2] Robert Dick, Regent since 1714, Professor of Natural Philosophy until 1751.

4. The attraction of new students

William Carstares 'Considerations and proposals for encouraging of parents in sending their sons to the University of Edinburgh'. Edinburgh University Library, MS La II 407/1–13.

As there's nothing of greater consequence to human societies, a church or nation, than the education of youth: so there is nothing of worse consequence to education than the discouraging of universities; which are the proper sources of learning, and have many advantages for improving of youth, that no private tutor or academy can pretend to.

But notwithstanding of this, many parents of the best sort are discouraged from sending their sons to universities and more especially to that of Edinburgh: considering upon the one hand the expense of keeping at home a particular tutor, to support perhaps one boy; and on the other hand, the visible hazard in sending a boy alone, and committing him wholly to his own management, who being in a strange place, and as yet unacquainted with the world; may fall into a thousand (juvenile curiosities?) and sink himself beyond recovery; before his parents can have the least notion thereof or apply any suitable remedies thereto.

Upon which considerations many parents are induced either to educate their sons at home or send them to private academies; by means of which, universities have fallen into decay, the improvement of youth is generally obstructed, and the general state of learning visibly threatened.

But if the forsaid discouragement could be removed, the university of Edinburgh would be more frequented by students. Not only from all parts of Scotland, but also from England and Ireland, where a great part of her nation's loyal and protestant subjects, are excluded all public universities by means of tests and oaths imposed upon youth.

And whereas proposals have been made at London for sending down the dissenting youths to be educated in the universities of Scotland, and several persons of good note have offered to mortify either to Edinburgh or Glasgow considerable sums of money for carrying on these designs, provided the forsaid difficulties could be removed; it is hoped that all good men who tend to the education of youth and the advancement of learning and the civil and religious interest of the three nations, and more especially the Right Honourable the Town Council of Edinburgh as patrons of the University there will think themselves concerned in a suggestion of so great consequence and contribute their endeavours to give parents all possible encouragement in sending their sons hither for a sober and virtuous education . . .

5. The establishment of a Faculty of Medicine

Minute of the Town Council of Edinburgh, 9 February 1726, MSS Minutes, Edinburgh City Archives, Vol 66, pp. 310–13. Published in Morgan (ed.) *The University of Edinburgh*, pp. 172–4.

The which day the Lord Provost, Baillies, Council and Deacons of Crafts Ordinary and Extraordinary [1] being convened in council anent the petition given in by John Rutherfoord, Andrew Sinclair, Andrew Plummer, and John Innes, Fellows of the Royal College of Physicians at Edinburgh[2], showing that the petitioners had under the Council's protection undertaken the professing and teaching of Medicine in this city, and by the encouragement which the Council had been pleased to grant them had carried it on with some success: That was Medicine professed and taught in the College by the petitioners it would tend more to promote it than to have it taught and professed in the manner hitherto undertaken, That the sole power of instituting such professions in the College and of electing of persons qualified to profess the same was vested in the Council, That the promoting the aforesaid profession was only what was intended by the petitioners, which would tend to the benefit and honour of this city and country, Craving therefore the Council to institute the profession in the College of Edinburgh and appoint the petitioners to teach and profess the same, as the petition bears: Which being maturely considered, and the Council, being fully convinced that nothing can contribute more to the flourishing of this or any other College than that all the parts of academical learning be professed and taught in them by able Professors, were of opinion that it would be of great advantage to this College, city and country that

Medicine in all its branches be taught and professed here by such a number of Professors of that science as may by themselves promote students to their Degrees with as great solemnity as is done in any other College or University at home or abroad. The Council further considering that the petitioners mentioned have given the clearest proof of their capacity and ability to reach the above valuable ends and purposes, they having already professed and taught Medicine with good success and advantage and with the approbation of all the learned in that science here, Do therefore unanimously constitute, nominate, and appoint Andrew Sinclair and John Rutherfoord, Doctors of Medicine, Professors of the Theory and Practice of Medicine, and Andrew Plummer and John Innes, Doctors of Medicine, Professors of Medicine and Chemistry in the College of Edinburgh, with full power to all of them to profess and teach Medicine in all its branches in the said College as fully and freely as the said science is taught in any University or College in this or any other country: And do, by these presents, give, grant, and bestow upon the said four Professors of Medicine and of the particular branches thereof above mentioned, all the liberties, privileges, and immunities that at present or hereafter are or may be enjoyed by the Professors of any other science in the foresaid College, and particularly with full power to them to examine candidates, and to do every other thing requisite and necessary to the graduation of Doctors of Medicine as amply and fully and with all the solemnities that the same is practised and done by the Professors of Medicine in any College or University whatsoever . . . And lastly, it is hereby expressly provided and declared that the said four Professors, or any of them, shall not have any fee or salary for their professing and teaching Medicine, as said is, by virtue of this present Act, or in time coming, which shall be payable out of the revenue or patrimony which does, or may at any time hereafter, belong to the city, whereanent these presents shall be a warrant.

[1] The Council was a complex mixture of representatives from mercantile and craft groups. The full Town Council of 33 members included 6 ordinary deacons and 8 extraordinary deacons, nominated by the trades corporations.

[2] These four men had been lecturing in Edinburgh since 1724, and had established a herb garden in the College Yard. The College already had a Professor of Anatomy, Alexander Monro primus, since 1720, so that it now had a medical faculty of five.

John Rutherfoord lectured on the Practice of Physic from 1726 to 1766, with John Innes, who retired in 1746.

Andrew Sinclair, physician, graduated Angers, took the Chair of the Institues of Medicine, retiring in 1747.

Andrew Plummer, graduate of Leyden and a pupil of Boerhaave, lectured, mainly on chemical pharmacy, till 1755.

6. The emergence of a new Chair: the appointment of Hugh Blair

a. Minute of the Town Council of Edinburgh, 27 June 1760, MSS Minutes, Vol. 76, p. 103. Published in Morgan (ed.) *The University of Edinburgh*, p. 177.

(The Town Council) considering that there is no Professor of Rhetoric in this city's University, And that the Reverend Doctor Hugh Blair, one of the ministers of this city, has for some time past taught that branch of literature with universal applause, And being satisfied that the teaching of Rhetoric in the University would be of singular use to the students and a great benefit to the city, and knowing by experience that the said Doctor Blair is fully qualified for exercising that office, Therefore did and hereby do, with and under the condition aforementioned, nominate and elect the said Dr Hugh Blair to be Professor of Rhetoric in this city's University, with power to him to exercise the said office as fully and freely in all respects as the other Professors in the said University do exercise their several Professions, but with and under this condition alwise, as it is hereby expressly provided and declared, that he shall not be entitled to any salary from the city on that account, And appoint a Commission to be made out in his favour accordingly.

b. Minute of the Town Council, 21 July 1762, MSS Minutes, Vol. 77, p. 245.

A commission by His Majesty under the Privy Seal bearing date the 27 day of April last nominating and present the Rev' d Hugh Blair one of the ministers of Edinburgh Regius Professor of Rhetoric and Belles Lettres in the University of Edinburgh during all the days of his lifetime, Requiring the Magistrates and Town Council of Edinburgh Patrons of the said University and the Principal and other Professors and masters thereof to admit and receive the said

Dr Hugh Blair to the peaceable exercise and possession of the said office in the usual form was read[1]. John Brown City Treasurer on behalf of himself the magistrates council and community did protest that the admission and reception of the said Dr Hugh Blair upon the foresaid commission should not prejudice their right to the patronage of the said college and thereupon took instruments in the Clerks hands[2].

And the Council having considered the foresaid commission and Protest, resolve that the said Dr Hugh Blair be admitted and received into the said office under the foresaid protestation saving and reserving to the city all their rights to the said college and appoint Baillie Hogg to instal him accordingly.

[1] The Regius Chair was endowed with a salary of £70 a year.
[2] 'to take instruments'—to enter. into the formal, authenticated, record.

7. The advantages of Scottish universities

Gilbert Elliot of Minto [1] to Adam Smith, London, 14th November, 1758. Glasgow University Library, MS Gen. 960/ 136. Printed in W. R. Scott, *Adam Smith as Student and Professor* (Glasgow, 1937) pp. 239-40.

London,
14th November 1758.

Dear Sir,

I have of late had a good deal of conversation with Lord Fitzmorris [2] about the education of his brother who is now at Eton and I believe about fifteen or sixteen years of age. He thinks his brother too young to go abroad and, as he left Oxford himself about two years ago, has no sort of inclination to send him to that University. After stating to him, as well as I could, the nature of our Universities and the advantages I thought his brother might draw from being put under your direction, he came to a resolution of advising his father, Lord Shelburne to follow that course. His Lordship has agreed to it, and I have undertaken to open it to you and to learn as soon as possible whether it be agreeable to you to undertake the charge. Lord Shelburne has an immense estate, and can afford if he pleases to settle ten thousand a year upon his second son without at all hurting Lord Fitzmorris, he tells me he will not spare money, but did not wish the boy should be indulged in too great an expense, which, I am afraid, has hitherto been the case. He proposes that he should be in your house and entirely under your direction, and to give you for his board and the inspection of his education a hundred pound a year, or more if it should be thought proper. I understand he is a very good school scholar, very lively, and tolerably ungovernable, but probably will not given you much trouble, as you will have the total charge and direction without any control. If you have no objection to taking him into your house, he will come to immediately, as Lord Fitzmorris tells me he may probably take that opportunity of running over Scotland, paying a visit to Lord Dunmore [3] and putting his brother upon a proper foot (ing). I think myself that a young man of this rank coming to your University may be of advantage to it, especially as I find every thinking man here begins to discover the very absurd constitution of the English Universities, without knowing what to do better. It is indeed possible that Oxford may a little recover itself, by having lately established there, a Professor for the common constitutional law of the Kingdom, and also admitted Masters for some of the exercises, which two last articles have some connection at least with the occupations of ordinary life, and I can hardly say so much for the usual academical institutions, little adapted for the improvement of young men either of rank or liberal views. I have very little doubt but you might soon draw a good many of the youth of this part of the world to pass a winter or two at Glasgow, notwithstanding the distance and disadvantage of the dialect, provided that to your real advantages you were to add the best Masters for the exercises and also for acquiring the French language, an accomplishment indispensably necessary, and which cannot be acquired either at Eton or Westminster, tho' all children, male and female bred in their fathers houses, are regularly taught both to speak and write French with tolerable facility. Pray let me have your answer as soon as possible.

Is your book in the Press, or will it be there soon?

Believe (me) Dear Sir

Yours very faithfully,

Gilbert Elliot

---

[1] Gilbert Elliot, later 3rd baronet of Minto (1722-77), MP and active politician from 1753-77, friendly with a number of the 'literati', and himself also a poet.

[2] Lord Fitzmaurice, better known as the second Earl of Shelburne (1737-

1805), Prime Minister 1782–3. He had one brother, the Hon. Thomas Fitzmaurice (1742–93), who matriculated at Glasgow in 1759, then graduated M.A. at Oxford in 1764. Barrister and M.P. 1763–80.

[3] John, 4th Earl of Dunmore.

PATRONAGE AND APPOINTMENTS

8. Glasgow: the choosing of a Professor of Oriental Languages

Alexander Dunlop[1] to Charles Mackie[2], Glasgow 22 October 1744. Edinburgh University Library, MS Dk. 1. 1.

. . . Dear Sir,
    . . . I know it will be a pleasure to you to be informed that my son was this day chosen to be Professor of Oriental Languages here[3]. We had a meeting this day eight days, in order to appoint a day for the election, when the Principal produced a letter he had received some days before from the Lord Advocate acquainting us that he was informed that Professions was in the gift of the Crown whose rights he was to support, but at the same time, did not at all incline to encroach on the *University's rights*. And therefore wanted to know how the affair stood. We appointed a committee to draw our answer to his letter and send a copy of the King's gift, and to signify our opinion that the Crown had no manner of right[4]; this was sent off on Wednesday, at the same time we appointed this day for the election. Who had occasioned this little squib to be thrown we know not, whatever we may suspect. We met this day, and the Rector having no return from the Lord Advocate, nor indeed did not request any. The election was unanimously in favour of my son, we were all present except Mr Loudon, the wind going easterly. Your servant can be at times unanimous as well as others. . . .

[1] Alexander Dunlop (1684–1747), Son of Principal Dunlop, and first fixed Professor of Greek at Glasgow, from 1704 to 1746.
[2] Charles Mackie (1688–1770) nephew of Principal Carstares, first Professor of Universal Civil History, holding the Chair from 1719 to 1765.
[3] The younger Alexander Dunlop was at the time of the election away from Glasgow tutoring the son of Sir James Campbell in Geneva; the Faculty allowed him to postpone entry to his office for a year. He held the Chair until 1751.
[4] The Chair of Oriental Languages was established in 1709, on receipt of a grant from Queen, and the salary was augmented from gifts by George I in 1716

and 1717. It was argued, however, that this was a revival of an older position, and not a new Regius Chair, in which the right of appointment lay with the Crown.

9. Patronage and the Duke of Argyll

a. John Stevenson [1] to Lord Milton, Edinburgh 2 November 1750. National Library of Scotland MSS SC 169.

My Lord,
Tho' I'm backward to ask favours of the great, I can bring myself to write where personal friendship and interests are less concerned than a public good.

A new vacancy in the University of Glasgow happening by the demise of Mr Loudon, I presume to name Mr George Muirhead [2] as a candidate. He is not only a man cut out for a blessing to a society of that kind; but of universal learning, particularly in all the branches of philosophy, as well as the best Greek scholar anywhere. As the Greek and Latin impressions of Glasgow exceed all the world at present; that branch of business would still rise to a greater height by his assistance to the Fouliss [3], with whom he is in close connexion. If the best principles, sweetest temper, and a grateful heart, recommend a man; he will deserve favour.

At present he is second minister of Dysart, but it's pity his talents were lost when he could be so useful elsewhere.

All I shall trouble your Lordship with further is, my knowledge of most of the masters of that University enables me to say that, if anybody who is thought to be in confidence with the Duke of Argyll, would intimate, in the most private way, never to be heard of; to Principal Campbell and Mr Simson [4], that his Grace would not be offended, if Mr Muirhead were elected; the affair could be done immediately.

I pretend to no claim to ask favours either of his Grace or your Lordship, but knowing that both love to do good, I shall at least be forgiven for having attempted to produce real merit. I am with the greatest respect and devotion
My Lord
Your Lordships most obedient
and most humble
servant,
John Stevenson

[1] John Stevenson (1694–1775) Professor of Logic at Edinburgh University from 1730 to 1775. A distinguished teacher who modernised the teaching of philosophy and introduced the teaching of modern rhetoric and literature into his classes.

[2] The vacant Chair of Logic on this occasion went to Adam Smith. But George Muirhead was elected as Professor of Oriental Languages at Glasgow in 1751, became Professor of Humanity there from 1754 to 1773. He fulfilled Stevenson's predictions by editing a number of works for the Foulis Press.

[3] Robert and Andrew Foulis.

[4] Neil Campbell (?–1761), Principal of Glasgow from 1728–61.
Robert Simson, Professor of Mathematics from 1711 to 1761, nephew of John Simson.

b. Lord Kames to Lord Milton, Kames, 6 September 1755.
National Library of Scotland MSS SC 188.

My Lord,

When anything occurs for the good of the Public, I naturally cast my eyes upon your Lordship, as the fittest person in Scotland for carrying on every word of this kind—Dr Plummer is dead and the properest man in Great Britain to succeed to the Profession of Chemistry is Dr Cullen—He will infallibly raise the reputation of that college which at present is sunk very low; and this in all probability will draw strangers in great abundance to study at Edinburgh. I am I confess the more solicitous about this matter that I know Cullen to be a fast adherent to the Duke of Argyll, and that his Grace has a good opinion of him. I know at the same time that the Doctor is so well esteemed in Edinburgh, that it will require no more to make the point effectual, than your Lordship declaring for him.

> I am with the greatest respect
> Your Lordships
> devoted servant
> Henry Home.

10. The interest of Lord Bute

Lord Bute to William Leechman, London June 10, 1761.
Glasgow University Archives, 31999.

Sir,

I receiv'd the letter you sent me in the name of the University of Glasgow, I have ever held that noble seminary of learning in the highest estimation; I shall be happy to contribute anything in my power towards its greater perfection; the present opportunity of supporting the applications of so many respectable personages, I embrace with real pleasure; and I hope in a few days to transmit the royal nomination; which from the character I have seen drawn of Mr Millar cannot fail to do honour to our young sovereign from whose parental eye the University of Glasgow is not concealed; I am Sir with great regard

> Your obedient
> humble servant
> Bute

Lord Bute to William Leechman, St James's, June 16 1761. Glasgow University Archives, MS 32001.

Sir,

I laid before the King the request you transmitted to me, in the name of the learned body, over which you preside, desiring that Mr John Millar, advocate, might be appointed to the vacant Professorship of Civil Law in your University, and I have the satisfaction to acquaint you that His Majesty has been graciously pleased to comply with your recommendation, and has already signed a warrant, directing a presentation to be issued in favour of Mr Millar[1].

In my own particular, I beg that you, Sir and the gentlemen of the University of Glasgow would believe, that I execute with pleasure the King's commands on this occasion, as I shall always take a great part in the success of whatever is agreeable to so respectable a society.

> Yours with great truth,
> Sir,
> Your most obedient
> humble servant,
> Bute.

[1] This Chair, founded in 1713, was founded as a Regius Chair.

NEW BOOKS, NEW CLUBS

11. The need for books

Thomas Harvie[1] 'Proposals for erecting a booksellers shop and a printing press within the University of Glasgow', Glasgow University Archives, MS 30662. Published in James Maclehose, *The Glasgow University Press, 1638–1931* (Glasgow, 1931) pp. 103–4.

Its needless to show how necessary and advantageous a well furnished shop with books, paper pens ink &c or a printing press within the University will be, or to observe that no learned society has ever flourished to any pitch without those helps. The common practice of all famous seminaries of learning makes this matter of fact evidence and our own experience here sufficiently confirms whatever can be said in its favours, every day teaches us what difficulty there is to get the books that are absolutely necessary for the scholars of all sorts, and how much we are imposed upon when we get them, and as to a printing press, the single consideration of our being obliged to go to Edinburgh in order to get one sheet right printed, make out the absolute necessity of one.

In order to have the University well accommodated with books and a printing press, it is proposed that before the next session of the College, there shall be a well furnish'd shop erected, with books of all sorts, paper, paper books, pens, ink, inkhorns, sealing wax and all other things sold wither in a booksellers or stationers shop, as also that sometime within four years after Whitsunday noon there shall be a printing press erected, with necessary founts and other materials for printing Hebrew Greek and Latin upon the conditions and manner after specified viz.

1. That the Undertaker shall be immediately declared University bookseller and printer, and that the privileges, immunities and advantages which the University can bestow on a bookseller or printer shall be assigned to the undertaker and his assignees whatsoever and that for 40 years.

2ly That a convenient shop and warehouse within the College be allowed gratis to the said undertaker, and the said shop shall be floored with dales[2] and shelves, tables, a brace[3] and chimney and large chace windows put in at the expence of the University.

3ly that when the printing press shall be erected the University furnish a convenient printing house, and for laying up books printed and drying the paper &c.

4ly (two lines deleted in the manuscript)

5 That the undertaker be obliged either to erect the press within the limit above mentioned or forfeit his privileges of bookseller and printer.

[1] A Thomas Harvie appeared as a member of Gershom Carmichael's class in 1704, and as a student of divinity in 1707; in 1714 he was given a bursary to study divinity abroad for one year. He received an appointment as master at the grammar school from 1734 to 1756.

[2] planks.

[3] chimney breast.

12. The Journal of the Easy Club

The Works of Allan Ramsay, edited by Alexander M. Kinghorn and Alexander Law, Vol. V, The Scottish Text Society, fourth series, 7 (Edinburgh and London, 1972) p. 5.

JOURNAL OF THE EASY CLUB
(established in Edinburgh May 1712)

The gentlemen who compose this society considering how much the unmaturity of years want of knowing the world and experience of living therein exposes them to the danger of being drawn away by unprofitable company to the waste of the most valuable part of their time, have resolved at some times to retire from all other business and company and meet in a society by themselves in order that by a mutual improvement in conversation they may become more adapted for fellowship with the politer part of mankind, and learn also from one anothers happy observations to abhor all such nauseous fops as are by their clamorous impertinencies the bane and destruction of all agreeable society, and also to ridicule these pedantic coxcombs who by their unthinking gravity peevish preciseness or modest folly demonstrate themselves the apish counterfeiters of such perfections as God by nature has utterly denied them the capacity of ever attaining to, which sorts of people are so industriously avoided by the Society and others of free tractable and ingenious tempers so carefully encouraged that on the second day of their meeting, after some deliberation it was unanimously determined their society should go under the name of the Easy Club, designing thereby that their denomination should be a check to all unruly and disturbing behaviour among their members. To prevent which also each of them are styled with a particular name taken from some eminent person whose character though they are sensible of their own insufficiency fully to maintain yet everyone knowing something of his patrons history have him before them as an example which as the wise say is more prevalent in reformation than precept. And each member being always called by his patron's name at the meeting makes it impossible he should forget to copy what is laudable in him and what is not so to reject.

May 12 1712. Those who founded the Club called one another by the names of Rochester, Isaac Bickerstaff and Tom Brown—they were in a few days joined by three who assumed the names of Sir Roger L'Estrange, Sir Isaac Newton and——Heywood[1].

[1] These names followed the pseudonyms used in the London *Spectator* and *Tatler*; later English names were renounced and those of famous Scots adopted.

13. The spread of student clubs

R. Wodrow[1], *Analecta; or, Materials for a history of Remarkable Providences; mostly relating to Scotch Ministers and Christians.* Printed for the Maitland Club, 4 vols (Edinburgh, 1842) III, p. 183. February, 1725.

I hear of new clubs setting up in Glasgow, or new names given to former clubs. The Triumpherian Club, known since by the name of Mr T. Harvey's Club[2], now in honour of Mr Wishart, have taken the name of the Sophocardian Club, Buchanan's name for Mr George Wishart. They have, I hear, given to Mr Wishart that subject, 'The rule of moral goodness'; and his brother, Mr G. at Edinburgh 'Whether it was possible for God to make this system of the sun better than it is'[3]. The students, who affect to be persons of bright parts, have a Club they call the Eleutherian Club, and some others affect the name of the Anti-Capadocian Club, because the Capadocians were willing to surrender their liberties tamely to the Romans[4]. The clubs are like to have a very ill influence on religion. People meet in them without any solid grave person to moderate, and give a loose to their fancy and enquiries, with (out) any stated rule of them or any solid principles. They declaim against reading, and cry up thinking.

[1] Robert Wodrow (1679–1734). Son of James Wodrow, Professor of Divinity at Glasgow University, he was educated at Glasgow, and in 1703 became minister of Eastwood, near Glasgow. A well known preacher, active in the Church courts, he was opposed to the law on patronage, and took the orthodox Calvinist view on theological matters. He published in 1721–2 the *History of the Sufferings of the Church of Scotland from the Restoration to the Revolution*; he also left a mass of MSS notes on the biographies of Scottish clergy, and his own reminiscences, from which the *Analecta* have been published.

[2] Possibly the T. Harvie of Document 12, otherwise unknown.

[3] An extremely confusing reference. The reference to 'Sophocardos' (Greek rendering of Wiseheart, or Wishart) is probably to George Wishart (?–1545–6), a distinguished Protestant martyr, and George Buchanan (1506–1582), political and religious reformer and historian. But the contemporary Wisharts involved in these clubs were William Wishart secundus (?–1753) and George Wishart, later minister of the Tron Church Edinburgh, both sons of William Wishart (1660–1729), Principal of Edinburgh University 1716–29.

[4] The Eleutherian Club was possibly called after St Eleutherius (?–189), Pope from 175 to 189, notable for opposing the heresy of the Montanists, who believed spiritual revelations could be achieved through the ecstatic trances of their prophets.

Cappadocia was a province of Eastern Anatolia, important as a Roman client and province.

14. The new Philosophical Society

Colin Maclaurin to Sir John Clerk of Penicuik[1], Edinburgh, May 5 1737. Scottish Record Office, GD 18/5097/1.

Sir,

I was much obliged to you for the observations concerning the comet [2]. I received some later from London, but have been so unlucky as not to have got a sight of it. I am at a great loss for want of a proper place for looking out for such appearances, my windows in the College having a view southwards only. I have delayed making up my account of the eclipses in expectation of some accounts from the North that might enable me to fix the northern limit of the annular appearance; and I do not incline to finish it till I see if I can learn anything concerning this from the ministers who are to be in town next week. I shall send you a copy as soon as I have finished it.

Some gentlemen of your acquaintance have been talking together of forming a society for promoting the study of natural knowledge in this country and for the advancement of the science as much as this may be in their power, in imitation of those that have been established of late in most countries where learning is cultivated. They always reckoned upon you, Sir, as one that would be a support and an ornament to such a society. I am enjoined to acquaint you that they have made some progress in sketching a plan for the society which they will communicate to you when they have an opportunity. In the mean time they would not proceed further without acquainting you and desiring to have your concurrence. Nobody has been as yet spoke to but Lord Aberdour, Lord Hope, Dr Plummer, Mr Munro, Dr Pringle, Mr Lynn and I[3]. But we have made a list of some persons whose inclinations we are to try, and if we find the gentlemen relish the design, we propose to bring them together the first of June, when we would wish to see you if we have not an opportunity more early. If you come to town before that time, please to acquaint me and I shall give you a particular account of what is proposed for a plan for the first year at least. I am also desired to tell you that it is thought to be expedient that the design be kept secret till it be ripe for execution. I am with the greatest respect

Hon'd Sir

Your most obedient

most humble servant

Colin Maclaurin.

[1] Sir John Clerk of Penicuik (1684–1755), lawyer, politician and landowner, with a wide interest in the arts and sciences, and a distinguished patron of learning.

[2] It was said of Colin Maclaurin, a keen astronomer, that 'if an eclipse or comet was to be observed, his telescopes were always in readiness', 'An Account of the Life and Writings of the Author', prefixed to his *Account of Sir Isaac Newton's Philosophical Discoveries*, in four books, 2nd edition, (London, 1750) vii.

[3] The list includes, besides Andrew Plummer and Alexander Monro primus, already mentioned as leading figures of the Edinburgh Medical School, John Pringle (1707–82), Professor of Moral Philosophy 1734–45, who later made an extremely distinguished career as a pioneer of military medicine in the British army, Lord Aberdour (1703–68), later 14th Earl of Morton, representative peer for Scotland 1739–68 and President of the Royal Society, 1764–8, and Lord Hope (1704–81), later 2nd Earl of Hopetoun. 'Mr Lynn' may have been Walter Lynn (1677–1763), English medical writer and inventor.

CHANGES WITHIN THE CHURCH

15. The charge against Professor Simson

Munimenta Alme Universitatis Glasguensis, II, pp. 441–6.

March 30, 1727.

The Presbytery (of Glasgow) having this day appointed their Clerk to draw out the Libel[1] against Professor Simson in mundo, the draft whereof was agreed upon by the Committee for Preserving Purity of Doctrine, and this Presbytery at their joint meeting in Glasgow the 17th of this instant post meridiem, he accordingly did the same . . . They also ordained the witnesses subjoined to that Libel to be cited . . . and the Clerk to give out warrants therefore, and the Libel to be recorded whereof the tenor follows:

The Libel against Professor Simson.

Forasmuch as, according to the Scriptures, and the doctrine of this Church contained in our Confession of Faith and Catechisms founded thereupon, our blessed Lord Jesus Christ, the Son of God, the Second Person of the most glorious and adorable Trinity, is Very and Eternal God, of one substance, and equal with the Father, and that in the Unity of the Godhead there be Three Persons of one substance, Power and Eternity, God the Father, God the Son, and God the Holy Ghost, the Father being of none, neither begotten nor proceeding, the Son Eternally begotten of the Father, and the Holy Ghost Eternally proceeding from the Father and the Son; and which three persons are one true eternal God, the same in substance, equal in power and glory, altho' distinguished by their personal properties, aforesaid. Like as, by the twelfth Act of the General Assembly of this Church, held in the year one thousand seven hundred and ten, all persons are discharged to vent any opinions contrary to any head or article of our Confession of Faith and Catechisms aforesaid, or to use any expressions in relation to the articles of faith, not agreeable to the form of sound words expressed in the Word of God, and the said Confession and Catechisms, which are most valuable pieces of our Reformation, and by the 5th Act of the General Assembly held in the year 1717, you, Mr John Simson, Minister of the Gospel and Professor of Divinity in the University of Glasgow, are particularly prohibited and discharged to use such expressions that do bear and are used by adversaries in any unsound sense, even tho' you should disown that unsound sense, or to teach, preach, or otherwise vent opinions, propositions, or hypotheses, not necessary to be taught in Divinity, and which give more occasion to strife, than to promote edification: Nevertheless it is of verity that you Mr John Simson . . . on one or other of . . . the months of one or other of the years 1725 or 1726 or of the bypast month of the year 1727 . . . used the expressions and proceeded as after-mentioned, . . . to wit, you did alter your teaching concerning the Blessed Trinity, and particularly, that whereas you formerly used to give your students the following caution, viz. That the term Person when applied to the Blessed Three in the Godhead was not to be taken in precisely the same sense as when spoken of creatures, you forbore to give them the same caution: As also you have owned and acknowledged that in speaking of our Lord Jesus Christ, you use not the terms Necessary existence nor Independency, and gave this pretended reason for it, That they are not mentioned concerning Christ in the Holy Scriptures, or our Confession of Faith, or the system you teach. And further in teaching your scholars you have said, That the independency and necessary existence of Lord Christ were things we knew not; that these terms were impertinent and not to be used in talking of the Trinity; and that they were philosophical niceties we knew nothing about, and are ambiguous terms of art; And when your students argued that if the Son was not independent he was not necessarily existent, and so might not have been, and the Father might possibly have been without him; you answered, How do you know, or, how do we know that? . . . As also in teaching you gave it as your own opinion and the judgment of the primitive Fathers that the Three Persons of the Trinity are not to be said to be either numerically or specifically one in substance or essence; but added, they were so the same as to be the One God in Three Persons; but gave not any name to, nor attempted to give any notion of that sameness or oneness; nor can there be any but numerical oneness of substance or essence consistent with the Godhead, who is but one in number and not more. And you having asserted that the Three Persons were all indeed one God, and had all the same infinite Divine perfections, you added, That whether the subject of these perfections was different was a metaphysical question we need not determine. And you likewise affirmed that in the Trinity there are Three intelligent agents or beings . . . All or any of which in so far as they may respectively infer all or any of the errors or unsound dangerous and unsafe ways of teaching or expressing as above libelled, being found proved, you the said Mr John Simson ought to be proceeded against with the censure of the Church, according to the demerit and quality of the offence which shall be proved . . . At appointment of the Presbytery this is signed by

Tho. Orr, Cls. Pres.

[1] Libel—in Scottish law, the complaint on which a prosecution takes place.

16. The impact of new religious ideas, according to Wodrow

R. Wodrow *Analecta*, III, pp. 514–6. 9 May 1728.

And the latitude and looseness in many of the younger sort may be ascribed to the unhappy clubs and meetings which, for many years, have been at Edinburgh, very much to the corrupting of the youth. From whatever this flows, it's certain that there are many sad tokens of wrath among many that are students of Divinity. When the most practical subjects are given, their discourses are general and desultory, and nothing like anything of seriousness or practical exercise, or anything of the old way of discoursing and preaching in this Church used; and when any have discourses of another sort, they are looked down on by the rest, and almost hissed. and there is nothing like meetings for prayer, conference on cases of conscience, or practical subjects, now for many years, as were in Mr Campbell and Mr Meldrum's time[1]; and many meet in other clubs, and for drinking. And, considering the burden of Patrons, and the recommendation of Professors, it's the lads of latitude and brightness, as it's called, and of the haranguing method of preaching, that are likely to get in to congregations; and, indeed, the very outward decency and gravity, proper for such as have their eye to Divinity, is not to be seen among them, as we had instances (in) abundance when they were admitted as witnesses to our Committee for Purity; and I am told several of them go openly to the dancing school at Edinburgh, and are very nice and exact as to that. The Lord appear, and help, and pity this poor Church in time to come!

This brings me to another very melancholy thing I am perfectly well informed of, and that is a terrible relaxation of discipline, and instilling of unaccountable and loose principles, and mocking at serious . . . [2] I thought there had been too much of this at Glasgow, but I find matters are much worse elsewhere. Mr Law, Mr R. Stewart, are noticed for their gravity and recommending religion; and Mr C. Drummond also, I believe, is grave. But I am well informed Mr Scott is quite otherwise, and turning intolerable [3]. He stands not openly to tell his scholars that, next to the New Testament, Homer is the most religious book he knows of in the world! When he comes to such places of the New Testament, in his Greek lessons, as relate to Christ's Divinity, he is sure to give them the most lax and loose sense. For instance 'There is one God, that is God'. He will ask the scholars, whether Christ denies himself to be the one God that is God there?—and boldly assert that God is, in another sense, (more?) good than Christ is, and goes that length as to mock at the common and sound sense of the words. When he comes to the Greek where justification is spoken of, he falls foul upon justification by Christ's righteousness; he tells his scholars, there is no justification but by obeying the commands of God, and any other justification than this is nonsense. To such lengths as these he runs, that the lads, though but young, will say openly enough that he is mad and raving. Alas! what can be expected after such nurture as the boys have when at their languages and philosophy?—and when they come to Divinity, we have seen what their carriage is.

Besides this profaneness is come to a great height, all the villainous profane and obscene books and plays printed at London by Curle and others, are got down from London by Allan Ramsay, and lent out, for an easy price, to young boys, servant women of the better sort, and gentlemen, and vice and obscenity dreadfully propagated. Ramsay has a book in his shop wherein all the names of those that borrow his plays and books, for two pence a night, or some such rate, are set down; and by these, wickedness of all kinds are dreadfully propagated among the youth of all sorts. My informer, my Lord Grange [4], tells me he complained to the magistrates of this, and they scrupled at meddling in it, till he moved that his book of borrowers should be inspected, which was done, and they were alarmed at it, and sent some of their number to his shop to look through some of his books; but he had notice an hour before, and had withdrawn a great many of the worst, and nothing was done to purpose. This, with the plays and interludes, come down from England this winter, of which before, dreadfully spreads all abominations, and profaneness, and lewdness; and a villainous, obscene thing is no sooner printed at London, that it's spread and communicated at Edinburgh.

[1] George Campbell (?-1701) Minister, deprived under the Restoration, returning in 1690 to be minister of the Old Kirk Edinburgh, and Professor of Divinity at Edinburgh University from 1690-1701.
George Meldrum (1634-1709) Minister, deprived of his living after 1681. He returned to be minister of Tron Church, Edinburgh, from 1692, and succeeded George Campbell as Professor of Divinity from 1701 to 1709.
[2] Several words missing in the MS here.
[3] William Law, Regent at the University of Edinburgh from 1690. In 1708 he took the Chair of Moral Philosophy, which he held until 1729.
Robert Stewart. Regent at Edinburgh from 1703, he held the Chair of Natural Philosophy from 1708 to 1742.
Colin Drummond, Regent at Edinburgh, appointed in 1707. From 1708 to 1730 he was Professor of Logic, and from 1730 to 1738 Professor of Greek. He taught Logic in the old fashioned way, but was probably a member of the Rankenian Club.
William Scott, Regent at Edinburgh from 1695, Professor of Greek from 1708 to 1729, and Professor of Moral Philosophy 1729-34.
[4] James Erskine, Lord Grange (1679-1754), Lord Justice Clerk, a strict and active presbyterian.

THE NEW TEACHING

17. On the hypotheses of philosophers

Colin Maclaurin, *An Account of Sir Isaac Newton's Philosophical Discoveries, in four books*, 2nd edition (London, 1750) pp. 7-9.[1]

Sir Isaac Newton saw how extravagant such attempts were, and therefore did not set out with any favourite principle or supposition, never proposing to himself the convention of a system. He saw that it was necessary to consult nature herself, to attend carefully to her manifest operations, and to extort her secrets from her by well chosen and repeated experiments. He would admit no objections against plain experience from metaphysical considerations, which, he saw, had often misled philosophers, and had seldom been of real use in their enquiries. He avoided presumption, he had the necessary patience as well as genius; and having kept steadily to the right path, he therefore succeeded.

Experiments and observations, tis true, could not alone have carried him far in tracing the causes from their effects, and explaining the effects from their causes: a sublime geometry was his guide in this nice and difficult enquiry. This is the instrument, by which alone the machinery of a work, made out with so much art, could be unfolded; and therefore he sought to carry it to the greatest height. Nor is it easy to discern, whether he has showed greater skill, and been more successful, in improving and perfecting the instrument, or in applying it to use. He used to call his philosophy *experimental philosophy*, intimating, by the name, the essential difference there is betwixt it and those systems that are the product of genius and invention only. These could not long subsist; but his philosophy, being founded on experiment and demonstration, cannot fail till reason or the nature of things are changed.

In order to proceed with perfect security, and to put an end for ever to disputes, he proposed that, in our enquiries into nature, the methods of *analysis* and *synthesis* should be both employed in a proper order; that we should begin with the phenomena, or effects, and from investigate the powers or causes that operate in nature; that, from particular causes, we should proceed to the more general ones, till the argument end in the most general: this is the method of analysis. Being once possesst of these causes, we should then descend in a contrary order; and from them, as established principles, explain all the phenomena that are their consequences, and prove our explications: and this is the *synthesis*. It is evident that, as in mathematics, so in natural philosophy, the investigation of difficult things by the method of *analysis* ought ever to precede the method of composition, or the *synthesis*. For in any other way, we can never be sure that we assume the principles which really obtain in nature; and that our system, after we have composed it with great labour, is not mere dream and illusion.

By proceeding according to this method, he demonstrated from observations, analytically, that gravity is a general principle; from which he afterwards explained the system of the world. By *analysis* he discovered new and wonderful properties of light, and from there, accounted for many curious phenomena in a *synthetic* way. But while he was thus demonstrating a great number of truths, he could not but meet with hints of many other things, that his sagacity and diligent observation suggested to him, which he was not able to establish with equal certainty: and as these were not to be neglected, but to be separated with care from the others, he therefore collected them together, and proposed them under the modest title of *queries*.

By distinguishing these so carefully from each other, he has done the greatest service to this part of learning, and has secured his philosophy against any hazard of being disproved or weakened by future discoveries. He has taken care to give nothing for demonstration but what must ever be found such; and having separated from this what he owns is not so certain, he has opened matter for the enquiries of future ages, which may confirm and enlarge his doctrines, but can never refute them.

[1] The *Account* was composed in 1728 while Maclaurin was lecturing at Edinburgh University, on the occasion of Newton's death, though it was first published only in 1748.

18. Newtonianism and moral philosophy

George Turnbull, *The Principles of Moral Philosophy. An Enquiry into the wise and good government of the moral world* (London, 1740) Preface, p. iii [1].

The great Master, to whose truly marvellous (I had almost said more than human) sagacity and accuracy, we are indebted for all the greatest improvements that have been made in Natural Philosophy, after pointing out in the clearest manner, the only way by which we can acquire real knowledge of any part of nature, corporeal or moral, plainly declares, that he looked upon the enlargement Moral Philosophy must needs receive, so soon as Natural Philosophy, in its full extent, being pursued in that only proper method of advancing it should be brought to any considerable degree of perfection, to be the principal advantage mankind and human society would then reap from such science.

It was by this important, comprehensive hint, I was led long ago to apply myself to the study of the human mind in the same way as to that of the human body, or any other part of *Natural Philosophy*: that is, to try whether due enquiry into moral nature would not soon enable us to account for *moral*, as the best of *Philosophers* teaches us to explain *natural* phenomena.

Now, no sooner had I conceived this idea of moral researches, than I began to look carefully at the better ancients, (into *Plato's* works in particular) to know their opinion of human nature, and of the order of the world. And by this research I quickly found, that they had a very firm persuasion of an infinitely wise and good administration, actually prevailing at present throughout the whole of nature, and therefore very likely to prevail for ever, founded partly, upon what they were able to comprehend in general of order in the government of the sensible world; but chiefly (for they had made no very great advances in what is now commonly called Natural Philosophy) upon the great insight they had acquired into the moral constitution of man, by applying themselves to moral enquiries. They were able to discern clearly from thence, that man is very well fitted and qualified for attaining to a very high degree of moral perfection even here; and being satisfied, that such care is taken of virtue, and such provision made for her in this life, as is most proper and best suited to her first state of formation and discipline, they could entertain any doubts of the kind concern of Heaven about *her* to be carried on, as may best serve the purpose of general good, by proper steps, for ever.

AND accordingly what I now publish, is an attempt (in consequence of such observations as I have been able to make or have been led to by others) *to vindicate human nature, and the ways of God to man*, by reducing the more remarkable appearances in the human system to excellent general laws; i.e. to powers and laws of powers admirably adapted to produce a very noble species of being in the rising scale of life and perfection.

[1] Turnbull wrote of his book: 'Let me just add, that tho' this enquiry hath not been very long by me in the shape it now appears, yet it is (a few things taken from late writers excepted) the substance of several *pneumatological* discourses (as they are called in the school language) read above a dozen years ago to students of moral philosophy, by way of preparative to a course of lectures, *on the rights and duties of mankind' Ibid*, p. xii.

2 The Ideas of Francis Hutcheson

The ideas of Francis Hutcheson (see Biographical Notes) seemed to many to embody the origins of the Scottish Enlightenment; the classic nineteenth century writer, T. H. Buckle, wrote that:

> Hutcheson . . . did not fear to construct a system of morals according to a plan entirely secular, and no example of which had been exhibited in Scotland before his time . . . Though he was a firm believer in revelation, he held that the best rules of conduct could be ascertained without its assistance, and could be arrived at by the unaided wit of man; and that, when arrived at, they were, in their aggregate to be respected as the Law of Nature. This confidence in the power of the human understanding was altogether new in Scotland and its appearance forms an epoch in the national literature.[1]

Few historians today would see Hutcheson in quite those terms; rather, he articulated, and brought together ideas which were already current in eighteenth century Scotland, encouraged by political and religious changes. His arguments were to have considerable effect within the Church of Scotland, providing a philosophical framework for those who were later to be called the Moderate party. Hutcheson himself was arraigned, in 1738, before the Presbytery of Glasgow, for teaching 'the following two false and dangerous doctrines: first, that the standard of moral goodness was the promotion of the happiness of others; and second, that we could have a knowledge of good and evil, without and prior to a knowledge of God'[2]. Both these propositions *could* be drawn from a very superficial study of Hutcheson's work, but fundamentally misrepresented his position. For him, the task of philosophy was 'to search accurately into the constitution of our nature, to see what sort of creatures we are; for what purposes nature has formed us; what

74

character God Our Creator requires us to maintain'[3]. The important point here is that Hutcheson proposed to base his moral philosophy on a thorough empirical study of human nature, a study which was intended to illuminate God's purpose for man, not to replace it. Nevertheless, in view of the contemporary concern over deism among orthodox circles, Hutcheson's thinking appeared suspect; though the complaints made against him were not upheld, and he was able to continue to educate the students of Glasgow.

The early documents included here are intended to illustrate the evolution of Hutcheson's view of man's moral faculty. Hutcheson rejected the view of some contemporary philosophers that men could discover moral rules by the use of their reason; he believed, rather, in the existence of a moral faculty, or sense, which perceived moral goodness, or in other words, a feeling of moral pleasure. This argument emerged partly from an analogy with the sense of beauty, and was certainly influenced by the writings on aesthetics of Lord Shaftesbury (Document 1). The moral sense was implanted in man by God (Document 3). But it is true that Hutcheson does also use the phrases 'the general interests of mankind', and 'the greatest happiness of the greatest number'; this might suggest that he was concerned to measure actions by their contribution to the general good, by their utility. The problem was that of distinguishing between judging an act by its motives and by its effects. Sometimes Hutcheson tends to assume that there will be no difference, and that an act that is benevolently motivated will automatically be for the good of society (Document 4). His discussion of social and political issues is based very much on those two assumptions: that man's moral sense will indicate what is right *and* that moral actions would be justified by the welfare and happiness of all. The tendency of his moral teaching was therefore to encourage the study of human nature, and of the moral sense, and towards optimism for the future progress of man, an optimism which left little scope for the understanding of the doctrine of original sin. The Divine plan, ordered and harmonious, once understood, could operate only for the further good of mankind. The tone of Hutcheson's work is very much that of the benevolent moralist, the teacher of ethics whose authorities are Aristotle and Cicero rather than Christian theologians. The impression is a misleading one, since Hutcheson did not fail to place his work within a Christian context—but it is one that it is very easy to gain.

Hutcheson drew heavily on the traditions of teaching already established for his Chair at Glasgow. Gershom Carmichael, his predecessor, had made considerable use of the work of the seventeenth century natural lawyers, and had himself edited and annotated Pufendorf's *De officio hominis et civis* in 1718. The importance of these writers was that they provided a framework within which discussion of man's role within society, regulated by natural law and natural rights, could take place, and purely legal concerns broadened to include material of political, social and economic importance. In his *Short Introduction to Moral Philosophy*, Hutcheson divided his subject matter into three books, 'The Elements of Ethics', 'The Elements of the Law of Nature', and 'The Principles of Economics and Politics'. If the ordering of this work is compared to Pufendorf's study (translated as *The Whole Duty of Man, according to the Law of Nature*[4]) there is certainly a correspondence in the ordering of the subject matter, and sometimes the direct derivation of material is clear. Document 10, which sets out the three contracts necessary to the entering of civil society, is derived directly from Pufendorf[5]. Yet there were very significant differences also. Hutcheson laid stress on the moral faculty as the means of perceiving the law of nature; Pufendorf stressed that:

> the law of nature asserts that this or that thing ought to be done, because from right reason it is concluded, that the same is necessary for the preservation of society amongst men[6].

Hutcheson's analysis of natural law depended more heavily on the perceptions of the moral sense than on the operation of reason. Yet throughout his later documents, in dealing with the foundations of the civil power (Document 10), with family relationships and the ordering of civil governments (Documents 8–10), Hutcheson clearly owes much to the view of the natural lawyers 'that mankind cannot be preserved without a sociable life',[7] that social institutions are natural to man.

But these discussions are also overlaid by a particular political emphasis, .by a Whiggish political outlook. It is clear from Documents 8, 12–14, that Hutcheson rejects authoritarian government within large and small societies. Within the family, he condemns patriarchy, defending the rights of wives in marriage, and limiting the powers of parents over their children. His comments on slavery are perhaps unexpected; though he rejects the very notion that any man may lose his 'natural rights' and become merely 'a piece of goods', yet he can see the alienation of a man's right to labour as a punishment for persistent idleness and indebtedness in the lower orders (Document 8). His discussion of political institutions, of monarchy, aristocracy and democracy, argues that there should be a close relationship between the holding of political power, and the distribution of landownership within a society; if necessary legislation should prevent the accumulation of over-large estates in a democracy, by an 'agrarian law'—the interests of the many should outweigh the selfishness of the few. This emphasis on the balance to be preserved between property and power was typical of writers who might see themselves as 're-publicans' or 'commonwealthsmen', who looked back to the gentry republic depicted in the *Oceana* (1656) of James Harrington (1611–77). Harrington argued that it was essential for the stability of society both that a balance should be preserved between the holding of property and political power, and that an equilibrium should be maintained between the different elements of government: the democratic aristocratic and executive branches. Hutcheson pro-posed constitutional mechanisms by which this equilibrium might be achieved; in his discussion of different forms of government he acknowledged that he owed most to the classic works of Aristotle, and to the 'republican' solutions of Harrington[8]. He was interested also in economic affairs, and distinguished between the advantages of a solid material prosperity, beneficial to all, and the corrupting effects of unlimited luxury; his detailed economic proposals are mentioned in Chapter 6. In general, his arguments were for a balanced, liberal society, in which authority was limited by law, in which 'natural liberties' were to be maintained, yet in which the privileges of the few could be restrained in the interests of the many. Documents 13 and 14 show that Hutcheson was not afraid to advocate the right to political resistance, and indeed that he saw the people as in general 'too tame and tractable'. Document 14 is included as an indication of Hutcheson's foresight; it was written some twenty years before the American colonists began to question their own situation.

Hutcheson's work is of considerable importance in the evolution of Enlightenment thought. It marks the real beginning of the serious tradition of moral philosophy in Scotland; and here it is merged with an analysis of social, political and economic institutions, derived at least in part from natural law theory. Hutcheson's insights were capable of further development, and later writers were to take up these themes. He himself was recognised as an outstanding teacher, and his views were inherited through students and followers, inside and outside the established Church of Scotland.

NOTES

1. Henry Thomas Buckle, *On Scotland and the Scotch Intellect*, edited and with an introduction by H. J. Hanham (Chicago, 1972) p. 245.

2. John Rae, *Life of Adam Smith* (London, 1895) pp. 12–13.

3. F. Hutcheson, *A Short Introduction to Moral Philosophy in three books containing the elements of ethicks and the law of nature*. Translated from the Latin (Glasgow, 1747) p. 2.

4. The edition used here is the fifth edition, translated by Andrew Tooke (London, 1735).

5. *The Whole Duty of Man*, pp. 221–2.

6. *Ibid.* p. 4.

7. *Ibid.* p. 41.

8. See, for example, *A System of Moral Philosophy, in three books*, 2 vols (London, 1755) II, pp. 243, 259, 266.

The Ideas of Francis Hutcheson: Documents

HUTCHESON ON THE MORAL SENSE

1. His aesthetic views: the understanding of beauty

An Inquiry into the Original of our Ideas of Beauty and Virtue; in two treatises. Second edition, corrected and enlarged (London, 1726) pp. 7–9.

Let it be observed, that in the following papers , the word beauty is taken for the idea raised in us, and a sense of beauty for our power of receiving this idea. Harmony also denotes our pleasant ideas arising from composition of sounds, and a good ear (as it is generally taken) a power of perceiving this pleasure. . . .

It is of no consequence whether we call these ideas of beauty and harmony perceptions of the external senses of seeing and hearing, or not. I should rather choose to call our power of perceiving these ideas, an internal sense, were it only for the convenience of distinguishing them from other sensations of seeing and hearing, which men may have without perception of beauty and harmony. It is plain from experience, that many men have in the common meaning, the senses of seeing, and hearing perfect enough; they perceive all the simple ideas separately, and have their pleasures; they distinguish them from each other, such as one colour from another, either quite different, or the stronger or fainter of the same colour, when they are placed beside each other, although they may often confound their names, when they occur apart from each other; as some do the names of green and blue: they can tell in separate notes, the higher, lower, sharper or flatter, when separately sounded; in figures they discern the length, breadth, wideness of each line, surface, angle; and may be as capable of hearing and seeing at great distances as any men whatsoever; and yet perhaps they shall find no pleasure in musical compositions, in painting, architecture, natural landscape; or but a very weak one in comparison of what others enjoy from the same objects. This greater capacity of receiving such pleasant ideas we commonly call a fine genius or taste: in music we seem universally to acknowledge something like a distinct sense from the external one of hearing, and call it a good ear; and the like distinction we should probably acknowledge in other objects, had we also got distinct names to denote these powers of perception by.

There will appear another reason perhaps afterwards, for calling this power of perceiving the ideas of beauty, an internal sense, from this, that in some other affairs, where our external senses are not much concerned, we discern a sort of beauty, very like, in many respects to that observed in sensible objects, and accompanied with like pleasure: such is that beauty perceived in theorems, or universal truths, in general causes, and in some extensive principles of action.

2. The existence of the 'moral sense'

A System of Moral Philosophy, in three books. 2 vols (London, 1755) I, pp. 58–61.

There is therefore, as each one by close attention and reflection may convince himself, a natural and immediate determination to approve certain affections, and actions consequent upon them; or a natural sense of immediate excellence in them, not referred to any other quality perceivable by our other senses or by reasoning. When we call this determination a *sense* or *instinct*, we are not supposing it of that low kind dependent on bodily organs, such as even the brutes have. It may be a constant settled determination in the soul itself, as much as our powers of judging and reasoning. And 'tis pretty plain that *reason* is only a subservient power to our ultimate determinations either of perceptions or will. The ultimate end is settled by some sense, and some determination of will: by some sense we enjoy happiness, and self-love determines to it without reasoning. Reason can only direct to the means; or compare two ends previously constituted by some other immediate powers . . .

As some others of our immediate perceptive powers are capable of culture and improvement, so is this moral sense, without presupposing any reference to a superior power of reason to which their perceptions are to be referred. We once had pleasure in the simple artless tunes of the vulgar. We indulge ourselves in music; we meet with finer and more complex compositions. In these we find a pleasure much higher, and begin to despise what formerly pleased us. A judge, from the notions of pity, gets many criminals acquitted; we approve this sweet tenderness of heart. But we find that violence and outrages abound; the sober, just and industrious are plagued, and have no security. A more extensive view of a public interest shows some sorts of pity to occasion more extensive misery, than arises from a strict execution of justice. Pity of itself never appears deformed; but a more extensive affection, a love to society, a zeal to promote general happiness, is a more lovely principle, and the want of this renders a character deformed. This only shows, what we shall presently confirm, that among the several affections approved there are many degrees: some much more lovely than others. Tis thus alone we correct any apparent disorders in this *moral faculty*, even as we correct our reason itself. As we improve and correct a low taste for harmony by inuring the ear to finer compositions; a low taste for beauty, by presenting larger systems to our mind, and more extensive affections towards them; and thus finer objects are exhibited to the moral faculty, which it will approve, even when these affections oppose the effect of some narrower affections, which considered by themselves would be truly lovely. No need here of reference to an higher power of perception, or to reason . . .

This moral sense from its very nature appears to be designed for regulating and controlling all our powers. This dignity and commanding nature we are immediately conscious of, as we are conscious of the power itself. Nor can such matters of immediate feeling be otherways proved but by appeals to our hearts. It does not estimate the good it recommends as merely differing in degree, though of the same kind with other advantages recommended by other senses, so as to allow us to practise smaller moral evils acknowledged to remain such, in order to obtain some great advantages of other sorts; or to omit what we judge in the present case to be our duty or morally good, that we may decline great evils of another sort. But as we immediately perceive the difference in kind, and that the dignity of enjoyment from fine poetry, painting, or from knowledge is superior to the pleasures of the palate, were they never so delicate; so we immediately discern moral good to be superior in kind and dignity to all others which are perceived by the other perceptive powers.

3. The origins of the moral sense

A Short Introduction to Moral Philosophy in three books containing the elements of ethicks and the law of nature. Translated from the Latin. (Glasgow, 1747) pp. 20–1.

Nor need we apprehend, that according to this scheme which derives all our moral notions from a sense, implanted however in the soul and not dependent on the body, the dignity of virtue should be impaired. For the constitution of nature is ever stable and harmonious: nor need we fear that any change in our constitution should also change the nature of virtue, more that we should dread the dissolution of the Universe by a change of the great principle of Gravitation. Nor will it follow from this scheme that all sorts of affections and actions were originally indifferent to the Deity, so that he could as well have made us approve the very contrary of what we now approve, by giving us senses of a contrary nature. For if God was originally omniscient, he must have foreseen, that by his implanting kind of affections, in an active species capable of profiting or hurting each other, he would consult the general good of all; and that implanting contrary affections would necessarily have the contrary effect: in like manner by implanting a sense which approved all kindness and beneficence, he foresaw that all these actions would be made immediately agreeable to the agent, which also on other accounts were profitable to the system; whereas a contrary sense . . . would have made such conduct immediately pleasing, as must in other respects be hurtful both to the agent and the system. If God therefore was originally wise and good, he must necessarily have preferred the present constitution of our sense approving all kindness and beneficence, to any contrary one; and the nature of virtue is thus as immutable as the divine Wisdom and Goodness. Cast the consideration of these perfections of God out of this question, and indeed nothing would remain certain or immutable.

NATURAL RIGHTS AND NATURAL LAW

4. The emergence of individual rights

System of Moral Philosophy, I, pp. 252–3.

From the constitution of our *moral faculty* above-explained, we have our notions of *right* and *wrong*, as characters of affections and actions. The affections approved as right, are either universal goodwill and love of moral excellence, or such particular kind affections as are consistent with these. The actions approved as *right*, are such as are wisely intended either for the general good, or such good of some particular society or individual as is consistent with it. The contrary affections and actions are *wrong* . . .

Our notion of *right* as a moral quality competent to some person, as when we say one has a *right* to such things, is a much more complex conception. Whatever action we would deem either as virtuous or innocent were it done by the agent in certain circumstances, we say he has a *right* to do it. Whatever one so possesses and enjoys in certain circumstances, that we would deem it a wrong action in any other to disturb or interrupt his possession, we say tis *his right*, or he has a *right* to enjoy or possess it. Whatever demand one has upon another in such circumstances that we would deem it wrong conduct in that other not to comply with it, we say one has a *right* to what is thus demanded. Or we may say more briefly, a man hath a *right* to do, possess, or demand anything 'when his acting, possessing, or obtaining from another in these circum-stances tends to the good of society, or to the interest of the individual consistently with the rights of others and the general good of society, and obstructing him would have the contrary tendency'.

5. The natural state of man

System of Moral Philosophy, I, pp. 280–1.

When we speak of the different states of men, by a *state* we do not mean any transient condition a man may be in for a little time, nor any obligation he may be under to one or two transient acts, but 'a permanent condition including a long series of rights and obligations.' The conditions men may be in as to sickness or health, beauty or deformity, or any other circumstances which are considered in the other arts, are foreign to our purpose. The moral states of men always include a series of moral obligations, and rights.

In the first state constituted by nature itself we must discern abundantly from the doctrine of the preceding book that there are many sacred rights competent to men, and many obligations incumbent on each one toward his fellows. The whole system of the mind, especially our *moral faculty*, shows that we are under natural bonds of beneficence and humanity toward all, and under many more special ties to some of our fellows, binding us to many services of an higher kind, than what the rest can claim: nor need we other proofs here that this first state founded by nature is so far from being that of war and enmity, that it is a state where we are all obliged by the natural feelings of our hearts, and by many tender affections, to innocence and beneficence toward all: and that war is one of the accidental states arising solely from injury, when we or some of our fellows have counteracted the dictates of their nature.

Tis true that in this state of liberty where there are no civil laws with a visible power to execute their sanctions, men will often do injurious actions contrary to the laws of their nature; and the resentments of the sufferers will produce wars and violence. But this proves nothing as to the true nature of that state, since all the laws and obligations of that state enjoin peace and justice and beneficence. In civil societies many disobey the law, by theft and violence, but we do not thence conclude that a political state is a state of war among men thus united.

6. The existence of a state of natural liberty

System of Moral Philosophy, I, pp. 283–4.

This state of natural liberty obtains among those who have no common superior or magistrate, and are only subject to *God* and the law of nature. Tis no fictitious state; it always existed and must exist among men, unless the whole earth should become one empire. The parental power of the first parents of mankind must soon have expired when their children came to maturity, as we shall show hereafter or at least when the parents died. This state of liberty probably continued a long time among the several heads of families before civil governments were constituted. And tis not improbable that it yet subsists in some ruder parts of the world. Nay it still must subsist among the several independent states with respect to each other, and among the subjects of different states who may happen to meet in the ocean, or in lands where no civil power is constituted. The laws of nature are the laws of this state, whether they be confirmed by civil power or not; and tis the main purpose of civil laws and their sanctions, to restrain men more effectually by visible punishments from the violation of them. The same reasons which justify the greater part of our civil laws, show the obligations of men to observe them as laws of nature abstracting from any motives from secular authority.

7. The natural rights of man

System of Moral Philosophy, I, pp. 293–300.

Private rights of individuals according to their different originals are neither *natural* or *adventitious*. The *natural* are such as each one has from the constitution of nature itself without the intervention of any human contrivance, institution, compact or deed. The *adventitious* arise from some human institution, compact or action.

The following natural rights of each individual seem of the perfect sort.

1. A right to life, and to that perfection of body which nature has given, belongs to every man as man, while no important public interest requires his being exposed to death, or wounds. This right is violated by unjust assaults, maiming or murdering . . .

2. As nature has implanted in each man a desire of his own happiness, and many tender affections towards others in some nearer relations of life, and granted to each one some understanding and active powers, with a natural impulse to exercise them for the purposes of these natural affections; tis plain each one has a natural right to exert his powers, according to his own judgement and inclination, for these purposes, in all such industry, labour, or amusements, as are not hurtful to others in their persons or goods, while no more public interests necessarily requires his labours, or requires that his actions should be under the direction of others.

This right we call *natural liberty*. Every man has a sense of this right, and a sense of the evil of cruelty in interrupting this joyful liberty of others without necessity for some more general good. . . . Let men instruct, teach, and convince their fellows as far as they can about the proper use of their natural powers, or persuade them to submit voluntarily to some wise plans of civil power where their important interests shall be secured. But till this be done, men must enjoy their natural liberty as long as they are not injurious, and while no great public interest requires some restriction of it.

This right of natural liberty is not only suggested by the selfish parts of our constitution but by many generous affections, and by our *moral sense*, which represents our own voluntary actions as the grand dignity and perfection of our nature.

3. A like natural right every intelligent being has about his own opinions, speculative or practical, to judge according to the evidence that appears to him. This right appears from the very constitution of the rational mind which can assent or dissent solely according to the evidence presented, and naturally desire knowledge . . .

4. As God, by the several affections and the moral faculty he has given us, has showed us the true ends and purposes of human life and all our powers; promoting the universal happiness, and, as far as is consistent with it, our own private happiness, and that of such as are dear to us; in conformity to his own gracious purposes; we must discern not only a right that each one has over his own life to expose it to even the greatest dangers when tis necessary for these purposes, but that it is frequently the most honourable and lovely thing we can do, and what we are sacredly obliged to out of duty to God and our fellow-creatures. . . .

5. Each one has a natural right to the use of such things as are in their nature fitted for the common use of all; (of which hereafter:) and has a like right, by any innocent means, to acquire property in such goods as are fit for occupation and property, and have not been occupied by others. The natural desires of mankind, both of the selfish and social kind, show this right. . . .

6. For the like reasons every innocent person has a natural right to enter into an intercourse of innocent offices or commerce with all who incline to deal with him. . . .

7. As we all have a strong natural desire of esteem, and the greatest aversion to infamy, every man has a natural right to the simple character of probity and honesty, and of dispositions fit for a

social life, until he has forfeited this right by an opposite conduct.

8. From the natural and strong desires of marriage and offspring we may discern the natural right each one has to enter into the matrimonial relations with anyone who consents, and is not in this matter subjected to the control of others or under a prior contract. In this matter, as much as any, an opinion of happiness and a mutual good liking is necessary to the happiness of the parties, and compulsion must create misery.

That all these rights are of the perfect sort, must appear from the great misery which would ensue from the violation of them to the person thus injured; and a general violation of them must break off all friendly society among men.

The natural equality of men consists chiefly in this, that these natural rights belong equally to all: this is the thing intended by the natural equality, let the term be proper or improper. Everyone is a part of that great system, whose greatest interest is intended by all the laws of *God* and nature. These laws prohibit the greatest or wisest of mankind to inflict any misery on the meanest, or to deprive them of any of their natural rights, or innocent acquisitions, when no public interest requires it. These laws confirm in the same manner to all their rights, natural or acquired, to the weak and simple their small acquisitions, as well as their large ones to the strong and artful. . . . There is *equality in right*, how different soever the objects may be; that *jus aequum*, in which the Romans placed true freedom.

THE INSTITUTIONS OF SOCIETY

8. Family relationships

a. HUSBAND AND WIFE

System of Moral Philosophy, II, p. 163.

The tender sentiments and affections which engage the parties into this relation of marriage, plainly declare it to be a state of equal partnership or friendship, and not such a one wherein the one party stipulates to himself a right of governing in all domestic affairs, and the other promises subjection. Grant that there were generally superior strength both of body and mind in the males, this does not give any perfect right of government in any society. It could at best only oblige the other party to pay a greater respect or honour to the superior abilities. And this superiority of the males in the endowments of mind does not at all hold universally. If the males more generally excel in fortitude, or strength of genius; there are other as amiable dispositions in which they are as generally surpassed by the females.

b. PARENTS AND CHILDREN

System of Moral Philosophy, II, pp. 188–90.

The intention of God in this matter, is manifest by this whole contrivance. The parental affection suggests the permanent obligation, on parents to preserve their children and consult their happiness to the utmost of their power . . . .

The manifestly disinterested nature of this affection shows at once the nature and duration of the parental power. The foundation of the right is the weakness and ignorance of childhood, which makes it absolutely necessary that they should be governed a long time by others: and the natural affection points out the parents as the proper governors, where no prudent civil institution has provided more effectually for their education. The generous nature of this affection shows that the power committed by nature is primarily intended for the good of the children, and, in consequence of their happiness, for the satisfaction also, and joy of the affectionate parent. The right therefore cannot extend so far as to destroy the children, or keep them in a miserable state of slavery. When they attain to mature years, and the use of reason, they must obtain that liberty which is necessary to any rational enjoyment of life. The parental affection naturally secures to them this emancipation, as the reason God has given them entitles them to it.

This foundation of the parental power plainly shows that it equally belongs to both parents; and that the mother is wronged when she is deprived of her equal share, unless where she has voluntarily consented, in dependence on the superior wisdom of her husband to submit all domestic matters to his last determination. But whenever the father does not interpose, or is absent, or dead, the whole right is in the mother.

C. MASTER AND SERVANT: AND THE INSTITUTION OF SLAVERY

System of Moral Philosophy, II, pp. 199–203.

The labours of any persons of tolerable strength and sagacity are of much more value than his bare maintenance. We see that the generality of healthy people can afford a good share of the profits of their labours for the support of a young family, and even for pleasure and gaiety. If a servant obliged himself by contract to perpetual labours for no other compensation than his bare maintenance, the contract is plainly unequal and unjust; and being of the onerous kind, where equality is professed on both sides, he has a perfect right to a further compensation, either in some *peculium*, or little stock for him and his family, or in a humane maintenance for his family.

Such a servant, whether for life or a term of years, is to retain all the rights of mankind, valid against his master, as well as all others, excepting only *that* to his labours, which he has transferred to his master: and in lieu of this he has a right to the maintenance as above mentioned, or to the wages agreed on. If by custom masters assume any reasonable jurisdiction over their domestics, not inconsistent with their safety and happiness, the servant, by voluntarily entering into the family, is deemed to have subjected himself to this jurisdiction; even as a foreigner who resides in a state, subjects himself to the laws of it as far as they relate to foreigners.

Where one has not transferred a right to all his labours, but only engaged for work of a certain kind; he is obliged to that work only; and in other respects is as free as his master. In none of these cases can the master transfer his right, or oblige the servant to serve another, unless this was expressly agreed on in the contract. . . .

Men may justly be placed in a much worse condition of servitude, in consequence of damages injuriously done, or of debts incurred, which they have by their gross vices made themselves incapable of discharging. The person whom they have thus injured has a perfect right to compensation by their labours during their lives, if they cannot sooner discharge the claim. A criminal too, by way of punishment, may justly be adjudged to perpetual labours of the severest sort. In these cases, a power is founded solely for the behoof of others, to make all the profit by their labours which they can yield. Whatever humanity may be due to such unhappy servants, as they are still our fellow-creatures, yet the master's power and right being constituted only for his behoof, it is naturally alienable without their consent. But, still, in this worst condition of servitude, neither the criminal, after he has endured any public punishment which the common safety may require, nor much less the debtor, have lost any of the natural rights of mankind beside that one to their own labours. . . .

As this sort of slavery has a just foundation, some nations favour liberty immoderately by never admitting the perpetual servitude of any citizen. And yet perhaps no law could be more effectual to promote general industry, and restrain sloth and idleness in the lower conditions, than making perpetual slavery of this sort the ordinary punishment of such idle vagrants as, after proper admonitions and trials of temporary servitude, cannot be engaged to support themselves and their families by any useful labours. Slavery would also be a proper punishment for such as by intemperance or other vices ruined themselves and families, and made them a public burden. . . .

As to the notions of slavery which obtained among the Grecians and Romans, and other nations of old, they are horridly unjust. No damage done or crime committed can change a rational creature into a piece of goods void of all right, and incapable of acquiring any, or of receiving any injury from the proprietor; unless one should maintain that doing useless mischief, and creating excessive misery unnecessarily, can tend to the general good; and occasion no diminution of the happiness in the system, which is contradictory in the very terms.

9. On the motives for forming civil governments

System of Moral Philosophy, II, pp. 212–3.

If all mankind were perfectly wise and good, discerning all the proper means of promoting the general happiness of their race, and inclined to concur in them, nothing further would be wanting; no other obligation or bonds than those of their own virtue and wisdom. The necessity of civil power therefore must arise either from the imperfection or depravity of men or both.

When many of the ancients speak of man as a species naturally fit for civil society, they do not mean that men as immediately desire a political union, or a state of civil subjection to laws, as they desire the free society of others in natural liberty, or as they desire marriage and offspring, from immediate instincts. Tis never for itself agreeable to any one to have his actions subject to the direction of others, or that they should have any power over his goods or his life. Men must have first observed some dangers or miseries attending a state of anarchy to be much greater, than any inconveniencies to be feared from submitting their affairs along with others to the direction of certain governors or councils concerned in the safety of all: and then they would begin to desire a political constitution for their own safety and advantage, as well as for the general good. As men are naturally endowed with reason, caution, and sagacity; and civil government, or some sort of political union must appear, in the present state of our nature, the necessary means of safety and prosperity to themselves and others, they must naturally desire it in this view; and nature has endowed them with active powers and understanding for performing all political offices. . . .

The evils to be feared in anarchy result plainly from the weakness of men, even of those who have no unjust intentions, and partly from the unjust and corrupt dispositions which may arise in many. Tis wrong to assert that there is no occasion for civil polity except from human wickedness. The imperfections of those who in the main are just and good may require it.

10. The foundations of civil power: the three contracts

System of Moral Philosophy, II, pp. 227.

Civil power is most naturally founded by these three different acts of a whole people. 1. An agreement or contract of each one with all the rest, that they will unite into one society or body, to be governed in all their common interests by one council. 2. A decree or designation, made by the whole people, of the form or plan of power, and of the persons to be entrusted with it. 3. A mutual agreement or contract between the governors thus constituted and the people, the former obliging themselves to a faithful administration of the powers vested in them for the common interest, and the latter obliging themselves to obedience.

11. The designing of a constitution

System of Moral Philosophy, II, pp. 244.

Tis obvious that when by any plan of polity these four advantages can be obtained, *wisdom* in discerning the fittest measures for the general interest; *fidelity*, with *expedition* and *secrecy* in the determination and execution of them, and *concord* or *unity*; a nation must have all that happiness which any plan of polity can give it; as sufficient *wisdom* in the governors will discover the most effectual means, and *fidelity* will choose them, by *expedition* and *secrecy* they will be most effectually executed, and unity will prevent one of the greatest evils, civil wars and sedition. The great necessity of taking sufficient precaution against these mischiefs of factions and civil war leads most writers in politics into another obvious maxim, viz.

That the several parts of supreme power if they are lodged by any complex plan in different subjects, some granted to a prince, others to a Senate, and others to a popular assembly, there must in such case be some *nexus imperii*, or some political bond upon them, that they may not be able or incline to act separately and in opposition to each other. Without this, two supreme powers may be constituted in the same state, which may give frequent occasions to civil wars.

12. On power and property

System of Moral Philosophy, II, pp. 245–8.

Another maxim is equally certain from reason and the experience of all nations, 'That property, and that chiefly in lands, is the natural foundation upon which power must rest; though it gives not any just right to power'. Where there is property there numbers of men can be supported, and their assistance obtained as they can be rewarded for it: and where they cannot be supported and rewarded, their assistance is not to be expected. When power wants this foundation, the state must always be restless, fluctuating, and full of sedition, until either the power draws property to itself, or property obtains power. Men who have property, and can therefore obtain force, will not be excluded from some share of power. And men in power will exert it one way or other in obtaining property to support themselves; which must occasion convulsions in a state.

Pure Monarchy will never continue long without crown-lands, or hereditary provinces, where the lands are either the property of the prince, or he has a power over them equivalent to property. . . .

An hereditary Aristocracy in like manner shall be exposed to constant seditions and fluctuations, unless a very large share of the lands are the property of the senators. . . .

A Democracy cannot remain stable unless the property be so diffused among the people that no such cabal of a few as could probably unite in any design, shall have a fund of wealth sufficient to support a force superior to that of the rest. And in the several complex forms of polity there must some suitable division of property be observed, otherwise they shall always be unstable and full of sedition; when power has its natural foundation of property it will be lasting, but may, in some forms be very pernicious and oppressive to the whole body of the people; and it must be the more pernicious that it will be very permanent, there being no sufficient force to overturn or control it. And this shows the great care requisite in settling a just plan, and a suitable division of property, and in taking precautions against any such change in property as may destroy a good plan: this should be the view of agrarian laws.

As 'tis manifest that in democracies, and in all democratic assemblies truly chosen by the people, and united in interest with them, there must ever be a faithful intention of the general interest, which is the interest of the whole assembly; no constitution can be good where some of the most important parts of the civil power are not committed in whole or in part to such an assembly, which ever must be faithful to that interest for which all civil polity is destined. And consequently when the situation of the people, their manners and customs, their trade or arts, do not sufficiently of themselves cause such a diffusion of property among many as is requisite for the continuance of the democratic part in the constitution; there should be such agrarian laws as will prevent any immoderate increase of wealth in the hands of a few, which could support a force superior to the whole body. Tis in vain to talk of invading the liberty of the rich, or the injury of stopping their progress in just acquisitions. No public interest hinders their acquiring as much as is requisite for any innocent enjoyments and pleasures of life. And yet if it did, the liberty and safety of thousands of millions is never to be put in the balance with even the innocent pleasures of a few families; much less with their vain ambition, or their unjust pleasures, from their usurped powers or external pomp and grandeur.

13. The right to resist

System of Moral Philosophy, II, pp. 279–80.

There is a popular outcry often raised against these tenets of the rights of resistance, as if they must cause continual seditions and rebellions: the contrary is abundantly known. Such mischiefs are more frequently occasioned by the opposite doctrines giving unbounded licence to vicious rulers, and making them expect and trust to the conscientious submission of a people, contrary to nature and common sense; when they are giving loose reins to all tyranny and oppression. Tis well known that men too often break through the justest persuasions of duty, under strong temptations; and much more readily will they break through such superstitious tenets, not founded in just reason. There is no hope of making a peaceful world or country, by means of such tenets as the unlimited powers of governors, and the unlawfulness of all resistance. And where the just rights of mankind are asserted and generally believed, yet there is such a general love of ease, such proneness to esteem any tolerable governors, such a fondness for ancient customs and laws, and abhorrence of what is contrary to them; such fear of dangers from any convulsions of state, and such advantages enjoyed or hoped for under the present administration, that it is seldom practicable to accomplish any changes, or to get sufficient numbers to concur in any violent efforts for that purpose, against a government established by long custom and law, even where there is just ground given for them. We see that they scarce ever are successful except upon the very grossest abuses of power, and an entire perversion of it to the ruin of a people. Mankind have generally been a great deal too tame and tractable; and hence so many wretched forms of power have always enslaved nine-tenths of the nations of the world, where they have the fullest rights to make all efforts for a change.

14. The relationship between mother-country and colonies

System of Moral Philosophy, II, pp. 308–9.

Nay as the end of all political unions is the general good of those thus united, and this good must be subordinated to the more extensive interests of mankind. If the plan of the mother-country is changed by force, or degenerates by degrees from a safe, mild, and gentle limited power, to a severe and absolute one; or if under the same plan of polity, oppressive laws are made with respect to the colonies or provinces; and any colony is so increased in numbers and strength that they are sufficient by themselves for all the good ends of a political union; they are not bound to continue in their subjection, when it is grown so much more burdensome than was expected. Their consent to be subject to a safe and gentle plan of power or laws, imports no subjection to the dangerous and oppressive ones. Not to mention that all the principles of humanity require that where the retaining any right or claim is of far less importance to the happiness or safety of one body than it is dangerous and oppressive to another, the former should quit the claim, or agree to all such restrictions and limitations of it as are necessary for the liberty and happiness of the other, provided the other makes compensation of any damage thus occasioned. Large numbers of men cannot be bound to sacrifice their own and their posterity's liberty and happiness, to the ambitious views of their mother-country, while it can enjoy all rational happiness without subjection to it; and they can only be obliged to compensate the expences of making the settlement and defending it while it needed such defence, and to continue, as good allies ready to supply as friends any loss of strength their old country sustained by their quitting their subjection to it. There is something so unnatural in supposing a large society, sufficient for all the good purposes of an independent political union, remaining subject to the direction and government of a distant body of men who know not sufficiently the circumstances and exigencies of this society; or in supposing this society obliged to be governed solely for the benefit of a distance country; that it is not easy to imagine there can be any foundation for it in justice or equity. The insisting on old claims and tacit conventions, to extend civil power over different nations, and form grand unwieldy empires, without regard to the obvious maxims of humanity, has been one great source of human misery.

3 Moral Philosophy and the Scottish Enlightenment: The Study of Human Nature

From the 1730s, and especially from 1739, the date at which David Hume (see Biographical Notes) published the *Treatise of Human Nature*, the problems of moral philosophy were actively explored and debated in Scotland; the study of human nature was seen as an essential pre-requisite to the wider study of man in society. This work Francis Hutcheson had already begun, and, as we shall see, his successors found much of value in his writings. But primarily the issues in the debate were those put forward by David Hume. Hume's position within the Scottish Enlightenment is not an easy one to gauge. His views were met with direct hostility and academic rejection, in spite of his personal friendship with many of the leading 'literati'. The study of Hume's philosophy is clearly a matter for the technically equipped philosopher; here it is possible only to indicate one or two of the major areas of debate, and the part that Hume played in provoking his contemporaries. In this chapter, the documents chosen deal with the fundamental question of epistemology: man's knowledge of the external world, and with the attempts made to develop a psychology of human nature.

Hume's first work, the *Treatise of Human Nature* was, according to his own autobiographical essay, *My Own Life*, projected in 1725–6, planned before 1732, and composed before 1736[1]. At an early stage, he emphasised that his aim was the application of experimental philosophy to moral subjects. In this, of course, he shared the same ambition as Francis Hutcheson; and like Hutcheson too, Hume aimed at a detailed analysis of the feelings and passions of man and at a demonstration of the limitations of human reason. But Hume went beyond Hutcheson in his extension of the analysis not only to the problems of ethics, but to the problem of knowledge itself: the nature of knowledge *and* the nature of belief. The three volumes of the *Treatise of Human Nature* were entitled 'Of the understanding', 'Of the Passions', and 'Of Morals'; Document 1 in this chapter, taken from *An Abstract of the Treatise of Human Nature*, attempts to summarise the contents of the first volume.

The *Abstract* was written in the face of what Hume saw as a seriously disappointing reception for the *Treatise*, the first two volumes of which were published in 1739, the third in 1740. In the summer of 1739 not a single review of the work had appeared in the London press; Hume therefore wrote a review of his own work anonymously. He probably intended to offer this for publication as a review, but instead it appeared as a separate pamphlet early in 1740[2]. It is a clear and masterful summary of the first volume of the *Treatise*, which expresses the basis of Hume's philosophy more effectively than anyone else's summary could. For Hume, experience reached man only through impressions of the outside world, which leave behind ideas; the only connections in our processes of thought come from the linking up or association of these ideas. The association of ideas must be based upon a nearness or contiguity in time or space, or on a pattern of constant conjunction in the past: Hume's example is, that one billiard-ball hitting another has always made the second ball move. Yet it is a matter of custom to suppose that the future movement of the ball will always follow that of the past, a custom reinforced by our belief that it will do so, a belief which is a *feeling* rather than a rational understanding. In the *Abstract*, Hume does not attempt to deny the sceptical consequences of these arguments, the implications of which were already being pointed out by his critics; though he did not reveal his authorship of the pamphlet until 1776. In his later works, which in the main expand and develop sections of the *Treatise*, he modified his position slightly.

Throughout his life he was only too conscious of the isolation of his intellectual position. In 1744 it seemed as if the Chair of Ethics and Pneumatical Philosophy at the University of Edinburgh might fall vacant; Hume and his friends optimistically campaigned for his candidature. Hume's reputation as a sceptic was one major reason for his failure to obtain the Chair, as it was again in 1751, when there was a possibility of obtaining the Professorship of Logic at Glasgow. And in 1752 Hume's own writings were publicly attacked by the General Assembly of the Church of Scotland. His reputation and his writings were notorious, in the full sense of the word; yet personally he was on the best of terms with the majority of his antagonists, and with leading moderate clergymen, and managed to keep controversy on the level of scholarly and amicable disagreement.

Hume's opponents fastened in particular on the argument set out in the *Abstract*. Those who directly opposed him became known as the 'common sense' school. Their leader was undoubtedly Thomas Reid (see Biographical Notes), Professor of Philosophy at Kings College Aberdeen, and later at Glasgow. James Beattie (see Biographical Notes), Professor at Marischall College, popularised the attack on scepticism. Early discussions of the questions raised by Hume in the Aberdeen Philosophical Society, founded in 1758, helped to shape and unite the reaction of these writers. Others belonging to this school included James Oswald (?–1793), who, in his *Appeal to Common Sense on behalf of religion*, Edinburgh, 1766, 1772, showed a grasp of the arguments rather similar to that of Beattie, and, more legitimately, Dugald Stewart (1753–1828), who is generally regarded as the follower of, and successor to, Thomas Reid, but whose career falls outside the limits of this study.

Document 2 illustrates the implications of the 'sceptical system' for Reid; his work is not for him merely part of an academic debate, but a more wide ranging one, for upon it will depend the defence of 'all religion and virtue'. Reid is a serious philosopher, and his detailed philosophical arguments are still of interest to philosophers today. Briefly, Document 3 points to the main lines of his argument, set out in his *Inquiry into the Human Mind on the Principles of Common Sense* (Edinburgh, 1764), a work which had been under consideration ever since the publication of Hume's *Treatise*. Reid's aim was the same as Hume's: the anatomy of human nature, carried out through careful observation and experiment, on Newtonian principles; but their observations were to lead them in entirely different directions. Reid used the term 'common sense' ambiguously, as in Document 4; he appears to see 'common sense' both as the name of a mental power, and as a set of self-evident, fundamental beliefs. His motive in writing is primarily to demonstrate how philosophy should be rooted in the 'common sense' beliefs of ordinary men, for whom there are some obvious and self-evident truths: in particular, that there is an external, material world. For Reid, it was necessary for him, as a philosopher, to state an alternative theory of perception, as the basis of his attack on scepticism. Document 3 is an account of Reid's discussion of the sense of smell, to illustrate this. There is a difference for Reid, between the sensation of smell felt by the individual, and the material existence of the smell. To Reid, the sensation is a 'natural sign', a sign which through experience we know signified the presence of a rose. Through a detailed analysis of this and other senses, Reid moves on to analyse 'original perceptions', through the operation of 'natural signs' via sensation, and 'acquired perceptions' in which sensations acquire new significance. Though individuals may misread signs, and therefore their perceptions may be false, they will be accompanied by a belief that the object exists, a belief which 'came fresh from the mint of Nature', or in other words is an ineradicable part of the human constitution. Reid dealt also with men's other faculties, and in particular with the ability to make judgements, which he believed to be an innate power of man—not merely a feeling of approbation or disapprobation, but a power of making moral distinctions. In this area, as in others, Reid ultimately withdrew his argument to the territory of 'common sense', interpreted as the original dictates of the human mind, the appeal to general consent and ordinary language. The documents from James Beattie's *Essay on Truth* suggest the possibilities of distortion and gross over-simplification, in the popular appeal against Hume. Yet Beattie's work sold extremely well, and its popularity was rapidly established. The philosophy of common sense remained dominant within the universities of Scotland until well into the nineteenth century.

Other writers were more concerned to explore the debate already begun by Hutcheson and continued by Hume, the exploration of the relationship between moral standards and the workings of human nature; where Hutcheson had analysed the moral faculty in relation to the natural law and divine law, Hume continued the arguments already put forward in the first two volumes of the *Treatise*:

> Our reasonings concerning *morals* will corroborate whatever has been said concerning the *understanding* and the *passions*[3].

His view of moral philosophy was consistent with his emphasis on impressions and feelings, and on the importance of experience:

> Morals excite passions, and produce or prevent actions. Reason of itself is utterly impotent in this particular. The rules of

morality, therefore, are not conclusions of our reason[4].

For Hume the main element in every value judgement was the distinction between pleasure and pain, a difference known through sensation, and appreciated by experience; it was man's moral sense which distinguished particular pleasures and pains. It was able to evaluate, to make moral judgements about particular acts, through sympathy with the feelings of others, where a spectator entered into those feelings, and to judge the appropriateness of a particular action. Hume distinguished between the 'natural' virtues, from which men felt agreeable and pleasant sensations, in matters touching them closely, and the 'artificial' virtues, the ability to correct the partiality of one's own affections in the interests of society as a whole (Document 7–8). Hume explores this concept of justice further in his account of man's entry into civil society (see Chapter 5). He refutes, therefore, any suggestion that man was able simply to perceive 'the eternal fitnesses or unfitnesses of things'; though he did believe that men living together in society had come to establish common standards of justice and morality.

Many other writers of the Scottish Enlightenment explored this kind of territory. Adam Ferguson (see Biographical Notes), in his *Institutes of Moral Philosophy* (Edinburgh, 1769), and his *Principles of Moral and Political Science*, 2 vols (Edinburgh, 1792), drawn from thirty years' experience of lecturing to Edinburgh students, shared the same commitment to the study of human nature:

As the study of human nature may refer to the actual state, or to the improveable capacity, of man, it is evident, that, the subjects being connected, we cannot proceed in the second, but upon the foundations which are laid in the first. Our knowledge of what any nature ought to be, must be derived from our knowledge of its faculties and powers; and the attainment to be aimed at must be of the kind which these faculties and powers are fitted to produce[5].

But, like Hutcheson, Ferguson was concerned to explore man's nature in the context of the Divine plan for mankind, and Ferguson's arguments owe much to Hutcheson, in their concern for the pursuit of virtue as the key to human fulfilment, in an ordered and harmonious universe. But further illustrations here have been limited to the work of Adam Smith (see Biographical Notes) who, as part of his ambitious attempt to encompass the range of human concerns, published in 1759 his *Theory of Moral Sentiments*; again this was drawn from the lectures which he was at that time offering his students at Glasgow. Smith's later work was to owe much to this firmly established base in moral philosophy. In Documents 9–11, Smith is grappling with one of the problems bequeathed to him by Hume: the way in which moral judgements may emerge from the transference of one's own feelings into another's. Our judgement of another person's action will depend on what we may feel is appropriate conduct in an identical situation; but because our powers of sympathy may be limited in any situation, the effort has to be made to suppose the judgement of 'the impartial spectator'. Ultimately, those moral rules known through sympathy with the feelings of others, and through the judgement of the impartial spectator, came to be known as the general rules of morality, and accepted as such.

Scottish moral philosophers had in common therefore both an approach to their subject, and a particular focus: the way in which men's senses, feelings, and understanding interacted to enable them to discern right and wrong. They shared a common method, although there were, even so, important differences between Hutcheson and Ferguson, on the one hand, and Hume on the other. They shared a common commitment to moral philosophy as the foundation for the study of man in society: and Hume, Ferguson, Smith, were not only philosophers, but also political scientists, economists, historians. Hume's 'attempt to introduce the experimental method of reasoning into moral subjects', the subtitle of the *Treatise*, had initiated a debate which was essential to the Enlightenment in Scotland.

NOTES

1. *My Own Life*, reprinted in J. Y. T. Greig (ed.), *The Letters of David Hume*, 2 vols (Oxford, 1932) I, pp. 1–3.

2. See J. M. Keynes and P. Sraffa, Introduction to David Hume, *An Abstract of a Treatise of Human Nature, 1740* (Cambridge 1938, reprinted Archon Books, Hamden, Connecticut, 1965).

3. David Hume, *A Treatise of Human Nature*, edited by L. A. Selby-Biggs, 1st edition 1888, numerous reprints, p. 455.

4. *Ibid.* p. 457.

5. Adam Ferguson, *Principles of Moral and Political Science, being chiefly a retrospect of lectures delivered in the College of Edinburgh*, 2 vols (Edinburgh, 1792) I, p. 5.

The Study of Human Nature: Documents

HUME'S CASE

1. David Hume's own summary of the argument of the *Treatise*

(David Hume) *An Abstract of a book lately published; entitled a Treatise of Human Nature &c.* . . . (London, 1740) pp. 5–20, 24.

This book seems to be wrote upon the same plan with several other works that have had a great vogue of late years in England. The philosophical spirit, which has been so much improved all over Europe within these last four score years, has been carried to as great length in this kingdom as in any other. Our writers seem even to have started a new kind of philosophy, which promises more both to the entertainment and advantage of mankind, than any other with which the world has been yet acquainted. Most of the philosophers of antiquity, who treated of human nature, have shown more of a delicacy of sentiment, a just sense of morals, or a greatness of soul, than a depth of reasoning and reflection. They content themselves with representing the common sense of mankind in the strongest lights, and with the best turn of thought and expression, without following out steadily a chain of propositions, or forming the several truths into a regular science. But 'tis at least worth while to try if the science of *man* will not admit of the same accuracy which several parts of natural philosophy are found susceptible of. There seems to be all the reason in the world to imagine that it may be carried to the greatest degree of exactness. If, in examining several phenomena, we find that they resolve themselves into one common principle, and can trace this principle into another, we shall at last arrive at those few simple principles, on which all the rest depend. And tho' we can never arrive at the ultimate principles, 'tis a satisfaction to go as far as our faculties will allow us.

This seems to have been the aim of our late philosophers, and, among the rest, of this author. He proposes to anatomize human nature in a regular manner, and promises to draw no conclusions but where he is authorized by experience. He talks with contempt of hypotheses; and insinuates, that such of our countrymen as have banished them from moral philosophy, have done a more signal service to the world, than *my Lord Bacon*, whom he considers as the father of experimental physics. He mentions, on this occasion, Mr. Locke, my Lord Shaftesbury, Dr. Mandeville, Mr. Hutcheson, Dr. Butler, who, tho' they differ in many points among themselves, seem all to agree in founding their accurate disquisitions of human nature entering upon experience.

Beside the satisfaction of being acquainted with what most nearly concerns us, it may be safely affirmed, that almost all the sciences are comprehended in the science of human nature, and are dependent on it. *The sole end of logic is to explain the principles and operations of our reasoning faculty, and the nature of our ideas*; morals and criticism *regard our tastes and sentiments; and* politics *consider men as united in society, and dependent on each other.* This treatise therefore of human nature seems intended for a system of the sciences. The author has finished what regards logic, and has laid the foundation of the other parts in his account of the passions.

. . . As his (the author's book) contains a great number of speculations very new and remarkable. It will be impossible to give the reader a just notion of the whole. We shall therefore chiefly confine ourselves to his explication of our reasoning from cause and effect. If we can make this intelligible to the reader, it may serve as a specimen of the whole.

Our author begins with some definitions. He calls a *perception* whatever can be present to the mind, whether we employ our senses, or are actuated with passion, or exercise our thought and reflection. He divides our perceptions into two kinds, viz. impressions and *ideas*. When we feel a passion or emotion of any kind, or have the images of external objects conveyed by our senses; the perception of the mind is what he calls an *impression*, which is a word that he employs in a new sense. When we reflect on a passion or an object which is not present, this perception is an *idea*. Impressions, therefore, are our lively and strong perceptions; *ideas* are the fainter and weaker. This distinction is evident; as evident as that betwixt feeling and thinking.

The first proposition he advances, is, that all our ideas, or weak perceptions, are derived from our impressions, or strong perceptions, and that we can never think of any thing which we have not seen without us, or felt in our own minds. This proposition seems to be equivalent to that which Mr. Locke has taken such pains to establish, *viz. that no ideas are innate*. Only it may be observed as an inaccuracy of that famous philosopher, that he comprehends all our perceptions under the term of idea, in which sense it is false, that we have no innate ideas. For it is evident our stronger perceptions or impressions are innate, and that natural affection, love of virtue, resentment, and all the other passions, arise immediately from nature. . . . .

Our author thinks, 'that no discovery could have been made more happily for deciding all controversies concerning ideas than this, that impressions always take the precedency of them, and that every idea with which the imagination is furnished, first makes its appearance in a correspondent impression. These latter perceptions are all so clear and evident, that they admit of no controversy; tho' many of our ideas are so obscure, that 'tis almost impossible even for the mind, which forms them, to tell exactly their nature and composition.' Accordingly, wherever any idea is ambiguous, he has always recourse to the impression, which must render it clear and precise. And when he suspects that any philosophical term has no idea annexed to it (as is too common) he always asks *from what impression that idea is derived*? And if no impression can be produced, he concludes that the term is altogether insignificant. 'Tis after this manner he examines our idea of *substance* and *essence*; and it were to be wished, that this rigorous method were more practised in all philosophical debates.

'Tis evident, that all reasonings concerning *matter of fact* are founded on the relation of cause and effect, and that we can never infer the existence of one object from another, unless they be connected together, either mediately or immediately. In order, therefore to understand these reasonings, we must be perfectly acquainted with the idea of a cause; and in order to that, must look about us to find something that is the cause of another.

Here is a billiard-ball lying on the table, and another ball moving towards it with rapidity. They strike; and the ball, which was formerly at rest, now acquires a motion. This is as perfect an instance of the relation of cause and effect as any which we know, either by sensation or reflection. Let us therefore examine it. 'Tis evident, that the two balls touched one another before the motion was communicated, and that there was no interval betwixt the shock and the motion. *Contiguity* in time and place is therefore a requisite circustance to the operation of all causes. 'Tis evident likewise, that the motion, which was the cause, is prior to the motion, which was the effect. *Priority* in time, is therefore another requisite circumstance in every cause. But this is not all. Let us try any other balls of the same kind in a like situation, and we shall always find, that the impulse of the one produces motion in the other. Here therefore is a *third* circumstance, *viz.* that of a *constant conjunction* between the cause and effect. Every object like the cause, produces always some object like the effect. Beyond these three circumstances of contiguity, priority, and constant conjunction, I can discover nothing in this cause. The first ball is in motion; touches the second; immediately the second is in motion: and when I try the experiment with the same or like balls, in the same or like circumstances, I find, that upon the motion and touch of the one ball, motion always follows in the other. In whatever shape I turn this matter, and however I examine it, I can find nothing farther.

This is the case when both the cause and effect are present to the senses. Let us now see upon what our inference is founded, when we conclude from the one that the other has existed or will exist. Suppose I see a ball moving in a straight line towards another, I immediately conclude, that they will shock, and that the second will be in motion. This is the inference from cause to effect; and of this nature are all our reasonings in the conduct of life: on this is founded all our belief in history and from hence is derived all philosophy, excepting only geometry and arithmetic. If we can explain the inference from the shock of two balls, we shall be able to account for this operation of the mind in all instances.

Were a man, such as *Adam*, created in the full vigour of understanding, without experience, he would never be able to infer motion in the second ball from the motion and impulse of the first. It is not anything that reason sees in the cause, which make us *infer* the effect. Such an inference, were it possible, would amount to a demonstration, as being founded merely on the comparison of ideas. But no inference from cause to effect amounts to a demonstration, as being founded merely on the comparison of ideas. But no inference from cause to effect amounts to a demonstration. Of which there is this evident proof. The mind can always *conceive* any effect to follow from any cause, and indeed any event to follow upon another: whatever·we *conceive* is possible, at least in a metaphysical sense: but wherever a demonstration takes place, the contrary is impossible, and implies a contradiction. There is no demonstration, therefore, for any conjunction of cause and effect. And this is a principle which is generally allowed by philosophers.

It would have been necessary, therefore, for *Adam* (if he was not inspired) to have had *experience* of the effect, which followed upon the impulse of these two balls. He must have seen, in several instances, that when the one ball struck upon the other, the second always acquired motion. If he had seen a sufficient number of instances of this kind, whenever he saw the one ball moving towards the other, he would always conclude without hesitation, that the second would acquire motion. His understanding would anticipate his sight, and form a conclusion suitable to his past experience.

It follows, then, that all reasonings concerning cause and effect, are founded on experience, and that all reasonings from experience are founded on the supposition, that the course of nature will continue uniformly the same. We conclude, that like causes, in like circumstances, will always produce like effects. It may now be worth while to consider, what determines us to form a conclusion of such infinite consequence.

'Tis evident, that *Adam* with all his science, would never have been able to *demonstrate*, that the course of nature must continue uniformly the same, and that the future must be conformable to the past. What is possible can never be demonstrated to be false; and 'tis possible the course of nature may change, since we can conceive such a change. Nay, I will go further, and assert, that he could not so much as prove by any *probable* arguments, that the future must be conformable to the past. All probable arguments are built on the supposition, that there is this conformity betwix the future and the past, and therefore can never prove it. This conformity is a *matter of fact*, and if it must be proved, will admit of no proof but from experience. But our experience in the past can be a proof of nothing for the future, but upon a supposition, that there is a resemblance betwixt them. This therefore is a point, which can admit of no proof at all, and which we take for granted without any proof.

We are determined by CUSTOM alone to suppose the future conformable to the past. When I see a billiard-ball moving towards another, my mind is immediately carried by habit to the usual effect, and anticipates my sight by conceiving the second ball in motion. There is nothing in these objects, abstractly considered, and independent of experience, which leads me to form any such conclusion: and even after I have had experience of many repeated effects of this kind, there is no argument, which determines me to suppose that the effect will be conformable to past experience. The powers, by which bodies operate, are entirely unknown. We perceive only their sensible qualities: and what *reason* have we to think, that the same powers will always be conjoined with the same sensible qualities?

'Tis not, therefore, reason, which is the guide of life, but custom. That alone determines the mind, in all instances, to suppose the future conformable to the past. However easy this step may seem, reason would never, to all eternity, be able to make it.

This is a very curious discovery, but leads us to others, that are still more curious. *When I see a billiard-ball moving towards another, my mind is immediately carried by habit to the usual effect, and anticipate my sight by conceiving the second ball in motion.* But is this all? Do I nothing but CONCEIVE the motion of the second ball? No surely. I also BELIEVE that it will move. What then is this *belief*? And how does it differ from the simple conception of any thing? Here is a new question unthought of by philosophers.

When a demonstration convinces me of any proposition, it not only makes me conceive the proposition, but also makes me sensible, that 'tis impossible to conceive any thing contrary. What is demonstratively false implies a contradiction; and what implies a contradiction cannot be conceived. But with regard to any matter of fact, however strong the proof may be from experience, I can always conceive the contrary, tho' I cannot always beleive it. The belief, therefore, makes some difference betwix the conception to which we assent, and that to which we do not assent.

To account for this, there are only two hypotheses. It may be said, that belief joins some new idea to those which we may conceive without assenting to them. But this hypothesis is false. For *first* no such idea can be produced. When we simply conceive an object, we conceive it in all its parts. We conceive it as it might exist, tho' we do not believe it to exist. Our belief of it would discover no new qualities. We may paint out the entire object in imagination without believing it. We may set it, in a manner, before our eyes, with every circumstance of time and place. 'Tis the very object conceived as it might exist; and when we believe it, we can do no more.

Secondly, The mind has a faculty of joining all ideas together, which involve not a contradiction; and therefore if belief consisted in some idea, which we add to the simple conception, it would be in a man's power, by adding this idea to it, to believe any thing, which he can conceive.

SINCE therefore belief implies a conception, and yet is something more; and since it adds no new idea to the conception; it follows, that it is a different MANNER of conceiving an object; *something* that is distinguishable to the feeling, and depends not upon our will, as all our ideas do. My mind runs by habit from the visible object of one ball moving towards another, to the usual effect of motion in the second ball. It not only conceives that motion, but *feels* something different in the conception of it from a mere reverie of the imagination. The presence of this visible object, and the constant conjunction of that particular effect, render the idea different to the *feeling* from those loose ideas, which come into the mind without any introduction. This conclusion seems a little surprising; but we are led into it by a chain of propositions which admit of no doubt. To ease the reader's memory I shall briefly resume them. No matter of fact can be proved but from its cause or its effect. Nothing can be known to be the cause of another but by experience. We can give no reason for extending to the future our experience in the past; but are entirely determined by custom, when we conceive an effect to follow, from its usual cause. But we also believe an effect to follow as well as conceive it. This belief joins no new idea to the conception. It only varies the manner of conceiving, and makes a difference to the feeling or sentiment. Belief, therefore, in all matters of fact arises only from custom, and is an idea conceived in a peculiar *manner*.

Our author proceeds to explain the manner or feeling, which renders belief different from a loose conception. He seems sensible, that 'tis impossible by words to describe this feeling, which every one must be conscious of in his own breast. He calls it sometimes a *stronger* conception, sometimes a more *lively*, a more *vivid*, a *firmer*, or a more *intense* conception. And indeed, whatever name we may give to this feeling, which constitutes belief, our author thinks it evident, that it has a more forcible effect on the mind than fiction and mere conception. This he proves by its influence on the passions and on the imagination; which are only moved by truth or what is taken for such . . .

. . . . By all that has been said the reader will easily perceive, that the philosophy contained in this book is very sceptical, and tends to give us a notion of the imperfections and narrow limits of human understanding. Almost all reasoning is there reduced to experience; and the belief, which attends experience, is explained to be nothing but a peculiar sentiment, or lively conception produced by habit. Nor is this all, when we believe anything of *external* existence, or suppose an object to exist a moment after it is no longer perceived, this belief is nothing but a sentiment of the same kind. Our author insists upon several other sceptical topics; and upon the whole concludes, that we assent to our faculties, and employ our reason only because we cannot help it. Philosophy would render us entirely *Pyrrhonian*, were not nature too strong for it.

THE OPPOSITION TO HUME

2. Thomas Reid, and the development of the 'common sense' school

Thomas Reid, *An Inquiry into the Human Mind, on the principles of Common Sense*, in *The Works of Thomas Reid* . . . with preface, notes and supplementary dissertations by Sir William Hamilton . . . Fourth edition (Edinburgh, 1854) pp. 95–6.

Dedication, to the Right Honourable James, Earl of Findlater and Seafield.
. . . I acknowledge, my Lord, that I never thought of calling in question the principles commonly received with regard to the human understanding, until the 'Treatise of Human Nature' was published in the year 1739. The ingenious author of that treatise upon the principles of Locke—who was no sceptic—hath built a system of scepticism, which leaves no ground to believe any one thing rather than its contrary. His reasoning appeared to me to be just; there was, therefore, a necessity to call in question the principles upon which it was founded, or to admit the conclusion.
But can any ingenuous mind admit this sceptical system without reluctance? I truly could not, my Lord; for I am persuaded that absolute scepticism is not more destructive of the faith of a Christian than of the science of a philosopher, and of the prudence of a man of

common understanding. I am persuaded, that the unjust *live by faith* as well as the *just*; that, if all belief could be laid aside, piety, patriotism, friendship, parental affection, and private virtue, would appear as ridiculous as knight-errantry; and that the pursuits of pleasure, of ambition, and of avarice, must be grounded upon belief, as well as those that are honourable or virtuous.

The day-labourer toils at his work, in the belief that he shall receive his wages at night; and, if he had not this belief, he would not toil. We may venture to say, that even the author of this sceptical system wrote it in the belief that it should be read and regarded. I hope he wrote it in the belief also that it would be useful to mankind; and, perhaps, it may prove so at last. For I conceive the sceptical writers to be a set of men whose business it is to pick holes in the fabric of knowledge wherever it is weak and faulty; and, when these places are properly repaired, the whole building becomes more firm and solid than it was formerly.

For my own satisfaction, I entered into a serious examination of the principles upon which this sceptical system is built; and was not a little surprised to find, that it leans with its whole weight upon a hypothesis, which is ancient indeed, and hath been very generally received by philosophers, but of which I could find no solid proof. The hypothesis I mean, is, That nothing is perceived but what is in the mind which perceives it: That we do not really perceive things that are external, but only certain images and pictures of them impressed upon the mind, which are called *impressions and ideas*.

If this be true, supposing certain impressions and ideas to exist in my mind, I cannot, from their existence, infer the existence of anything else: my impressions and ideas are the only existences of which I can have any knowledge or conception; and they are such fleeting and transitory beings, that they can have no existence at all, any longer than I am conscious of them. So that, upon this hypothesis, the whole universe about me, bodies and spirits, sun, moon, stars, and earth, friends and relations, all things without exception, which I imagined to have a permanent existence, whether I thought of them or not, vanish at once;

> And, like the baseless fabric of a vision,
> Leave not a rack behind.

I thought it unreasonable, my Lord, upon the authority of

philosophers to admit a hypothesis which, in my opinion, overturns all philosophy, all religion and virtue, and all common sense—and, finding that all the systems concerning the human understanding which I was acquainted with, were built upon this hypothesis, I resolved to inquire into this subject anew, without regard to any hypothesis.

3. An example: the smell of a rose

Thomas Reid, *An Inquiry into the Human Mind*, in *The Works of Thomas Reid*, p. 114.

The vulgar are commonly charged by philosophers, with the absurdity of imagining the smell in the rose to be something like to the sensation of smelling; but I think unjustly; for they neither give the same epithets to both, nor do they reason in the same manner from them. What is smell in the rose? It is a quality or virtue of the rose, or of something proceeding from it, which we perceive by the sense of smelling; and this is all we know of the matter. But what is smelling? It is an act of the mind, but is never imagined to be a quality of the mind. Again, the sensation of smelling is conceived to infer necessarily a mind or sentient being; but smell in the rose infers no such thing. We say, this body smells sweet, that stinks; but we do not say, this mind smells sweet and that stinks. Therefore, smell in the rose, and the sensation which it causes, are not conceived, even by the vulgar, to be things of the same kind, although they have the same name.

From what hath been said, we may learn that the smell of a rose signifies two things: *First*, a sensation, which can have no existence but when it is perceived, and can only be in a sentient being or mind; *Secondly*, it signifies some power, quality, or virtue, in the rose, or in effluvia proceeding from it, which hath a permanent existence, independent of the mind, and which, by the constitution of nature, produce the sensation in us. By the original constitution of our nature, we are both led to believe that there is a permanent cause of the sensation, and prompted to seek after it; and experience determines us to place it in the rose.

4. Philosophy and 'common sense'

Thomas Reid, *An Inquiry into the Human Mind*, in *The Works of Thomas Reid*, pp. 126-7.

Upon the whole, it appears that our philosophers have imposed upon themselves and upon us, in pretending to deduce from sensation the first origin of our notions of external existences, of space, motion, and extension, and all the primary qualities of body—that is, the qualities whereof we have the most clear and distinct conception. These qualities do not at all tally with any system of the human faculties that hath been advanced. They have no resemblance to any sensation, or to any operation of our minds; and, therefore, they cannot be ideas either of sensation or of reflection. The very conception of them is irreconcilable to the principles of our philosophic systems of the understanding. The belief of them is no less so . . .

It is beyond our power to say when, or in what order, we came by our notions of these qualities. When we trace the operations of our minds as far back as memory and reflection can carry us, we find them already in possession of our imagination and belief, and quite familiar to the mind: but how they came first into its acquaintance, or what has given them so strong a hold of our belief, and what regard they deserve, are, no doubt, very important questions in the philosophy of human nature. . . .

. . . the wisdom of *philosophy* is set in opposition to the *common sense* of mankind. The first pretends to demonstrate, *a priori*, that there can be no such thing as a material world; that sun, moon, stars, and earth, vegetable and animal bodies, are, and can be nothing else, but sensations in the mind, or images of those sensations in the memory and imagination; that, like pain and joy, they can have no existence when they are not thought of. The last can conceive no otherwise of this opinion, than of a kind of metaphysical lunacy, and concludes that too much learning is apt to make men mad; and that the man who seriously entertains this belief, though in other respects he may be a very good man, as a man may be who believes that he is made of glass; yet, surely he hath a soft place in his understanding, and hath been hurt by much thinking . . .

If this is wisdom, let me be deluded with the vulgar. I find something within me that recoils against it, and inspires more reverent sentiments of the human kind, and of the universal administration. Common Sense and Reason have both one author; that Almighty Author in all whose other works we observe a consistency, uniformity, and beauty which charm and delight the understanding: there must, therefore, be some order and consistency in the human faculties, as well as in other parts of his workmanship. A man that thinks reverently of his own kind, and esteems true wisdom and philosophy, will not be fond, nay, will be very suspicious, of such strange and paradoxical opinions. If they are false, they disgrace philosophy; and, if they are true, they degrade the human species, and make us justly ashamed of our frame.

To what purpose is it for philosophy to decide against common sense in this or any other matter? The belief of a material world is older, and of more authority, than any principles of philosophy. It declines the tribunal of reason, and laughs at all the artillery of the logician. It retains its sovereign authority in spite of all the edicts of philosophy, and reason itself must stoop to its orders. Even those philosophers who have disowned the authority of our notions of an external material world, confess that they find themselves under a necessity of submitting to their power . . .

In order, therefore, to reconcile Reason to Common Sense in this matter, I beg leave to offer to the consideration of philosophers these two observations. First, that, in all this debate about the existence of a material world, it hath been taken for granted on both sides, that this same material world, if any such there be, must be the express image of our sensations; that we can have no conception of any material thing which is not like some sensation in our minds; and particularly that the sensations of touch are images of extension, hardness, figure, and motion. Every argument brought against the existence of a material world, either by the Bishop of Cloyne [1], or by the author of the 'Treatise of Human Nature', supposeth this. If this is true, their arguments are conclusive and unanswerable; but, on the other hand, if it is not true, there is no shadow of argument left. Have those philosophers, then, given any solid proof of this hypothesis, upon which the whole weight of so strange a system rests? No. They have not so much as attempted to do it. But, because ancient and modern philosophers have agreed in this opinion, they have taken it for granted. But let us, as becomes philosophers, lay aside authority; we need not, surely, consult Aristotle or Locke, to know whether pain be like the point of a sword. I have as clear a conception of extension, hardness, and motion as I have of the point of a sword; and with some pains and practice, I can form as clear a notion of the other sensations of touch as I have of pain. When I do so, and compare them together, it appears to me clear as daylight, that the former are not of kin to the latter, nor resemble them in any one feature. They are as unlike, yea as certainly and manifestly unlike, as pain is to the point of a sword. It may be true, that those sensations first introduced the material world to our acquaintance; it may be true, that it seldom or never appears without their company; but, for all that, they are as unlike as the passion of anger is to those features of the countenance which attend it.

So that, in the sentence those philosophers have passed against the material world, there is an *error personae*. Their proof touches not matter, or any of its qualities; but strikes directly against an idol of their own imagination, a material world made of ideas and sensations, which never had, not can have an existence.

Secondly, The very existence of our conceptions of extension, figure and motion, since they are neither ideas of sensation nor reflection, overturns the whole ideal system by which the material world hath been tried and condemned; so that there hath been likewise in this sentence an *error juris*.

It is a very fine and a just observation of Locke, that as no human art can create a single particle of matter, and the whole extent of our power over the material world consists in compounding, combining, and disjoining the matter made to our hands; so, in the world of thought, the materials are all made by nature, and can only be variously combined and disjoined by us. So that it is impossible for reason or prejudice, true or false philosophy, to produce one simple notion or conception, which is not the work of nature, and the result of our constitution. The conception of extension, motion, and the other attributes of matter, cannot be the effect of error or prejudice; it must be the work of nature. And the power of faculty by which we acquire those conceptions, must be something different from any power of the human mind that hath been explained, since it is neither sensation or reflection.

[1] Bishop Berkeley.

5. The popularisation of common-sense

James Beattie, *An Essay on the Nature and Immutability of Truth, in Opposition to sophistry and scepticism*, 6th edition, revised and carefully corrected (Edinburgh, 1777) pp. 24–6.

On hearing these propositions,—I exist, Things equal to one and the same thing are equal to one another, The sun rose today, there is a God, Ingratitude ought to be blamed and punished. The three angles of a triangle are equal to two right angles &c,—I am conscious, that my mind admits and acquiesces in them.

I say, that I believe them to be true, that is, I conceive them to express something conformable to the nature of things. Of the contrary proposition I should say, that my mind does not acquiesce in them, but disbelieves them, and conceives them to express something not conformable to the nature of things. My judgment in this case, I conceive to be the same that I should form in regard to these proposition, if I were perfectly acquainted with all nature, in all its parts, and in all its laws.

If I be asked, what I mean by *the nature of things*, I cannot otherwise explain myself, than by saying, that there is in my mind something which induces me to think, that every thing existing in nature is determined to exist, and to exist after a certain manner, in consequence of established laws; and that whatever is agreeable to those laws is agreeable to the nature of things, because by those laws the nature of all things is determined. Of those laws I do not pretend to know anything, except in so far as they seem to be intimated to me by my own feelings, and by the suggestions of my own understanding. But these feelings and suggestions are such, and affect me in such a manner, that I cannot help receiving them, and trusting in them, and believing that their intimations are not fallacious, but such as I should approve of if I were perfectly acquainted with every thing in the universe, and such as may approve, and admit of, and regulate my conduct by, without danger of any inconvenience.

It is not easy on this subject to avoid identical expressions. I am not certain that I have been able to avoid them. And perhaps I might have expressed my meaning more shortly and more clearly, by saying that I account that to be *truth* which the constitution of our nature determines us to believe.* Believing and disbelieving are simple acts of the mind; I can neither define nor describe them in words; and therefore the reader must judge of their nature from his own experience. We often believe what we afterwards find to be false; but while belief continues, we think it true; when we discover its falsity, we believe it no longer.

*   I might have said more explicitly, but the meaning is the same, 'That I account that to be *truth* which the constitution of human nature determines man to believe, and that to be *falsehood* which the constitution of human nature determines man to disbelieve'.

6. The attack on scepticism

James Beattie, *Essay on Truth*, Postscript, added November 1770, pp. 448–9.

In the whole circle of human sciences, real or pretended, there is not any thing to be found which I think more perfectly contemptible, than the speculative philosophy of the moderns. It is indeed a most wretched medley of ill-digested notions, indistinct perceptions, inaccurate observations, perverted language, and sophistical argument; distinguishing where there is no difference, and confounding where there is no similitude; feigning difficulties where it cannot find them, and overlooking when real. I know no end that the study of such jargon can answer, except to harden and stupify the heart, bewilder the understanding, sour the temper, and habituate the mind to irresolution, captiousness and falsehood.

THE KNOWLEDGE OF MORALITY

7. Hume's view of the moral sense

David Hume *A Treatise of Human Nature*, edited by L. A. Selby-Biggie, 1st edition 1888, numerous reprints, pp. 470–1.

Thus the course of the argument leads us to conclude, that since vice and virtue are not discoverable merely by reason, or the comparison of ideas, it must be by means of some impression or sentiment they occasion, that we are able to mark the difference betwixt them. Our decisions concerning oral rectitude and depravity are evidently perceptions; and as all perceptions are either impressions or ideas, the exclusion of the one is a convincing argument for the other. Morality, therefore, is more properly felt than judged of; tho' this feeling or sentiment is commonly so soft and gentle, that we are apt to confound it with an idea, according to our common custom of taking all things for the same, which have any near resemblance to each other.

The next question is, Of what nature are these impressions, and after what manner do they operate upon us? Here we cannot remain long in suspense, but must pronounce the impression arising from virtue, to be agreeable, and that proceeding from vice to be uneasy. Every moment's experience must convince us of this. There is no spectacle so fair and beautiful as a noble and generous action; nor any which gives us more abhorrence than one that is cruel and treacherous . . .

Now since the distinguishing impressions, by which moral good or evil is known, are nothing but *particular* pains or pleasures; it follows, that in all enquiries concerning these moral distinctions, it will be sufficient to show the principles, which make us feel a satisfaction or uneasiness from the survey of any character, in order to satisfy us why the character is laudable or blameable. An action, or sentiment, or character is virtuous or vicious; why? because its view causes a pleasure or uneasiness of a particular kind. In giving a reason, therefore, for the pleasure or uneasiness, we sufficiently explain the vice or virtue. To have the sense of virtue, is nothing but to *feel* a satisfaction of a particular kind from the contemplation of a character. The very *feeling* constitutes our praise or admiration. We go no farther; nor do we enquire into the cause of the satisfaction. We do not infer a character to be virtuous, because it pleases: But in feeling that it pleases after such a particular manner, we in effect feel that it is virtuous.

8. The origin of justice

Hume, *Treatise of Human Nature*, edited by Selby-Bigge, pp. 488–9.

Now it appears that in the original frame of our mind, our strongest attention is confined to ourselves; our next is extended to our relations and acquaintance; and 'tis only the weakest which reaches to strangers and indifferent persons. This partiality, then, and unequal affection, must not only have an influence on our behaviour and conduct in society, but even on our ideas of vice and virtue; so as to make us regard any remarkable transgression of such a degree of partiality, either by too great an enlargement, or contraction of the affections, as vicious and immoral. This we may observe in our common judgments concerning actions, where we blame a person, who either centres all his affections in his family, or is so regardless of them, as, in any opposition of interest, to give the preference to a stranger, or mere chance acquaintance. From all which it follows, that our natural uncultivated ideas of morality, instead of providing a remedy for the partiality of our affections, do rather conform themselves to that partiality, and give it an additional force and influence.

The remedy, then, is not derived from nature, but from *artifice*; or more properly speaking, nature provides a remedy in the judgment and understanding, for what is irregular and commodious in the affections. For when men, from their early education in society, have become sensible of the infinite advantages that result from it, and have besides acquired a new affection to company and conversation; and when they have observed that the principal disturbance in society arises from those goods, which we call external, and from their looseness and easy transition from one person to another; they must seek for a remedy, by putting these goods, as far as possible, on the same footing with the fix'd and constant advantages of the mind and body. This can be done after no other manner, than by a convention entered into by all the members of the society to bestow stability on the possession of those external goods, and leave every one in the peaceable enjoyment of what he may acquire by his fortune and industry. By this means, every one knows what he may safely possess; and the passions are restrained in their partial and contradictory motions.

9. Adam Smith and the doctrine of sympathy

a. Adam Smith, *The Theory of Moral Sentiments*, in *The Works of Adam Smith* 5 vols (London, 1812) I, p. 2.

As we have no immediate experience of what other men feel, we can form no idea of the manner in which they are affected, but by conceiving what we ourselves should feel in the like situation. Though our brother is upon the rack, as long as we ourselves are at our ease, our senses will never inform us of what he suffers. They never did, and never can, carry us beyond our own person, and it is by the imagination only that we can form any conception of what are his sensations. Neither can that faculty help us to this any other way, than by representing to us what would be our own, if we were in his case. It is the impressions of our own senses only, not those of his, which our imaginations copy. By the imagination we place ourselves in his situation, we conceive ourselves enduring all the same torments, we enter as it were into his body, and become in some measure the same person with him, and thence form some idea of his sensations, and even feel something which, though weaker in degree, is not altogether unlike them.

b. *ibid.* I, pp. 4–5

Neither is it those circumstances only, which create pain or sorrow, that call forth our fellow-feeling. Whatever is the passion which arises from any object in the person principally concerned, an analogous emotion springs up, at the thought of his situation, in the breast of every attentive spectator. Our joy for the deliverance of those heroes of tragedy or romance who interest us, is as sincere as our grief for their distress, and our fellow-feeling with their misery is not more real than that with their happiness. We enter into their gratitude towards those faithful friends who did not desert them in their difficulties; and we heartily go along with their resentment against those perfidious traitors who injured, abandoned, or deceived them. In every passion of which the mind of man is susceptible, the emotions of the by-stander always correspond to what, by bringing the case home to himself, he imagines should be the sentiments of the sufferer.

Pity and compassion are words appropriated to signify our fellow-feeling with the sorrow of others. Sympathy, though its meaning was, perhaps, originally the same, may now, however, without much impropriety, be made use of to denote our fellow-feeling with any passion whatever.

c. *ibid.* I, pp. 19–21

The sentiment or affection of the heart from which any action proceeds, and upon which its whole virtue or vice must ultimately depend, may be considered under two different aspects, or in two different relations; first, in relation to the cause which excites it, or the motive which gives occasion to it; and secondly, in relation to the end which it proposes, or the effect which it tends to produce.

In the suitableness or unsuitableness, in the proportion or disproportion which the affection seems to bear to the cause or object which excites it, consists the propriety or impropriety, the decency or ungracefulness of the consequent action.

In the beneficial or hurtful nature of the effects which the affection aims at, or tends to produce, consists the merit or demerit of the action, the qualities by which it is entitled to reward, or is deserving of punishment.

Philosophers have, of late years, considered chiefly the tendency of affections, and have given little attention to the relation which they stand in to the cause, which excites them. In common life, however, when we judge of any person's conduct, and of the sentiments which directed it, we constantly consider them under both these aspects. When we blame in another man the excesses of love, of grief, of resentment, we not only consider the ruinous effects which they tend to produce, but the little occasion which was given for them. The merit of his favourite, we say, is not so great, his misfortune is not so dreadful, his provocation is not so extraordinary, as to justify so violent a passion. We should have indulged, we say; perhaps, have aproved of the violence of his emotion, had the cause been in any respect proportioned to it.

When we judge in this manner of any affection as proportioned or disproportioned to the cause which excites it, it is scarce possible that we should make use of any other rule or canon but the correspondent affection in ourselves. If, upon bringing the case home to our own breast, we find that the sentiments which it gives occasion to, coincide and tally with our own, we necessarily approve of them as proportioned and suitable to their objects; if otherwise, we necessarily disapprove of them, as extravagant and out of proportion.

Every faculty in one man is the measure by which he judges of the like faculty in another. I judge of your sight by my sight, of your ear by my ear, of your reason by my reason, of your resentment by my resentment, of your love by my love. I neither have, nor can have, any other way of judging about them.

10. The impartial spectator

Adam Smith, *The Theory of Moral Sentiments*, in *The Works of Adam Smith*, I, pp. 219–21.

The all-wise Author of Nature has, in this manner, taught man to respect the sentiments and judgments of his brethren; to be more or less pleased when they approve of his conduct, and to be more or less hurt when they disapprove of it. He had made man, if I may say so, the immediate judge of mankind; and has, in this respect, as in many others, created him after his own image, and appointed him his vicegerent upon earth, to superintend the behaviour of his brethren. They are taught by nature, to acknowledge that power and jurisdiction which has been thus conferred upon him, to be more or less humbled and mortified when they have incurred his censure, and to be more or less elated when they have obtained his applause.

But though man has, in this manner, been rendered the immediate judge of mankind, he has been rendered so only in the first instance; and an appeal lies from his sentence to a much higher tribunal, to the tribunal of their own consciences, to that of the supposed impartial and well-informed spectator, to that of the man within the breast, the great judge and arbiter of their conduct. The jurisdictions of those two tribunals are founded upon principles which, though in some respects resembling and akin, are, however, in reality different and distinct. The jurisdiction of the man without, is founded altogether in the desire of actual praise, and in the aversion to actual blame. The jurisdiction of the man within, is founded altogether in the desire of praise-worthiness, and in the aversion to blame-worthiness; in the desire of possessing those qualities, and performing those actions, which we love and admire in other people; and in the dread of possessing those qualities, and performing those actions, which we hate and despise in other people.

11. The general rules of morality

Adam Smith, *The Theory of Moral Sentiment*, in *The Works of Adam Smith*, I, pp. 269–71.

. . . Our continual observations upon the conduct of others, insensibly lead us to form to ourselves certain general rules concerning what is fit and proper either to be done or to be avoided. Some of their actions shock all our natural sentiments. We hear everybody about us express the same detestation against them. This still further confirms, and even exasperates our natural sense of their deformity. It satisfies us that we view them in the proper light, when we see other people view them in the same light. We resolve never to be guilty of the like, nor ever, upon any account, to render ourselves in this manner the objects of universal disapprobation. We thus naturally lay down to ourselves a general rule, that all such actions are to be avoided, as tending to render us odious, contemptible, or punishable, the objects of all those sentiments for which we have the greatest dread and aversion. Other actions, on the contrary, call forth our approbation, and we hear everybody around us express the same favourable opinion concerning them. Everybody is eager to honour and reward them. They excite all those sentiments for which we have by nature the strongest desire; the love, the gratitude, the admiration of mankind. We become ambitious of performing the like; and thus naturally lay down to ourselves a rule of another kind, that every opportunity of acting in this manner is carefully to be sought after.

It is thus that the general rules of morality are formed. They are ultimately founded upon experience of what, in particular instances, our moral faculties, our natural sense of merit and propriety, approve, or disapprove of. We do not originally approve or condemn particular actions; because, upon examination, they appear to be agreeable or inconsistent with a certain general rule. The general rule, on the contrary, is formed, by finding from experience, that all actions of a certain kind, or circumstances in a certain manner, are approved or disapproved of.

4 The Principles of 'Natural History'

There were certain underlying assumptions shared, in different degrees, by those who wrote about the study of society in eighteenth century Scotland. 'Natural history' or 'philosophical' history, was based firmly on moral philosophy, on a close examination of human nature; it also presupposed a certain methodological approach, and assumptions about the social nature of man, and about the direction of human progress. The principal writers on this subject were Lord Kames, Adam Smith, Adam Ferguson, William Robertson and John Millar (see Biographical Notes); a number of other minor writers, including Sir John Dalrymple (1726–1810), Lord Monboddo (1714–99), James Dunbar (?–1798), and Gilbert Stuart (1742–86) shared their interests and wrote on similar subjects.

The aims of their historical writing are described in Documents 1–3: a comprehensive charting of human development through certain common stages, through the close study both of existing contemporary societies, including the most primitive, such as the American Indian, and through the evidence of historians, travellers, and missionaries. What is interesting here is the assumption of a common progress from rudeness to refinement, which all societies and nations would share. This is certainly the view shared by Smith, Robertson, and Millar; Adam Ferguson's position is rather different. Although Ferguson also believed in the comparative approach to the history of man, he was less concerned with the evaluation of each stage of society in terms of the final result, more concerned with the approach towards the perfecting of human nature, by each individual society, at whatever stage in its development. The more orthodox view stressed the overwhelming importance of different modes of production in determining the character of a society; for Ferguson, the critical point was the scope given by any society to man's active nature, to fulfil its own potential.

The comparative method first emerges, as a conscious tool for the use of historians, in the mid-eighteenth century. In France, Montesquieu had, in *L'Esprit des Lois* (1749), attempted to relate the government of a society to its other aspects: to economy, climate, manners, and social institutions; and he had used much comparative material. Yet Montesquieu had not used his evidence to present any *progressive* view of the different stages of human society. From the mid-1750s the major elements of a distinctively Scottish version of man's past were becoming clearer; and in France, too, other writers followed the indications left by Montesquieu.

One important factor which strongly influences these writers' view of primitive peoples was the increasing accessibility of knowledge of the American Indian. One much used source of information was the work by the Abbe Lafitau (1670–1740), *Moeurs des Sauvages Ameriquains, comparee aux moeurs des premiers temps* (1724); though previous works had also studied American Indian tribes, none were so acceptable—Lafitau's book was thorough, detailed, and contained much comparative insight. Other sources included the Bible, used as an anthropological and historical source, the works of classical authors, and the medieval past. Clearly most of this material had been available for a very long time; but new questions were now being asked of it[1]. First, the new questions were built on an assumption that man was a *social* being, that there were necessary bonds which linked man to his fellow beings. Adam Ferguson put most effectively a view shared by almost all his contemporaries: the view that 'mankind are to be taken in groups' (Document 7). The solitary savage that was idealised in the imagination of Jean-Jacques Rousseau (see his *Discourse on the Origin of Inequality*, first published 1755) was a meaningless fiction; the evidence of this lay in the demonstration that language, and therefore communication, was natural to man (Document 5). For Ferguson, man as a species had a place at the head of that scale of being which placed each created species, of human, animal and plant life, in a divinely established hierarchy. Man shared certain characteristics with the animal kingdom; but was clearly distinguished from them by his intelligence, which offered man a capacity for personal fulfilment denied to other species. Man like other animals was gregarious; his habits were social, and he had had, from the beginning, the capacity to communicate through language, an ability which 'even the rudest tribes' possessed. Other contemporaries were less emphatic, but shared the same belief in the natural sociality of man, a position derived both from Hutcheson and ultimately from the natural law school. In David Hume's *Treatise*, however, it is not always easy to distinguish between the admittedly fictitious savage in the fictitious state of nature, used merely as an intellectual construct, and the savage for whom the life of the family was the major social bond, (Document 8).

Lord Monboddo's arguments are included here for their notoriety, and for their place within this debate (Document 6); though Monboddo's approach differed from all the other contemporary writers discussed here. He believed that man's distinction from the animal kingdom was by no means as clearcut as Ferguson has stated; the evidence of individual savages, without the power of speech, proved this. He went further in his discussion of the Orangoutang as 'a nation without speech', and agreed with Rousseau on the existence of the solitary savage. But his assertions brought him little but ridicule from the literary world.

Smith, Millar, and Robertson, however, saw the 'savage' state of human development as the first of the four stages through which each society had in its own way to pass. The nature of each state was determined in the main by its mode of production; and the institutions, manners, and style of any society would depend upon its economic base. In Scotland, perhaps the first to publish such an analysis was Sir John Dalrymple, in his *Essay towards a General History of Feudal Property in Great Britain* (1757), in which he postulated three stages of property ownership, though drawing no very firm conclusions from this. He was followed by Lord Kames, who, in his *Historical Law Tracts* (1758), described four stages of social development, and used these stages to illustrate the development of legal institutions. However, it is possible that both these men were anticipated by Adam Smith's lectures at the University of Glasgow. It is known that Smith was delivering a well developed version of this view by 1762–3 (Document 10); and it seems likely from the evidence of those who attended Smith's earlier classes, including John Millar, that the same lectures were being delivered in the mid–1750s[2]. Smith himself, lecturing on 'natural jurisprudence and politics', followed the progress of government and legal institutions in the light of the different stages of social development. Like Hutcheson, his predecessor, he was concerned to spell out the rights and obligations of man in society; unlike Hutcheson he placed changing personal and property rights within their historical context, and within the framework of changing economic structures. After Smith, John Millar, holder of the Chair of Roman Law at Glasgow, carried on the analysis of social institutions within the framework established by Smith.

Ferguson's version of this approach to the past differed in several respects. He divided the stages of society not into four, but into three: savagery, barbarism, and the 'polished' society. The savage state, in which property was almost unknown, corresponded to Smith's; the barbarian society might be a pastoral or an agricultural one. In his treatment of all societies Ferguson was most concerned to evaluate the chances which each kind of society offered for man to fulfil his own moral potential; his view of human progress therefore depended on fundamentally different assumptions from those of Smith, for whom material progress was inevitable, and, for the most part, beneficial for man. Ferguson's standards are explicitly those of the moralist.

Other influences could also affect the material environment which shaped men's lives, in particular the climate and geography of a society. Smith nods in this direction; Millar and Ferguson spell out in more detail the way in which climatic conditions may influence the distribution of property, and men's own ability to improve their condition. Robertson, in his *History of America*, 1777, did illustrate this by examining the variations in life among the Indian tribes from different parts of the American continent[3].

This analysis of the 'natural history' of man needed also to establish the means by which a society moved from one stage in its development to the next. There was common agreement on the capacity of man to search for infinite improvement, on the direct involvement of man's active powers in economic growth. But at the same time, the study of social and economic history was leading to the view that progress and change came about not necessarily through the deliberate planning of human wisdom, but often in spite of it, sometimes through accident, sometimes through the clash of opposed interests. Ferguson put the case most clearly, that 'men stumble upon establishments'; and Ferguson in his discussion of what has been called 'the law of unintended outcomes' was led to the conclusion that men's ability to direct their own affairs was limited, and that conflict could be as fruitful as harmony (Document 13). Social institutions were moulded by the circumstances and the inheritance of particular societies—and especially by the economic base of that society; this chapter is intended to illustrate certain of these principles of 'natural history'.

NOTES

1. There is a full recent treatment of this aspect of the writers of the Scottish Enlightenment in Ronald L. Meek, *Social Science and the Ignoble Savage* (Cambridge, 1976).

2. Meek, *op. cit.* pp. 109–12; and see also Andrew S. Skinner, 'Adam Smith: an Economic Interpretation of History' in *Essays on Adam Smith*, edited by Andrew S. Skinner and Thomas Wilson (Oxford, 1975).

3. See especially Books IV and VII of the *History of America*, first published in 1777 and reprinted in *The Works of William Robertson, D. D.* New edition (London, 1817).

The Principles of
'Natural History': Documents

APPROACHES TO THE STUDY OF SOCIETY

1. The methods of 'natural history': two examples

a. John Millar, *The Origin of the Distinction of Ranks, or, an inquiry into the circumstances which give rise to influence and authority in the different ranks of society*, third edition, corrected and enlarged (London, 1779) pp. 14–15.

The following inquiry is intended to illustrate the natural history of mankind in several important articles. This is attempted, by pointing out the more obvious and common improvements which gradually arise in the state of society, and by showing the influence of these upon the manners, the laws and the government of a people.

With regard to the facts made use of in the following discourse, the reader, who is conversant in history, will readily perceive the difficulty of obtaining proper materials for speculations of this nature. Historians of reputation have commonly overlooked the transactions of early ages, as not deserving to be remembered; and even in the history of later and more cultivated periods, they have been more solicitous to give an exact account of battles, and public negotiations, than of the interior police and government of a country. Our information, therefore, with regard to the state of mankind in the rude parts of the world, is chiefly derived from the relations of travellers, whose character and situation in life, neither set them above the suspicion of being easily deceived, nor of endeavouring to misrepresent the facts which they have related. From the number, however, and the variety of those relations, they acquire, in many cases, a degree of authority, upon which we may depend with security, and to which the narration of any single person, how respectable soever, can have no pretension. When illiterate men, ignorant of the writings of each other, and who, unless upon religious subjects, had no speculative systems to warp their opinions, have, in distant ages and countries, described the manners of people in similar circumstances, the reader has an opportunity of comparing their several descriptions, and from their agreement or disagreement is enabled to ascertain the credit that is due to them.

b. W. Robertson, 'The History of America', 1777, reprinted in *The Works of William Robertson, D. D.* New edition, 12 vols (London, 1817), IX, pp. 50–4.

The condition and character of the American nations, at the time when they became known to the Europeans, deserve more attentive consideration than the inquiry concerning their original. The latter is merely an object of curiosity; the former is one of the most important as well as instructive researches which can occupy the philosopher or historian. In order to complete the history of the human mind, and attain to a perfect knowledge of its nature and operations, we must contemplate man in all those various situations wherein he has been placed. We must follow him in his progress through the different stages of society, as he gradually advances from the infant state of civil life towards its maturity and decline. We must observe, at each period, how the faculties of his understanding unfold, we must attend to the efforts of his active powers, watch the various movements of desire and affection, as they rise in his breast, and mark whither they tend, and with what ardour they are exerted. The philosophers and historians of ancient Greece and Rome, our guides in this as well as every other disquisition, had only a limited view of this subject, as they had hardly any opportunity of surveying man in his rudest and most early state. In all those regions of the earth, with which they were well acquainted, civil society had made considerable advances, and nations had finished a good part of their career before they began to observe them. The Scythians and Germans, the rudest people of whom any ancient author has transmitted to us an authentic account, possessed flocks and herds, had acquired property of various kinds, and, when compared with mankind in their primitive state, may be reckoned to have attained to a great degree of civilisation.

But the discovery of the New World enlarged the sphere of contemplation, and presented nations to our view, in stages of their progress, much less advanced than those wherein they have been observed in our continent. In America, man appears under the rudest form in which we can conceive him to subsist. We behold communities just beginning to unite, and may examine the sentiments and actions of human beings in the infancy of social life, while they feel but imperfectly the force of its ties, and have scarcely relinquished their native liberty. That state of primaeval simplicity, which was known in our continent only by the fanciful description of pets, really existed in the other. The greater part of its inhabitants were strangers to industry and labour, ignorant of arts, imperfectly acquainted with the nature of property, and enjoying almost without restriction or control the blessings which flowed spontaneously from the bounty of nature. There were only two nations in this vast continent which had emerged from this rude state, and had made any considerable progress in acquiring the idea, and adopting the institutions, which belong to polished societies. Their government and manners will fall naturally under our review in relating the discovery and conquest of the Mexican and Peruvian empires; and we shall have there an opportunity of contemplating the Americans in the state of highest improvement to which they ever attained . . .

It is extremely difficult to procure satisfying and authentic information concerning nations while they remain uncivilised. To discover their true character under this rude form, and to select the features by which they are distinguished, requires an observer possessed of no less impartiality than discernment. For, in every stage of society, the faculties, the sentiments, and desires of men are so accommodated to their own state, that they become standards of excellence to themselves, they affix the idea of perfection and happiness to those attainments which resemble their own, and wherever the objects and enjoyments to which they have been accustomed are wanting, confidently pronounce a people to be barbarous and miserable. Hence the mutual contempt with which the members of communities, unequal in their degrees of improvement, regard each other. Polished nations, conscious of the advantages which they derive from their knowledge and arts, are apt to view rude nations with peculiar scorn, and, in the pride of superiority, will hardly allow either their occupations, their feelings, or their pleasures, to be worthy of men. It had seldom been the lot of communities, in their early and unpolished state, to fall under the observation of persons endowed with force of mind superior to vulgar prejudices, and capable of contemplating man, under whatever aspect he appears, with a candid and discerning eye.

2. Man's progressive nature

Adam Ferguson, *Principles of Moral and Political Science*, I, pp. 192–5.

For our purpose, however, it is sufficient to observe, that the state of nature or the distinctive character of any progressive being is to be taken, not from its description at the outset, or at any subsequent stage of its progress: but from an accumulative view of its movement throughout. The oak is distinguishable from the pine, not merely by its seed leaf; but by every successive aspect of its form; by its foliage in every successive season; by its acorn; by its spreading top; by its lofty growth, and the length of its period. And the state of nature, relative to every tree in the wood, includes all the varieties of form or dimension through which it is known to pass in the course of its nature.

By parity of reason, the natural state of a living creature includes all its known variations, from the embryo and the foetus to the breathing animal, the adolescent and the adult, through which life in all its varieties is known to pass.

The state of nature, relative to man, is also a state of progression equally real, and of greater extent. The individual receives the first stamina of his frame in a growing state. His stature is waxing, his limbs and his organs gain strength, and he himself a growing faculty in the use of them. His faculties improve by exercise, and are in a continual state of exertion . . .

The state of nature relative to the species is differently constituted, and of different extent. It consists in the continual succession of one generation to another; in progressive attainments made by different ages; communicated with additions from age to age; and in periods, the farthest advanced, not appearing to have arrived at any necessary limit. This progress indeed is subject to interruption, and may come to a close, or give way to vicissitudes at any of its stages; but not more necessarily at the period of highest attainment than at any other.

So long as the son continues to be taught what the father knew, or the pupil begins where the tutor has ended, and is equally bent on advancement; to every generation the state of art and accommodations already in use serves but as ground work for new inventions and successive improvement. As Newton did not acquiesce in what was observed by Kepler and Galileo; no more have successive astronomers restricted their view to what Newton has demonstrated. And with respect to the mechanic and commercial arts, even in the midst of the most laboured accommodations, so long as there is any room for improvement, invention is busy as if nothing had yet been done to supply the necessities, or complete the conveniencies of human life: But even here, and in all its steps of progression, this active nature, in respect to the advantages, whether of knowledge or art, derived from others, if there be not a certain effort to advance, is exposed to reverse and decline. The generation, in which there is no desire to know more or practise better than its predecessors, will probably neither know so much nor practise so well. And the decline of successive generations, under this wane of intellectual ability, is not less certain than the progress made under the operation of a more active and forward disposition.

3. Man's distinction from the animal world

Adam Ferguson, *Principles of Moral and Political Science*, I, p. 48.

Man, whether considered in respect to the range of his active nature, or the result of his disposition to society, notwithstanding the superior powers of communication and intercourse we have mentioned, appears to be no more than a variety in the system of life. With the other parts of this system he partakes in all the principles of vegetable and animal natures, discoverable in him as well as in them, only, by external phenomena or apparent effects.

But there is a principle, in respect to which man differs from the other animals, not only in measure or degree, but totally, and in kind. This principle we term his intelligence or mind, intimately conscious of itself, as it exists in thought, discernment, and will.

4. On the progressive nature of man's intelligence

Adam Ferguson, *Principles of Moral and Political Science*, I, p. 54.

To the mere animal, the Author of nature appears to have said 'Such I have made you, and such you shall be, and no more': To man 'I have given you intelligence and freedom; I have not set bounds to what you may attain, in the proper use of your faculties; and, as the good you attain shall be your own, so, for the talent you misplace, you must be accountable'.

Such is the sum of that distinction, which subsists between man and the other animals; a distinction which it is of great consequence to retain in our thoughts, at every step of the argument relating to him.

THE NATURAL CONDITION OF MAN

5. The origins of language

Adam Ferguson, *Principles of Moral and Political Science*, I, pp. 42–3.

If we are asked, therefore, who was the inventor of articulate sounds? and, without being led by any degree of connection between the sign and the thing signified, taught mankind a name for every known subject, a name for every quality, for every relation of things, for every thought or sentiment of the mind, a form for every proposition, whether interrogatory, affirmative or negative, whether doubtful or certain, general, or particular, who taught the tongue to vary the inflections of sound, to keep pace with the variations of meaning? We may venture to answer that Mind, or the principle of life in man, is competent to this effect; as fire, wherever it be lodged in any corporeal mass, is competent to expansion, fusion, or evaporation. In natures stationary, like those of most animal species, an original stock of instinctive expression may be sufficient for every purpose of life: But, in the progressive nature of man, it is necessary that the stock of language should wax with the growing occasions on which it is employed. And, although no single genius, however vast, is equal to the invention of a language, such as even the vulgar speak, we may yet conceive that a talent for the use of arbitrary signs, such as the ordinary race of men possess, operating in the detail of occasions, struggling to express a meaning in such signals as occurred, or were nearest at hand, has enabled the parties mutually to understand, and be understood, so as to give to the vernacular dialect of every society, in the result of their efforts, its degree of enlargement and use . . .

Parts of speech, which, in speculation, cost the grammarian so much study, are in practice familiar to the vulgar: The rudest tribes, even the idiot and the insane are possessed of them: They are soonest learned in childhood; insomuch, that we must suppose human nature, in its lowest state, competent to the use of them; and, without the intervention of uncommon genius, mankind, in a succession of ages, qualified to accomplish in detail this amazing fabric of language, which, when raised to its height, appears so much above what could be ascribed to any simultaneous effort of the most sublime and comprehensive abilities.

We are apt to treat the origin of language, as we treat that of society itself, by supposing a time when neither existed; but, from the facts now stated, we may venture to infer, that, since mankind were fairly entered on this scene of human life, there never was any such time; that both associating and speaking, in however rude a form, are coeval with the species of man.

6. A notorious dissenting view: Lord Monboddo and the origins of language

James Burnet, Lord Monboddo, *Of the Origin and Progress of Language*, first volume (Edinburgh, 1773), pp. 171–6; 5 later volumes were subsequently published.

We are now to descend from those high speculations concerning ideas which constitute the *form* of language, to sounds, which are the *matter* of it. And though I may have failed in my endeavours to convince the reader, that the operation of abstracting the perceptions of sense, and forming of them generals and universals . . . is not performed by any natural instinct, but has arisen, like the arts that are founded upon it, from experience and observation, and by use has been formed into habit; I cannot doubt but that I shall convince every one who will think it worth his while to read what follows, that articulation is altogether the work of art, at least of a habit acquired by custom and exercise, and that we are truly by nature the *mutum pecus* that Horace makes us to be. This I think I am able to prove, both from theory and facts. I will begin with the facts which will serve to explain my theory.

It is a clear case, that we do not speak in that state which, of all others, best deserves the appellation of *natural*, I mean when we are born, nor for a considerable time after; and even then we learn but slowly, and with a great deal of labour and difficulty. About the same time also we begin to form ideas. But the same answer, I know, is made to serve for both; namely, That our minds as well as our bodily organs, are then weak, and therefore are unable to perform several of their natural functions; but as soon as they become strong and confirmed by age, then we both think and speak. That this is not true with respect to *thinking*, I have already endeavoured to show; and with respect to speaking, I say, in the first place, that of all those savages which have been caught in different parts of Europe[1], not one had the use of speech, though they had all the organs of pronunciation such as we have them and the understanding of a man, as least as much as was possible, when it is considered, that their minds were not cultivated by any kind of conversation or intercourse with their own species; nor had they come the length, according to my hypothesis, of forming ideas, or thinking at all. One of these was catched in the woods of Hanover as late as the reign of George I and for any thing I know is yet alive; at least I am sure he was so some years ago. He was a man in mind as well as body, as I have been informed by a person who lived for a considerable time in the neighbourhood of a farmer's house where he was kept, and had an opportunity of seeing him almost every day; not an idiot, as he has been represented by some who cannot make allowance for the difference that education makes upon men's minds; yet he was not only mute when first caught, but he never learned to speak, though at the time the gentleman from whom I have my information saw him, he had been above thirty years in England.

Further, not only solitary savages, but a whole nation, if I may call them so, have been found without the use of speech. This is the case of the Ouran Outangs that are found in the kingdom of Angola in Africa, and in several parts of Asia. They are exactly of the human form; walking erect, not upon all-four, like the savages that have been found in Europe; they use sticks for weapons; they live in society; they make huts of branches of trees, and they carry off negro girls, whom they make slaves of, and use both for work and pleasure.· These facts are related of them by Mons. Buffon in his natural history: and I was further told by a gentleman who had been in Angola, that there were some of them seven feet high, and that the negroes were extremely afraid of them; for when they did any mischief to the Ouran Outangs they were sure to be heartily cudgelled, when they were catched. But though from the particulars above mentioned it appears certain, that they are of our species, and though they have made some progress in the arts of life, they have not come the length of language; and accordingly none of them that have been brought to Europe could speak, and what seem strange, never learned to speak. I myself saw at Paris one of them, whose skin was stuffed, standing upon a shelf in the King's cabinet of natural curiosities. He had exactly the shape and features of a man; and particularly I was informed, that he had organs of pronunciation as perfect as we have. He lived several years at Versailles, and died by drinking spirits. He had as much of the understanding of a man as could be expected from his education, and performed many little offices to the lady with whom he lived; but never learned to speak. I was well informed too, of one of them belonging to a French gentleman in India, who used to go market for him, but was likewise mute [2].

[1] See an account of them in Rousseau's *treatise sur l'inegalite des hommes*, note 3. The first of these savages was catched near Hesse-Cassel in 1344, and was taught to speak. Another was found in the forests of Lithuania in the year 1694. He too was mute when he was found; and whether he ever learned to speak, does not appear. In 1719, two savages were found in the Pyrenaen mountains, and the Hanoverian savage was catched and brought to England in the reign of George I. All these, when they were first catched, were not only mute, that is, had no articulation, but appeared to be truly quadrupeds; and the first mentioned, our author says, was taught with much difficulty to walk upright. When we join to this a fact which Mons. Rousseau likewise avers, that the children of the Hottentots and Caribbees walk so long upon their hands, that they are with much difficulty taught to walk upright, it would seem that we must add to man's other acquired habits his quality of *biped*, which has always been thought an essential part of his original nature, and accordingly is made part of some definitions of him. But Aristotle knew better; for all that he has said is that by nature man is *more* a biped than any other animal— . . . *De animalium incessu*, cap 5. The meaning of which I take to be that he has by nature a greater aptitude to acquire the habit of walking *on two* than any other animal. And Mons. Rousseau's arguments in support of his natural erectness appear to me to prove no more.

[2] Mons. Rousseau, in his work above quoted, note 10 has collected the several accounts given of this animal by travellers, and agrees with me in opinion, that he

belongs to our species; rejecting with great contempt the notion of those who think that speech is natural to man. Now if we get over that prejudice, and do not insist, that other arts of life, which the Ouran Outangs want, are likewise natural to man, it is impossible we can refuse them the appellation *men*.

7. 'Mankind are to be taken in groups . . .'

Adam Ferguson, *Essay on the History of Civil Society*, second edition, corrected (London, 1768) pp. 6–9.

Mankind are to be taken in groups, as they have always subsisted. The history of the individual is but a detail of the sentiments and thoughts he has entertained in the view of his species: and every experiment relative to this subject should be made with entire societies, not with single men. We have every reason, however, to believe, that in the case of such an experiment made, we shall suppose, with a colony of children transplanted from the nursery, and left to form a society apart, untaught and undisciplined, we should only have the same things repeated, which in so many different parts of the earth have been transacted already. The members of our little society would feed and sleep, would herd together and play, would have a language of their own, would quarrel and divide, would be to one another the most important objects of the scene, and, in the ardour of their friendships and competitions, would overlook their personal danger, and suspend the care of their self-preservation. Has not the human race been planted like the colony in question? Who has directed their course? whose instruction have they heard? or whose example have they followed?

   Nature, therefore, we shall presume, having given to every animal its mode of existence, its dispositions and manner of life, has dealt equally with those of the human race; and the natural historian who would collect the properties of this species, may fill up every article now, as well as he could have done in any former age. Yet one property by which man is distinguished, has been sometimes overlooked in the account of his nature, or has only served to mislead our attention. In other classes of animals, the individual advances from infancy to age or maturity; and he attains, in the compass of a single life, to all the perfection his nature can reach: but in the human kind, the species has a progress as well as the individual; they build in every subsequent age on foundations formerly laid; and, in a succession of years, tend to a perfection in the application of their faculties, to which the aid of long experience is required, and to which many generations must have combined their endeavours. We observe the progress they have made; we distinctly enumerate many of its steps; we can trace them back to a distant antiquity; of which no record remains, nor any monument is preserved, to inform us what were the openings of this wonderful scene. The consequence is, that instead of attending to the character of our species, where the particulars are vouched by the surest authority, we endeavour to trace it through ages and scenes unknown; and, instead of supposing that the beginning of our story was nearly of a piece with the sequel, we think ourselves warranted to reject every circumstance of our present condition and frame, as adventitious and foreign to our nature. The progress of mankind from a supposed state of animal sensibility, to the attainment of reason, to the use of language, and to the habit of society, has been accordingly painted with a force of imagination, and its steps have been marked with a boldness of invention, that would tempt us to admit, among the materials of history, the suggestions of fancy, and to receive, perhaps, as the model of our nature in its original state, some of the animals whose shape has the gretst resemblance to ours.[1]

It would be ridiculous to affirm, as a discovery, that the species of the horse was probably never the same with that of the lion; yet, in opposition to what has dropped from the pens of eminent writers, we are obliged to observe, that men have always appeared among animals a distinct and a superior race; that neither the possession of similar organs, nor the approximation of shape, nor the use of the hand, nor the continued intercourse with this sovereign artist, has enabled any other species to blend their nature or their inventions with his; that in his rudest state, he is found to be above them; and in his greatest degeneracy, never descends to their level. He is, in short, a man in every condition; and we can learn nothing of his nature from the analogy of other animals. If we would know him, we must attend to himself, to the course of his life, and the tenor of his conduct. With him the society appears to be as old as the individual, and the use of the tongue as universal as that of the hand or the foot. If there was a time in which he had his acquaintance with his own species to make, and his faculties to acquire, it is a time of which we have no record, and in relation to which our opinions can serve no purpose, and are supported by no evidence.

[1] Rousseau, *Sur l'origine de l'inegalite parmi les hommes.*

8. The origins of society: the family

D. Hume, *Treatise of Human Nature*, edited by Selby-Bigge, pp. 484–6.

Of all the animals, with which this globe is peopled, there is none towards whom nature seems, at first sight, to have exercised more cruelty than towards man, in the numberless wants and necessities, with which she has loaded him, and in the slender means, which she affords to the relieving these necessities. In other creatures these two particulars generally compensate each other. If we consider the lion as a voracious and carnivorous animal, we shall easily discover him to be very necessitous; but if we turn our eye to his make and temper, his agility, his courage, his arms, and his force, we shall find, that his advantages hold proportion with his wants. The sheep and ox are deprived of all these advantages; but their appetites are moderate, and their food is of easy purchase. In man alone, this unnatural conjunction of infirmity, and of necessity, may be observed in its greatest perfection. Not only the food, which is required for his sustenance, flies his search and approach, or at least requires his labour to be produced, but he must be possessed of clothes and lodging, to defend him against the injuries of the weather; tho' to consider him only in himself, he is provided neither with arms, nor force, nor other natural abilities, which are in any degree answerable to so many necessities.

'Tis by society alone he is able to supply his defects, and raise himself up to an equality with his fellow-creatures, and even acquire a superiority above them. By society all his infirmities are compensated; and tho' in that situation his wants multiply every moment upon him, yet his abilities are still more augmented, and leave him in every respect more satisfied and happy, than 'tis possible for him, in his savage and solitary condition, ever to become. When every individual person labours a-part, and only for himself, his force is too small to execute any considerable work; his labour being employed in supplying all his different necessities, he never attains a perfection in any particular art; and as his force and success are not at all times equal, the least failure in either of these particulars must be attended with inevitable ruin and misery. Society provides a remedy for these *three* inconveniences. By the conjunction of forces, our power is augmented: By the partition of employments, our ability increases: And by mutual succour we are less exposed to fortune and accidents. 'Tis by this additional *force*, *ability* and *security*, that society becomes advantageous.

But in order to form society, 'tis requisite not only that it be advantageous, but also that men be sensible of these advantages; and 'tis impossible, their wild uncultivated state, that by study and reflexion alone, they should ever be able to attain this knowledge. Most fortunately, therefore, there is conjoined to those necessities, whose remedies are remote and obscure, another necessity, which having a present and more obvious remedy, may justly be regarded as the first and original principle of human society. This necessity is no other than that natural appetite betwixt the sexes, which unites them together, and preserves their union, till a new tie takes place in their concern for their common offspring. This new concern becomes also a principle of union betwixt the parents and offspring, and forms a more numerous society; where the parents govern by the advantage of their superior strength and wisdom, and at the same time are restrained in the exercise of their authority by that natural affection, which they bear their children. In a little time, custom and habit operating on the tender minds of the children, makes them sensible of the advantages, which they may reap from society, as well as fashions them by degrees for it, by rubbing off those corners and untoward affections, which prevent their coalition.

THE DEVELOPMENT OF AN EVOLUTIONARY VIEW

9. Three stages of economic growth

Lord Kames, *Historical Law Tracts*, second edition (Edinburgh, 1761), pp. 50–1, note.

Hunting and fishing, in order for sustenance, were the original occupations of man. The shepherd life succeeded; and the next stage was that of agriculture. These progressive changes, in the order now mentioned, may be traced in all nations, so far as we have any remains of their original history. The life of a fisher or hunter is averse to society, except among the members of single families. The shepherd life promotes larger societies, if that can be called a society, which hath scarce any other than a local connection. But the true spirit of society, which consists in mutual benefits, and in making the industry of individuals profitable to others as well as to themselves, was not known till agriculture was invented. Agriculture requires the aid of many other arts. The carpenter, the blacksmith, the mason, and other artificiers contribute to it. Thus, circumstance connects individuals in an intimate society of mutual support, which again compacts them within a narrow space. Now in the first state of man, viz, that of hunting and fishing, there obviously is no place for government, except that which is exercised by the heads of families over children and domestics. The shepherd life in which societies are formed by the conjunction of families for mutual defence, requires some sort of government; slight indeed in proportion to the slightness of the mutual connection. But it was agriculture which first produced a regular system of government. The intimate union among a multitude of individuals, occasioned by agriculture, discovered a number of social duties, formerly unknown. These behoved to be ascertained by laws, the observance of which must be enforced by punishment. Such operations cannot be carried on otherwise than by lodging power in one or more persons, to direct the resolutions, and apply the force of the whole society. In short, it may be laid down as an universal maxim, that in every society, the advances of government towards perfection are strictly proportioned to the advances of the society towards intimacy of union.

10. The four stage theory of development

Adam Smith, MSS Notes of his Lectures on Jurisprudence, 6 vols, December 24 1762—12 April 1763 (Glasgow University Library, MS Gen. 94/1), Vol. I, entry for 24 December 1762.

There are four distinct states which mankind passes through. 1st the age of Hunters; 2nd, the age of Shepherds; 3rd, the age of Agriculture; 4th, the age of Commerce.

If one should suppose ten or twelve persons of different sexes settled in an uninhabited island, the first method they would fall upon for their sustenance would be to support themselves by the wild fruits and wild animals which the country afforded. Their sole business would be hunting the wild beasts or catching the fishes. The pulling of a wild fruit can hardly be called an employment. The only thing amongst them which deserved the appellation of a business would be the chase. This is the age of hunters. In process of time, as their numbers multiplied, they would find the chase too precarious for their support. They would be necessitated to contrive some other method whereby to support themselves. At first perhaps they would try to lay up at one time, when they had been successful, what would support them for a considerable time. But this would go no great length. The contrivance they would think of most naturally would be to tame some of those wild animals they caught, and by affording them better food than what they could get elsewhere, they would induce them to continue about their land themselves and multiply their kind.

Hence would arise the age of shepherds. They would more probably begin first by multiplying animals than vegetables, as less skill and observation would be required: nothing more than to know what food suited them. We find accordingly that in almost all countries the age of shepherds preceded that of agriculture. The Tartars and Arabians subsist almost entirely by their flocks and herds. The Arabs have a little agriculture, but the Tartars none at all. The whole of the savage nations which subsist by flocks have no notion of cultivating the ground. The only instance that has the appearance of an objection to this rule is the state of the North American Indians. They, though they have no conception of flocks and herds, have nevertheless some notion of agriculture. Their women plant a few stalks of Indian corn at the back of their huts: but this can hardly be called agriculture. This corn does not make any considerable part of their food: it serves only as a seasoning or something to give a relish to their common food, the flesh of those animals they have caught in the chase. Flocks and herds, therefore, are the first resource men would take themselves to when they found difficulty in subsisting by the chase.

But when a society becomes numerous they would find a difficulty in supporting themselves by herds and flocks. Then they would naturally turn themselves to the cultivation of land and the raising of such plants and trees as produced nourishment fit for them: they would observe that those weeds which fell on the dry, bare soil or on the rock, seldom came to anything, but that those which entered the soil generally produced a plant and bore seed similar to that which was sown. These observations they would extend to the different plants and trees they found produced agreeable and nourishing food. And by this means they would gradually advance into the age of Agriculture. As society was farther improved the several arts, which at first would be exercised by each individual as far as was necessary for his welfare, would be separated; some persons would cultivate one and others, as they severally inclined. They would exchange with one another what they produced more than was necessary for their support, and get in exchange for them the commodities they stood in need of and did not produce themselves. This exchange of commodities extends in time not only betwixt the individuals of the same society, but betwixt those of different nations. Thus we send to France our cloths, iron-work and other trinkets, and get in exchange their wines. To Spain and Portugal we send our superfluous corn, and bring from thence the Spanish and Portuguese wines. Thus at last the age of Commerce arises. When therefore a country is stored with all the flocks and herds it can support, the land cultivated so as to produce all the grain and other commodities necessary for our subsistence it can be brought to bear, or at least as much as supports the inhabitants when the superfluous products, whether of nature or art, are exported and other necessary ones brought in exchange, such as society has done all in its power towards its ease and convenience.

11. The savage and the barbarian

Adam Ferguson, *Essay on the History of Civil Society*, second edition 1768, pp. 123–4.

Of the nations who dwell in . . . the less cultivated parts of the earth, some entrust their subsistence chiefly to hunting, fishing, or the natural produce of the soil. They have little attention to property, and scarcely any beginnings of subordination or government. Others having possessed themselves of herds, and depending for their provision on pasture, know what it is to be poor and rich. They know the relations of patron and client, of servant and master, and suffer themselves to be classed according to their measures of wealth. This distinction must create a material difference of character, and may furnish two separate heads under which to consider the history of mankind in their rudest state; that of the savage, who is not yet acquainted with property; and that of the barbarian, to whom it is, although not ascertained by laws, a principal object of care and desire.

It must appear very evident, that property is a matter of progress. It requires, among other particulars which are the effect of time, some method of defining possession. The very desire of it proceeds from experience; and the industry by which it is gained, or improved, requires such a habit of acting with a view to distant objects, as may overcome the present disposition either to sloth or enjoyment. This habit is slowly acquired, and is in reality a principal distinction of nations in the advanced state of mechanic and commercial arts.

12. From savagery to civilisation

John Millar, *The Origin of the Distinction of Ranks*, third edition, 1779, pp. 3–6.

When we survey the present state of the globe, we find that, in many parts of it, the inhabitants are so destitute of culture, as to appear little above the condition of brute animals; and even when we peruse the remote history of polished nations, we have seldom any difficulty in tracing them to a state of the same rudeness and barbarism. There is, however, in man a disposition and capacity for improving his condition, by the exertion of which, he is carried on from one degree of advancement to another; and the similarity of his wants, as well as of the faculties by which those wants are supplied, has everywhere produced a remarkable uniformity in the several steps of his progression. A nation of savages, who feel the want of almost everything requisite for the support of life, must have their attention directed to a small number of objects, to the acquisition of food and clothing, or the procuring shelter from the inclemencies of the weather; and their ideas and feelings, in conformity to their situation, must, of course, be narrow and contracted. Their first efforts are naturally calculated to increase the means of subsistence, by catching or ensnaring wild animals, or by gathering the spontaneous fruits of the earth; and the experience, acquired in the exercise of these employments, is apt, successively to point out the methods of taming and rearing cattle, and of cultivating the ground. According as men have been successful in these great improvements, and find less difficulty in the attainment of bare necessaries, their prospects are gradually enlarged, their appetites and desires are more and more awakened and called forth in pursuit of the several conveniencies of life; and the various branches of manufacture, together with commerce, its inseparable attendant, and with science and literature, the natural offspring of ease and affluence, are introduced and brought to maturity. By such gradual advances in rendering their situation more comfortable, the most important alterations are produced in the state and condition of a people: their numbers are increased; the connections of society are extended; and men, being less oppressed with their own wants, are more at liberty to cultivate the feelings of humanity: property, the great source of distinction among individuals, is established; and the various rights of mankind, arising from their multiplied connections, are recognised and protected: the laws of a country are thereby rendered more numerous; and a more complex form of government becomes necessary, for distributing justice, and for preventing the disorders which proceed from the jarring interests and passions of a large and opulent community. It is evident, at the same time, that these and such other effects of improvement, which have so great a tendency to vary the state of mankind, and their manner of life, will be productive of suitable variations in their taste and sentiments, and in their general system of behaviour.

There is thus, in human society, a natural progress from ignorance to knowledge, and from rude, to civilized manners, the several stages of which are usually accompanied with peculiar laws and customs. Various accidental causes, indeed, have contributed to accelerate, or to retard this advancement in different countries. It has even happened that nations, being placed in such unfavourable circumstances as to render them long stationary at a particular period, have been so habituated to the peculiar manners of that age, as to retain a strong tincture of those peculiarities, through every subsequent revolution. This appears to have occasioned some of the other varieties which take place in the maxims and customs of nations equally civilized.

13. On progress: the 'law of unintended outcomes'

Adam Ferguson, *Essay on the History of Civil Society*, second edition, 1768, pp. 187–8.

Every step and every movement of the multitude, even in what are termed enlightened ages, are made with equal blindness to the future; and nations stumble upon establishments, which are indeed the result of human action, but not the execution of any human design. If Cromwell said, That a man never mounts higher, than when he knows not whither he is going; it may with more reason be affirmed of communities, that they admit of the greatest revolutions where no change is intended, and that the most refined politicians do not always know whither they are leading the state by their projects.

If we listen to the testimony of modern history, and to that of the most authentic parts of the ancient; if we attend to the practice of nations in every quarter of the world, and in every condition, whether that of the barbarian or the polished, we shall find very little reason to retract this assertion. No constitution is formed by concert, no government is copied from a plan. The members of a small state contend for equality; the members of a greater, find themselves classed in a certain manner that lays a foundation for monarchy. They proceed from one form of government to another, by easy transitions, and frequently under old names adopt a new constitution. The seeds of every form are lodged in human nature; they spring up and ripen with the season. The prevalence of a particular species is often derived from an imperceptible ingredient mingled in the soil.

14. On the influence of climate

a. Adam Ferguson, *Essay on the History of Civil Society*, second edition, 1768, pp. 170–1.

If we pass from these general representations of what mankind have done, to the more minute descriptions of the animal himself, as he has occupied different climates, and is diversified in his temper, complexion, and character, we shall find a variety of genius corresponding to the effects of his conduct and the result of his story.

Man, in the perfection of his natural faculties, is quick and delicate in his sensibility; extensive and various in his imaginations and reflections; attentive, penetrating and subtle, in what relates to his fellow creatures; firm and ardent in his purposes; devoted to friendship or to enmity; jealous of his independence and his honour, which he will not relinquish for safety or for profit: under all his corruptions or improvements, he retains his natural sensibility, if not his force; and his commerce is a blessing or a curse, according to the direction his mind has received.

But under the extremes of heat or of cold, the active range of the human soul appears to be limited; and men are of inferior importance, either as friends, or as enemies. In the one extreme, they are dull and slow, moderate in their desires, regular and pacific in their manner of life; in the other, they are feverish in their passions, weak in their judgments, and addicted by temperament to animal pleasure. In both the heart is mercenary, and makes important concessions for childish bribes: in both the spirit is prepared for servitude: in the one it is subdued by the fear of the future; in the other it is not roused even by its sense of the present.

b. John Millar, *The Origin of the Distinction of Ranks*, third edition, 1779, p. 9.

Among the several circumstances which may affect the gradual improvements of society, the difference of climate is one of the most remarkable. In warm countries, the earth is often extremely fertile, and with little culture is capable of producing whatever is necessary for subsistence. To labour under the extreme heat of the sun is, at the same time, exceedingly troublesome and oppressive. The inhabitants, therefore, of such countries, while they enjoy a degree of affluence, and while by the mildness of the climate they are exempted from many inconveniencies and wants, are seldom disposed to any laborious exertion, and thus, acquiring habits of indolence, become addicted to sensual pleasure, and liable to all those infirmities which are nourished by idleness and sloth. The people who live in a cold country find, on the contrary, that little or nothing is to be obtained without labour; and being subjected to numberless hardships, while they are forced to contend with the ruggedness of the soil, and the severity of the seasons, in earning their scanty provisions, they become active and industrious, and acquire those dispositions and talents which proceed from the constant and vigorous exercise both of the mind and body.

5 Social Institutions

The approach of these Scottish writers to the study of social institutions combined assumptions about human nature, derived from the study of moral philosophy, with the principles of 'natural history' illustrated in the last chapter. Each of the writers represented here, David Hume, Lord Kames, Adam Ferguson, Adam Smith and John Millar, held their own views about 'the constant and universal principles of human nature', the universal elements in human psychology; yet this belief in an underlying uniformity did not necessarily prevent the application of the idea of four stages of human progress, or the illustration of the range and complexity of human institutions over time and place. These writers aimed, however, not only at illustrating this range, but at charting the laws which governed the growth and progress of social institutions.

Of those writers represented here, David Hume's work, in the *Treatise of Human Nature* and in the *Essays*,[1] was the earliest. In some respects it did foreshadow later aspects of 'natural' or 'philosophical' history; Hume believed that it was possible to consider and to chart the evolution of social institutions. For Hume the most important tool which the 'philosophical' historian could wield was, however, his knowledge of human psychology. It would be far too crude to suggest that Hume assumed human behaviour would always follow unvarying laws; he was indeed very conscious of the way in which environment might mould human nature[2]. Nevertheless Hume never really explores the theme of economic development as a primary factor in the making of human institutions—and there are very few indications of anything approaching the four stage theory of economic progress in his work[3]. For Hume the key to social institutions lay not in any single pattern of economic life, but rather in the relationship between the political world and the laws of human psychology. Hume's view of political science will be raised in Chapter 6.

Lord Kames was the first of these writers to publish an account of the relationship between institutions (in this case, legal institutions) and the economic life of a people. Kames had already, in 1747 published his *Essays . . . concerning British Antiquities*; this work in some ways anticipated the arguments of the *Historical Law Tracts*, published in 1758[4]. Starting from the dry ground of Scottish law, Kames had broadened his perspective, until in 1758 he presented a clear case for the historical study of law, for the weaving together of an evolutionary chain of development from the range of evidence available to the comparative historian (Documents 7a, b).

It is, however, in the work of Adam Smith and John Millar that the work of the 'philosophical' historian is seen at its clearest. The subject matter of their work was at least partly dictated by their own situation, by the lectures which they gave to their students. As suggested in the last chapter, Adam Smith was already, by the 1750s and 60s turning the framework established by Hutcheson into a descriptive account of the growth of government. Our source for Smith's ideas here can only be the lecture notes taken by his students; these are of great value in providing a coherent account of Smith's thinking, sometime before the publication of the *Wealth of Nations* in 1776.[5] John Millar, in his *Origin of the Distinction of Ranks* (first published 1771, revised edition 1779), and in his *Historical View of the English Government*, (1787) used material accumulated over years of lecturing[6]. *The Origin of the Distinction of Ranks* is a closely knit and coherent work which analyses the growth of social bonds within families, tribes and nations, constantly relating their development to the economic life of society. It is perhaps the formal culmination of this line of approach, the most schematic statement produced by the Scottish Enlightenment, of the content of 'natural history'.

Adam Ferguson's *Essay on the History of Civil Society* is distinctive, because, although it appears to share the same concerns as those of Smith and Millar, it is nevertheless primarily the work of a moralist. Ferguson's *Essay* is also a meditation of the progress of man from rudeness to refinement; yet Ferguson is less interested merely in charting that progress, than in recording the potential of each stage of society, and its institutions, for the fulfilment of the individual man; as he put it, 'it is of more importance to know the condition to which we ourselves should aspire, than that which our ancestors may be supposed to have left'[7].

The first problem which confronted all these writers was that all political theorists in the seventeenth and early eighteenth centuries had found it necessary to reconstruct the origin of government.

Hobbes, Locke, Rousseau, all in varying ways, postulated a state of nature prior to the formation of government, and a positive entry into a governed society through an original contract; in effect this was largely an explanatory device, through which it was possible to explore the rationale of authority. Hutcheson, as was seen in Chapter 2, preserved the traditional formulation. David Hume's analysis, first found in Book 3 of the *Treatise*, and later in the *Essays*, does not altogether depart from this, but adds interesting elements. For Hume, government was a device which enabled men to resist their own violent and partial interests, to erect the artificial rules of justice into an institutional form, setting up a government with a personal interest in the observance of those rules, which ensured the protection of private property, of trade, and the enforcement of contracts. Government had, therefore, for Hume, a utilitarian justification; but that (for Hume) was not quite the same as its historical origins. Governments, though advantageous, were not absolutely essential to man; their origins lay in the immediate need of leadership under the threat of war.

Others, too, saw the military origins of established governments as of considerable importance. For Adam Smith and John Millar the 'state of nature' and the 'original contract' are fictions no longer of use even as an explanatory device. It is clear (see Documents 3–6) that it was change in the economic basis of society which created circumstances favourable to leadership and the erection of governments: for which the occasion might well be the immediate threat of war. For Smith the principle of authority was one which met a permanent human need; and like Hume he emphasised, too, the utilitarian function of governments, as a means of preserving uniform and enforceable rules. Underlying these permanent aspects of government, however, lay the changing economic world; changes in production were inevitably accompanied by growth and sophistication in government. From the tribal life of hunters, to the nomadic pastoral tribes and the settled agricultural world, the Scottish historians traced the laws that governed the exercise of power in different societies. Adam Ferguson, too, considered the 'original contract' a meaningless myth, and set out the stages through which governments would pass; yet he lays more stress on its accidental development through the unforeseen consequences of human actions and human conflicts than either Smith or Millar.

Further examples are given here of the application of the methods of the 'philosophical' historian to the study of the law, to the history of the family (which received original and pioneering treatment), and to the study of religious belief and establishments. In all these examples it is possible to analyse the way in which these different historians balance their study of human psychology with the comparative methods of analysis of the historian.

NOTES

1. The bibliography of Hume's essays is a complicated matter; the *Essays, Moral, Political and Literary*, reprinted in David Hume *The Philosophical Works*, edited by T. H. Green and T. H. Grose, 4 vols (London, 1882) were drawn from a number of Hume's publications. Most important were the *Essays Moral and Political*, 2 vols (Edinburgh, 1741 and 1742), *Essays Moral and Political*, Third edition, corrected with additions in 1748, *Political Discourses* (Edinburgh, 1752), *Four Dissertations* (Edinburgh, 1757), *Essays and Treatises on several Subjects* (London, 1758)—this was the first full consolidated edition, with some late additions. A few pieces unpublished during Hume's lifetime (including 'Of the Immortality of the Soul', and 'Of Suicide') have been added to *The Philosophical Works*. For a convenient checklist, see J. B. Stewart, *The Moral and Political Philosophy of David Hume* (New York, 1963) pp. 405–8; for a detailed discussion see T. H. Grose, 'History of the Editions' in the *Philosophical Works*, III, pp. 15–86.

2. D. Forbes, *Hume's Philosophical Politics* (Cambridge, 1975), pp. 102ff.

3. Ronald L. Meek, *Social Science and the Ignoble Savage*, pp. 30–1.

4. I. S. Ross *Lord Kames and the Scotland of his Day* (Oxford, 1972), pp. 205–6.

5. The edition used here is that published by Edwin Cannan in 1896, of the lecture notes made by an unknown student in 1762–3; however the publication is awaited of the *Lectures on Jurisprudence*, edited by R. L. Meek, D. D. Raphael, and P. G. Stein, to include both a new edition of these lecture notes, and a set of lecture notes recently discovered (from which Doc. 10, Ch. 4, was extracted).

6. W. C. Lehmann John Millar of Glasgow, 1735–1801, *His life and thought and his contribution to sociological analysis* (Cambridge, 1960) pp. 57–8, 407–9; *idem* 'Some observations on the law lectures of Professor Millar at the University of Glasgow (1760–1801)', *Juridical Review*, new series, 15 (1970) pp. 56–77.

7. Adam Ferguson, *Essay on the History of Civil Society*, second edition, (1768) p. 15.

Social Institutions: Documents

THE ROOTS OF POLITICAL AUTHORITY

1. The origins of government

David Hume, *Treatise of Human Nature*, edited by Selby-Bigge, pp. 536–41.

In reflecting on any action, which I am to perform a twelve-month hence, I always resolve to prefer the greater good, whether at that time it will be more contiguous or remote; not does any difference in that particular make a difference in my present intentions and resolutions. My distance from the final determination makes all those minute differences vanish, nor am I affected by any thing, but the general and more discernable qualities of good and evil. But on my nearer approach, those circumstances, which I at first overlooked, begin to appear, and have an influence on my conduct and affections. A new inclination to the present good springs up, and makes it difficult for me to adhere inflexibly to my first purpose and resolution. This natural infirmity I may very much regret, and I may endeavour, by all possible means, to free myself from it. I may have recourse to study and reflexion within myself; to the advice of friends; to frequent meditation, and repeated resolution: And having experienced how ineffectual all these are, I may embrace with pleasure any other expedient, by which I may impose a restraint upon myself, and guard against this weakness.

The only difficulty, therefore, is to find out this expedient, by which men cure their natural weakness, and lay themselves under the necessity of observing the laws of justice and equity, notwithstanding their violent propension to prefer contiguous to remote. 'Tis evident such a remedy can never be effectual without correcting this propensity; and as 'tis impossible to change or correct any thing material in our natures, the utmost we can do is to change our circumstances and situation, and render the observance of the laws of justice our nearest interest, and their violation our most remote. But this being impracticable with respect to all mankind, it can only take place with respect to a few, whom we thus immediately interest in the execution of justice. These are the persons, whom we call civil magistrates, kings and their ministers, our governors and rulers, who being indifferent persons to the greatest part of the state, have no interest, or but a remote one, in any act of injustice; and being satisfied with their present condition, and with their part in society, have an immediate interest in every execution of justice, which is so necessary to the upholding of society. Here then is the origin of civil government and society. Men are not able radically to cure, either in themselves or others, that narrowness of soul, which makes them prefer the present to the remote. They cannot change their natures. All they can do is to change their situation, and render the observance of justice the immediate interest of some particular persons, and its violation their more remote. These persons, then, are not only induc'd to observe these rules in their own conduct, but also to constrain others to a like regularity, and enforce the dictates of equity thro' the whole society. And if it be necessary, they may also interest others more immediately in the execution of justice, and create a number of officers, civil and military, to assist them in their government.

But this execution of justice, tho' the principal, is not the only advantage of government. As violent passion hinders men from seeing distinctly the interest they have in an equitable behaviour towards others; so it hinders them from seeing that equity itself, and gives them a remarkable partiality in their own favours. This inconvenience is corrected in the same manner as that above-mentioned. The same persons, who execute the laws of justice, will also decide all controversies concerning them; and being indifferent to the greatest part of the society, will decide them more equitably, than every one would in his own case . . .

Though government be an invention very advantageous, and even in some circumstances absolutely necessary to mankind; it is not necessary in all circumstances, nor is it impossible for men to preserve society for some time, without having recourse to such an invention. Men, 'tis true, are always much inclin'd to prefer present interest to distant and remote; nor is it easy for them to resist the temptation of any advantage, that they may immediately enjoy, in apprehension of an evil, that lies at a distance from them: But still this weakness is less conspicuous, where the possessions and the pleasures of life are few, and of little value, as they always are in the infancy of society. An Indian is but little tempted to dispossess another of his hut, or to steal his bow, as being already provided of the same advantages; and as to any superior fortune, which may attend one above another in hunting and fishing, 'tis only casual and temporary, and will have but small tendency to disturb society. And so far am I from thinking with some philosophers, that men are utterly incapable of society without government, that I assert the first rudiments of government to arise from quarrels, not among men of the same society, but among those of different societies. A less degree of riches will suffice to this latter effect, than is requisite for the former. Men fear nothing from public war and violence but the resistance they meet with, which, because they share it in common, seems less terrible; and because it comes from strangers, seems less pernicious in its consequences, than when they are exposed singly against one whose commerce is advantageous to them, and without whose society 'tis impossible they can subsist . . .

This we find verified in the American tribes, where men live in concord and amity among themselves without any established government; and never pay submission to any of their fellows, except in time of war, when their captain enjoys a shadow of authority, which he loses after their return from the field, and the establishment of peace with the neighbouring tribes. This authority, however, instructs them in the advantages of government, and teaches them to have recourse to it, when either by the pillage of war, by commerce, or by any fortuitous inventions, their riches and possessions have become so considerable as to make them forget, on every emergence, the interest they have in the preservation of peace and justice. Hence we may give a plausible reason, among others, why all governments are at first monarchical, without any mixture and variety; and why republics arise only from the abuses of monarchy and despotic power. Camps are the true mothers of cities; and as war cannot be administered, by reason of the suddenness of every exigency, without some authority in a single person, the same kind of authority naturally takes place in that civil government, which succeeds the military. And this reason I take to be more natural, than the common one derived from patriarchal govern-ment, or the authority of a father, which is said first to take place in one family, and to accustom the members of it to the government of a single person. The state of society without government is one of the most natural states of men, and must subsist with the conjunction of many families, and long after the first generation. Nothing but an increase of riches and possessions could oblige men to quit it; and so barbarous and uninstructed are all societies on their first formation, that many years must elapse before these can increase to such a degree, as to disturb men in the enjoyment of peace and concord.

But tho' it be possible for men to maintain a small uncultivated society without government, 'tis impossible they should maintain a society of any kind without justice . . .

2. The principles of authority and utility

Lectures on Justice, Police, Revenue and Arms, delivered in the University of Glasgow by Adam Smith, reported by a student in 1763, and edited by Edwin Cannan (Oxford, 1896) pp. 9–11.

There are two principles which induce men to enter into a civil society which we shall call the principles of authority and utility. At the head of every small society or association of men, we find a person of superior abilities. In a warlike society he is a man of superior strength, and in a polished one of superior mental capacity. Age and a long possession of power have also a tendency to strengthen authority. Age is naturally in our imagination connected with wisdom and experience, and a continuance in power bestows a kind of right to the exercise of it. But superior wealth still more than any of these qualities contributes to confer authority. This proceeds not from any dependence that the poor have upon the rich, for in general the poor are independent, and support themselves by their labour, yet, though they expect no benefit from them, they have a strong propensity to pay them respect. This principle is fully explained in the Theory of Moral Sentiments, where it is shown that it arises from our sympathy with our superiors being greater than that with our equals or inferiors: we admire their happy situation, enter into it with pleasure, and endeavour to promote it.

Among the great, as superior abilities of body and mind are not so easily judged of by others, it is more convenient, as it is more common, to give the preference to riches. It is evident that an old family, that is, one which has been long distinguished by its wealth, has more authority than any other. An upstart is always disagreeable, we envy his superiority over us and think ourselves are well entitled to wealth as he. If I am told that a man's grandfather was very poor and dependent on my family, I will grudge very much to see his grandson in a station above me, and will not be very much disposed to submit to his authority. Superior age, superior abilities of body and of mind, ancient family and superior wealth seem to be the four things that give one man authority over another.

The second principle which induces men to obey the civil magistrate is utility. Every one is sensible of the necessity of this principle to preserve justice and peace in the society. By civil institutions the poorest may get redress of injuries from the wealthiest and most powerful; and though there may be some irregularities in particular cases, as undoubtedly there are, yet we submit to them to avoid greater evils. It is the sense of public utility, more than of private, which influences men to disobedience. It may sometimes be for my interest to disobey, and to wish government overturned, but I am sensible that other men are of a different opinion from me, and would not assist men in the enterprise. I therefore submit to its decision for the good of the whole.

3. Adam Ferguson on the foundation of political establishments

Adam Ferguson, *Essay on the History of Civil Society*, second edition (1768) pp. 185–6.

We have hitherto observed mankind, either united together on terms of equality, or disposed to admit of a subordination founded merely on the voluntary respect and attachment which they paid to their leaders; but, in both cases, without any concerted plan of government, or system of laws.

The savage, whose fortune is comprised in his cabin, his fur, and his arms, is satisfied with that provision, and with that degree of security, he himself can procure. He perceives, in treating with his equal, no subject of discussion that should be referred to the decision of a judge; nor does he find in any hand the badges of magistracy, or the ensigns of a perpetual command.

The barbarian, though induced by his admiration of personal qualities, the lustre of a heroic race, or a superiority of fortune, to follow the banners of a leader, and to act a subordinate part in his tribe, knows not, that what he performs from choice, is to be made a subject of obligation. He acts from affections unacquainted with forms; and when provoked, or when engaged on disputes, he recurs to the sword, as the ultimate means of decision, in all questions of right.

Human affairs, in the mean time, continue their progress. What was in one generation a propensity to herd with the species, becomes, in the ages which follow, a principle of national union. What was originally an alliance for common defence, becomes a concerted plan of political force; the care of subsistence becomes an anxiety for accumulating wealth, and the foundation of commercial arts.

Mankind, in following the present sense of their minds, in striving to remove inconveniencies, or to gain apparent and contiguous advantages, arrive at ends which even their imagination could not anticipate, and pass on, like other animals, in the track of their nature, without perceiving its end. He who first said, 'I will appropriate this field: I will leave it to my heirs'; did not perceive, that he was laying the foundation of civil laws and political establishments. He who first ranged himself under a leader, did not perceive, that he was setting the example of a permanent sub-ordination, under the pretence of which, the rapacious were to seize his possessions, and the arrogant to lay claim to his service.

EARLY FORMS OF GOVERNMENT

4. The stages of government, in early societies

Adam Smith, *Lectures on Justice, Police, Revenue and Arms*, pp. 14–16.

In a nation of hunters there is properly no government at all. The society consists of a few independent families who live in the same village and speak the same language, and have agreed among themselves to keep together for their mutual safety, but they have no authority one over another. The whole society interests itself in any offence; if possible they make it up between the parties, if not they banish from their society, kill or deliver up to the resentment of the injured him who has committed the crime. But this is no regular government, for though there may be some among them who are much respected, and have great influence in their determinations, yet he never can do anything without the consent of the whole.

Thus among hunters there is no regular government, they live according to the laws of nature.

The appropriation of herds and flocks which introduced an inequality of fortune, was that which first gave rise to regular government. Till there be property there can be no government, the very end of which is to secure wealth, and to defend the rich from the poor. In this age of shepherds, if one man possessed 500 oxen, and another had none at all, unless there were some government to secure them to him, he would not be allowed to possess them. This inequality of fortune, making a distinction between the rich and the poor, gave the former much influence over the latter, for they who had no flocks or herds must have depended on those who had them, because they could not now gain a subsistence from hunting, as the rich had made the game, now become tame, their own property. They therefore who had appropriated a number of flocks and herds, necessarily came to have great influence over the rest; and accordingly we find in the Old Testament that Abraham, Lot and the other patriarchs were like little petty princes . . .

We come now to explain how one man came to have more authority than the rest, and how chieftains were introduced. A nation consists of many families who have met together, and agreed to live with one another. At their public meetings there will always be one of superior influence to the rest, who will in a great measure direct and govern their resolutions, which is all the authority of a chieftain in a barbarous country. As the chieftain is the leader of the nation, his son naturally becomes the chief of the young people, and on the death of his father succeeds to his authority. Thus chieftainship becomes hereditary. This power of chieftainship comes in the progress of society to be increased by a variety of circumstances . . .

5. The emergence of monarchy

John Millar, *The Origin of the Distinction of Ranks*, third edition (1779) pp. 215–8.

The improvement of agriculture, as it increases the quantity of provisions, and renders particular tribes more numerous and flourishing, so it obliges them at length to send out colonies to a distance, who occupy new seats wherever they can find a convenient situation, and are formed into separate villages, after the model of those with which they are acquainted. Thus, in proportion as a country is better cultivated, it comes to be inhabited by a greater number of distinct societies, whether derived from the same or from a different original, agreeing in their manners, and resembling each other in their institutions and customs.

These different communities being frequently at war, and being exposed to continual invasions from their neighbours, are in many cases determined, by the consideration of their mutual interest, to unite against their common enemies, and to form a variety of combinations, which from the influence of particular circumstances, are more or less permanent. Having found the advantage of joining their forces in one expedition, they are naturally disposed to continue the like association in another, and by degrees are encouraged to enter into a general alliance. The intercourse which people, in such a situation, have maintained in war will not be entirely dissolved even in time of peace . . .

An alliance for mutual defence and security is a measure suggested by such obvious views of expediency that it must frequently take place, not only among tribes of husbandmen, but also among those of shepherds, and even of mere savages. Many instances of it are, accordingly, to be found in Tartary, upon the coast of guinea, in the history of the ancient Germans, and among the Indians of America. But such alliances are not likely to produce a permanent union, until the populousness of a country has been increased by agriculture, and the inhabitants, in consequence of that employment, have taken up a fixed residence in the same neighbourhood.

From a confederacy of this kind, a very simple form of government is commonly established. As every village or separate community, is subjected to its own leader, their joint measures fall naturally under the direction of all those distinguished personages; whose frequent meeting and deliberation gives rise, in a short time, to a regular council or senate . . .

The same considerations however which determine the individuals of a single tribe to be guided by a particular person in their smaller expeditions must recommend a similar expedient in conducting a numerous army, composed of different clans, often disagreeing in their views, and little connected with each other. While every chief has the conduct of his own dependents, it is found convenient that some one leader should be instructed with the supreme command of their united forces; and as that dignity is commonly bestowed upon the person who, by his opulence, is most capable of supporting it, he is frequently enabled to maintain it during life, and even in many cases to render it hereditary. In this manner a great chief, or *king*, is placed at the head of a nation, and is permitted to assume the inspection and superintendence of what relates to its defence and security . . .

6. The development of monarchical authority

John Millar, *The Origin of the Distinction of Ranks*, third edition (1779) pp. 238-41.

The continued union of rude tribes, or small societies, has a tendency to produce a great alteration in the political system of a people. The same circumstances, by which, in a single tribe, a chief is gradually advanced over the different heads of families, contribute, in a kingdom, to exalt the sovereign above the chiefs, and to extend his authority throughout the whole of his dominions.

As the king is placed at the head of the nation, and acts the most conspicuous part in all their public measures, his high rank and station reflect upon him a degree of splendour, which is apt to obscure the lustre of every inferior chief; and the longer he has remained in a situation where he excites the admiration and respect of the people, it is to be supposed that their habits of submission to him will be the more confirmed.

From the opulence, too, of the sovereign, which is generally much greater than that of any other member of the community, as well as from the nature of his office, he has more power to reward and protect his friends, and to punish or depress those who have become the objects of his resentment or displeasure. The consideration of this must operate powerfully upon individuals, as a motive to court his favour, and, of consequence, to support his interest. It is therefore to be concluded that, from the natural course of things, the immediate followers and dependents of the king will be constantly increasing, and those of every inferior leader will be diminishing in the same proportion.

In a government so constituted as to introduce a continual jealousy between the crown and the nobles, it must frequently happen that the latter, instead of prosecuting a uniform plan for aggrandizing their own order, should be occupied with private quarrels and dissensions among themselves; so that the king, who is ready to improve every conjuncture for extending his power, may often employ and assist the great lords in destroying each other, or take advantage of those occasions when they have been weakened by their continued struggles, and are in no condition to oppose his demands.

According as the real influence and authority of the crown are extended, its prerogatives are gradually augmented. When the king finds that the original chiefs have become in a great measure dependent upon him, he is not solicitous about consulting them in the management of public affairs; and the meetings of the national council, being seldom called, or being attended only by such members as are entirely devoted to the crown, dwindle away from time to time, and are at last laid aside altogether. The judicial power of the heads of different tribes is gradually subjected to similar encroachments; and that jurisdiction, which they at first held in virtue of their own authority, is rendered subordinate to the tribunal of the monarch, who, after having established the right of appeal from their courts to his own court, is led to appoint the judges in each particular district. The power of making laws, as well as that of determining peace and war, and of summoning all his subjects to the field, may come in like manner to be exercised at the discretion of the prince.

This progress of government, towards monarchy, though it seems to hold universally, is likely to be accompanied with some diversity of appearances in different countries; and, in particular, is commonly more rapid in a small state than in a large one; in which point of view the ancient Greeks and Romans are most remarkably distinguished from the greater part of the feudal kingdoms in Europe.

LEGAL INSTITUTIONS

7. The history of the law

a. Lord Kames, *Historical Law Tracts*, second edition (1761)
Preface, pp. iii–v.

The history of man is a delightful subject. A rational enquirer is
no less entertained than instructed, in tracing the progress of
manners, of laws, of arts, from their birth to their present maturity.
Events and subordinate incidents are, in each of these, linked
together and connected in a regular chain of causes and effects. Law
in particular, becomes then only a rational study, when it is traced
historically, from its first rudiments among savages, through
successive changes, to its highest improvements in a civilized
society. And yet the study is seldom conducted in that manner. Law,
like geography, is taught as if it were a collection of facts merely: the
memory is employed to the full, rarely the judgment. This method,
were it not rendered familiar by custom, would appear strange and
unaccountable. With respect to the political constitution of Britain,
how imperfect must the knowledge be of that man who confines his
reading to the present times? If he follow the same method in
studying its laws, have we reason to hope that his knowledge of them
will be more perfect?

Such neglect of the history of law, is the more strange, that in
place of a dry, intricate and crabbed science, law treated historically becomes an entertaining study: entertaining not only to those
whose profession it is, but to every person who hath any thirst for
knowledge. With the generality of men, it is true, the history of law
makes it not so great a figure, as the history of wars and conquests.
Singular events, which by the prevalence of chance or fortune excite
much wonder, are much relished by the vulgar. But readers of solid
judgment find more entertainment, in studying the constitution of a
state, its government, its laws, the manners of its peoples; where
reason is exercised in discovering causes and tracing effects through
a long train of dependencies.

b. Lord Kames, *Historical Law Tracts*, second edition (1761) p. 22.

In tracing the history of law through dark ages unprovided with records, or so slenderly provided as not to afford any regular historical chain, we must endeavour, the best way we can, to supply the broken links, by hints from poets and historians, by collateral facts and by cautious conjectures drawn from the nature of the government, of the people, and of the times. If we use all the light that is afforded, and if the conjectural facts correspond with the few facts that are distinctly vouched, and join all in one regular chain, nothing further can be expected from human endeavours. The evidence is compleat, so far at least as to afford conviction, if it be the best of the kind. This apology is necessary with regard to the subject under consideration. In tracing the history of the criminal law, we must not hope that all its steps and changes can be drawn from the archives of any one nation. In fact, many steps were taken, and many changes made before archives were kept, and even before writing was a common art. We must be satisfied with collecting the facts and circumstances as they may be gathered from the laws of different countries: and if these put together make a regular system of causes and effects, we may rationally conclude that the progress has been the same among all nations, in the capital circumstances at least; for accidents, or the singular nature of a people, or of a government, will always produce some pecularities.

8. The origins of punishment

Adam Smith, *Lectures on Justice, Police, Revenue and Arms*, pp. 14–16.

Injury naturally excites the resentment of the spectator, and the punishment of the offender is reasonable as far as the indifferent spectator can go along with it. This is the natural measure of punishment. It is to be observed that our first approbation of punishment is not founded upon the regard to public utility which is commonly taken to be the foundation of it. It is our sympathy with the resentment of the sufferer which is the real principle. That it cannot be utility is manifest from the following example. Wool in England was conceived to be the source of public opulence, and it was made a capital crime to export that commodity. Yet though wool was exported as formerly and men were convinced that the practice was pernicious, no jury, no evidence could be got against the offenders. The exportation of wool is naturally no crime, and men could not be brought to consider it as punishable with death. In the same manner, if a sentinel be put to death for leaving his post, though the punishment be just and the injury that might have ensued be very great, yet mankind can never enter into this punishment as if he had been a thief or a robber.

Resentment not only prompts to punishment, but points out the manner of it. Our resentment is not gratified unless the offender be punished for the particular offence done ourselves, and unless he be made sensible that it is for that action. A crime is always the violation of some right, natural or acquired, real or personal. The non-performance of a contract indeed is not a crime, unless it be through some fraudulent intention.

The greatest crime that can be done against any person is murder, of which the natural punishment is death, not as a compensation, but as a reasonable retaliation. In every civilised nation death has been the punishment of the murderer, but in barbarous nations a pecuniary compensation was accepted of, because then government was weak, and durst not meddle in the quarrels of individuals unless in the way of mediation. In the age of hunters particularly there was little more than the name of authority, and a man of superior influence can do no more than persuade the parties to an agreement. When one man killed another, the whole society met, and advised the one party to give, and the other to take, a compensation. In America when one member of a family kills another, the society does not intermeddle with them, as this cannot hurt the peace of the society; they only take notice of it when one family attacks another. It was long before the government could call a man before them and tell him what he must do, because it was long before people would submit to such absolute authority.

THE HISTORY OF THE FAMILY

9. The family, and the condition of women in savage societies

A. Ferguson, *Essay on the History of Civil Society*, second edition (1768) pp. 125–6.

Where savage nations, as in most parts of America, mix with the practice of hunting some species of rude agriculture, they still follow, with respect to the soil and the fruits of the earth, the analogy of their principal object. As the men hunt, so the women labour together; and, after they have shared the toils of the seed-time, they enjoy the fruits of the harvest in common. The field in which they have planted, like the district over which they are accustomed to hunt, is claimed as a property by the nation, but is not parcelled in lots to its members. They go forth in parties to prepare the ground, to plant, and to reap. The harvest is gathered into the public granary, and from thence, at stated times, is divided into shares for the maintenance of separate families. Even the returns of the market, when they trade with foreigners, are brought home to the stock of the nation.

As the fur and the bow pertain to the individual, the cabin and its utensils are appropriated to the family; and as the domestic cares are committed to the women, so the property of the household seems likewise to be vested in them. The children are considered as pertaining to the mother, with little regard to descent on the father's side. The males, before they are married, remain in the cabin in which they are born; but after they have formed a new connection with the other sex, they change their habitation, and become an accession to the family in which they have found their wives. The hunter and the warrior are numbered by the matron as a part of her treasure; they are reserved for perils and trying occasions; and in the recess of public councils, in the intervals of hunting or war, are maintained by the cares of the women, and loiter about in mere amusement or sloth.

While one sex continue to value themselves chiefly on their courage, their talent for policy, and their warlike achievements, this species of property which is bestowed on the other, is in reality a mark of subjection; not, as some writers allege, of their having acquired an ascendant. It is the care and trouble of a subject with which the warrior does not choose to be embarrassed. It is a servitude, and a continual toil, where no honours are won; and they whose province it is, are in fact the slaves and the helots of their country. If in this destination of the sexes, while the men continue to indulge themselves in the contempt of sordid and mercenary arts, the cruel establishemnt of slavery is for some ages deferred; if in this tender, though unequal alliance, the affections of the heart prevent the severities practised on slaves; we have in the custom itself, as perhaps in many other instances, reason to prefer the first suggestions of nature, to many of her after refinements.

10. The duties of marriage

Adam Smith, *Lectures on Justice, Police, Revenue and Arms*, pp. 73–5.

. . . In every species of animals the connexion between the sexes is just as much as is necessary for the propagation and support of the species. Quadrupeds, whenever the female impregnates, have no farther desire for each other; the support of the young is no burden to the female, and there is no occasion for the assistance of the male. Among birds some such thing as marriage seems to take place, they continue the objects of desire to each other, their connexion remains for a considerable time, and they jointly support the young; but whenever the young can shift for themselves all further inclination ceases. In the human species women by their milk are not capable of providing long for their children. The assistance of the husband is therefore necessary for their sustenance, and this ought to make marriage perpetual. In countries, however, where Christianity is not established, the husband possesses an unlimited power of divorce, and is not accountable for his conduct. In ancient Rome, though they had the power of doing it, yet it was thought contrary to good manners. We may observe an utility in this constitution of our nature that children have so long a dependence upon their parents, to bring down their passions to theirs, and thus be trained up at length to become useful members of society. Every child gets this piece of education, even under the most worthless parent.

On this subject it is proposed to consider the duties of each of the two parties during their union, how this union should be begun and ended, and what are the particular rights and privileges of each.

The first duty is fidelity of the wife to the husband; breach of chastity is the greatest of offences. Spurious children may be introduced into the family, and come to the succession instead of lawful ones. This real utility, however, is not the proper foundation of the crime. The indignation of the public against the wife arises from their sympathy with the jealousy of the husband, and accordingly they are disposed to resent and punish it. The sentiment of jealousy is not chiefly founded, or rather not at all, upon the idea of a spurious offspring. It is not from the particular act that the jealousy arises, but he considers her infidelity as an entire alienation of that preference to all other persons which she owes him. This is the real idea he has of it, as may appear from the following consideration. The idea we have of a father does not arise from the voluptuous act which gave occasion to our existence, for this idea is partly loathsome, partly ridiculous. The real idea that a son has of a father is the director of his infancy, the supporter of his helplessness, his guardian, pattern and protector. These are the proper filial sentiments. The father's idea of a son is of one that depends upon him, and was bred in his house or at his expense, by which connexion there should grow up an affection towards him; but a spurious offspring is disagreeable from the resentment that arises against the mother's infidelity.

In those countries where the manners of the people are rude and uncultivated, there is no such thing as jealousy, every child that is born is considered as their own. The foundation of jealousy is that delicacy which attends the sentiment of love, and it is more or less in different countries, in proportion to the rudeness of their manners. In general, wherever there is little regard paid to the sex, infidelity is little regarded, and there will be the greatest looseness of manners . . . When manners became more refined, jealousy began, and rose at length to such a heights that wives were shut up, as they are among the Turks at this day. As mankind became more refined, the same fondness which made them shut up women made them allow liberties. In the latter ages of Greece women were allowed to go anywhere. This same fondness, carried to a high degree, gives as great a licence as when infidelity was disregarded. In no barbarous country is there more licentiousness than in France. Thus we may observe the prejudice of manners, with respect to women, in the different periods of society.

11. The role of women in a commercial society

John Millar, *The Origin of the Distinction of Ranks*, third edition
(1779) pp. 107–111.

The advancement of a people in manufactures and commerce has
a natural tendency to remove those circumstances which prevented
the free intercourse of the sexes, and contributed to heighten and
inflame their passions . . .

When men begin to disuse their ancient barbarous practices,
when their attention is not wholly engrossed by the pursuit of
military reputation, when they have made some progress in arts,
and have attained to a proportional degree of refinement, they are
necessarily led to set a value upon those female accomplishments
and virtues which have so much influence upon every species of
improvement, and which contribute in so many different ways to
multiply the comforts of life. In this situation, the women become,
neither the slaves, nor the idols of the other sex, but the friends and
companions. The wife obtains that rank and station which appears
most agreeable to reason, being suited to her character and talents.
Loaded by nature with the first and most immediate concern in
rearing and maintaining the children, she is endowed with such
dispositions as fit her for the discharge of this important duty, and is
at the same time particularly qualified for all such employments as
require skill and dexterity more than strength, which are so
necessary in the interior management of the family. Possessed of
peculiar delicacy, and sensibility, whether derived from original
constitution, or from her way of life, she is capable of securing the
esteem and affection of her husband, by dividing his cares, by
sharing his joys, and by soothing his misfortunes.

The regard, which is thus shown to the useful talents and
accomplishments of the women, cannot fail to operate in directing
their education, and in forming their manners. They learn to suit
their behaviour to the circumstances in which they are placed, and
to that particular standard of propriety and excellence which is set
before them. Being respected upon account of their diligence and
proficiency in the various branches of domestic economy, they
naturally endeavour to improve and extend those valuable
qualifications. They are taught to apply with assiduity to those
occupations which fall under their province, and to look upon
idleness as the greatest blemish in the female character. They are

instructed betimes in whatever will qualify them for the duties of their station, and is thought conducive to the ornament of private life. Engaged in these solid pursuits, they are less apt to be distinguished by such brilliant accomplishments as make a figure in the circle of gaiety and amusement. Accustomed to live in retirement, and to keep company with their nearest relations and friends, they are inspired with all that modesty and diffidence which is natural to persons unacquainted with promiscuous conversation; and their affections are neither dissipated by pleasure, nor corrupted by the vicious customs of the world. As their attention is principally bestowed upon the members of their own family, they are led in a particular manner to improve those feelings of the heart which are excited by these tender connections, and they are trained up in the practice of all the domestic virtues.

THE STUDY OF RELIGION

12. The origins of polytheism

Adam Smith, 'The Principles which lead and direct Philosophical Enquiries; illustrated by the history of Astronomy', *Essays on Philosophical Subjects*, to which is prefixed an account of the life and writings of the author, by Dugald Stewart (London, 1795) pp. 24-5.

. . . a savage, whose notions are guided altogether by wild nature and passion, waits for no other proof that a thing is the proper object of any sentiment, than that it excites it. The reverence and gratitude, with which some of the appearances of nature inspire him, convince him that they are the proper objects of reverence and gratitude, and therefore proceed from some intelligent beings, who take pleasure in the expressions of those sentiments. With him, therefore, every object of nature, which by its beauty or greatness, its utility or hurtfulness, is considerable enough to attract his attention, and whose operations are not perfectly regular, is supposed to act by the directions of some invisible and designing power. The sea is spread out into a calm or heaved into a storm, according to the good pleasure of Neptune. Does the earth pour forth an exuberant harvest? It is owing to the indulgence of Ceres. Does the vine yield a plentiful vintage? It flows from the bounty of Bacchus. Do either refuse their presents? It is ascribed to the displeasure of those offended deities . . . Hence the origin of Polytheism, and of that vulgar superstition which ascribes all the irregular events of nature to the favour or displeasure of intelligent, though invisible beings, to gods, demons, witches, genii, fairies. For it may be observed, that in all Polytheistic religions, among savages as well as in the early ages of Heathen antiquity, it is the irregular events of nature only that are ascribed to the agency and power of their gods . . . Man, the only designing power with which they were acquainted, never acts but either to stop, or to alter the course, which natural events would take, if left to themselves. Those other intelligent beings, whom they imagined, but knew not, were naturally supposed to act in the same manner; not to employ themselves in supporting the ordinary course of things, which went on of its own accord, but to stop, to thwart, and to disturb it. And thus, in the first ages of the world, the lowest and most pusill-animous superstition supplied the place of philosophy.

13. Polytheism and theism

David Hume, 'The Natural History of Religion' first published in *Four Dissertations* (London, 1757), reprinted in *The Philosophical Works*, edited by T. H. Green and T. H. Grose, 4 vols (London, 1882) IV, pp. 334–6.

It is remarkable, that the principles of religion have a kind of flux and reflux in the human mind, and that men have a natural tendency to rise from idolatry to theism, and to sink again from theism into idolatry. The vulgar, that is, indeed, all mankind, a few excepted being ignorant and uninstructed, never elevate their contemplation to the heavens, or penetrate by their disquisitions into the secret structure of vegetable or animal bodies; so far as to discover a supreme mind or original providence, which bestowed order on every part of nature. They consider these admirable works in a more confined and selfish view; and finding their own happiness and misery to depend on the secret influence and unforeseen concurrence of external objects, they regard, with perpetual attention, the *unknown causes* which govern all these natural events, and distribute pleasure and pain, good and ill, by their powerful, but silent, operation. The unknown causes are still appealed to on every emergence; and in this general appearance or confused image, are the perpetual objects of human hopes and fears, wishes and apprehensions. By degrees, the active imagination of men, uneasy in this abstract conception of objects, about which it is incessantly employed, begins to render them more particular, and to clothe them in shapes more suitable to its natural comprehension. It represents them to be sensible, intelligent beings like mankind; actuated by love and hatred, and flexible by gifts and entreaties, by prayers and sacrifices. Hence the origin of religion: And hence the origin of idolatry or polytheism.

But the same anxious concern for happiness, which begets the idea of these invisible intelligent powers, allows not mankind to remain long in the first simple conception of them; as powerful but limited beings; masters of human fate, but slaves to destiny and the course of nature. Men's exaggerated praises and compliments still swell their idea upon them; and elevating their deities to the utmost bounds of perfection, at last beget the attributes of unity and infinity, simplicity and spirituality. Such refined ideas, being somewhat disproportioned to vulgar comprehension, remain not long in their original purity; but require to be supported by the notion of inferior mediators or subordinate agents, which interpose between mankind and their supreme deity. These demigods or middle beings, partaking more of human nature, and being more familiar to us, become the chief objects of devotion, and gradually recall that idolatry which had been formerly banished by the ardent prayers and panegyrics of timorous and indigent mortals. But as these idolatrous religions fall every day into grosser and more vulgar conceptions, they at last destroy themselves, and by the vile representations, which they form of their deities, make the tide turn again towards theism. But so great is the propensity, in this alternate revolution of human sentiments, to return back to idolatry, that the utmost precaution is not able effectually to prevent it. And of this, some theists, particularly the Jews and Mahometans, have been sensible; as appears by their banishing all the arts of statuary and painting, and not allowing the representations, even of human figures, to be taken by marble or colours; lest the common infirmity of mankind should thence produce idolatry. The feeble apprehensions of men cannot be satisfied with conceiving their deity as a pure spirit and perfect intelligence; and yet their natural terrors keep them from imputing to him the least shadow of limitation and imperfection. They fluctuate between these opposite sentiments. The same infirmity still drags them downwards, from an omnipotent and spiritual Deity to a limited and corporeal one, and from a corporeal and limited deity to a statue or visible representation. The same endeavour at elevation still pushes them upwards, from the statue or material image to the invisible power; and from the invisible power to an infinitely perfect Deity, the creator and sovereign of the universe.

14. Enthusiasm and superstition

David Hume, 'Of Superstition and Enthusiasm', first published in *Essays Moral and Political* (Edinburgh, 1741) and reprinted in *The Philosophical Works*, III, pp. 144–50.

That the corruption of the best of things produces the worst, is grown into a maxim, and is commonly proved, among other instances, by the pernicious effects of *superstition* and *enthusiasm*, the corruptions of true religion.

These two species of false religion, though both pernicious, are yet of a very different, and even of a contrary nature. The mind of man is subject to certain unaccountable terrors and apprehensions, proceeding either from the unhappy situation of private or public affairs, from ill health, from a gloomy or melancholy disposition, or from the concurrence of all these circumstances. In such a state of mind, infinite unknown evils are dreaded from unknown agents; and where real objects of terror are wanting, the soul, active to its own prejudice, and fostering its predominant inclination, finds imaginary ones, to whose power and malevolence it sets no limits. As these enemies are entirely invisible and unknown, the methods taken to appease them are equally unaccountable, and consist in ceremonies, observances, mortifications, sacrifices, presents, or in any practice, however absurd or frivolous, which either folly or knavery recommends to a blind and terrified credulity. Weakness, fear, melancholy, together with ignorance, are, therefore, the true sources of SUPERSTITION.

But the mind of man is also subject to an unaccountable elevation and presumption, arising from prosperous success, from luxuriant health, from strong spirits, or from a bold and confident disposition. In such a state of mind, the imagination swells with great, but confused conceptions, to which no sublunary beauties or enjoyments can correspond. Every thing mortal and perishable vanishes as unworthy of attention; and a full range is given to the fancy in the invisible regions or world of spirits, where the soul is at liberty to indulge itself in every imagination, which may best suit its present taste and disposition. Hence arise raptures, transports, and surprising flights of fancy; and confidence and presumption still increasing, these raptures, being altogether unaccountable, and seeming quite beyond the reach of our ordinary faculties, are attributed to the immediate inspiration of that Divine Being, who is the object of devotion. In a little time, the inspired person comes to regard himself as a distinguished favourite of the Divinity; and when this frenzy once takes place, which is the summit of enthusiasm, every whimsy is consecrated: Human reason, and even morality are rejected as fallacious guides: and the fanatic madman delivers himself over, blindly, and without reserve, to the supposed illapses of the spirit, and to inspiration from above. Hope, pride, presumption, a warm imagination, together with ignorance, are, therefore, the true sources of ENTHUSIASM.

These two species of false religion might afford occasion to many speculations; but I shall confine myself, at present to a few reflections concerning their different influence on government and society.

My *first* reflection is, *that superstition is favourable to priestly power, and enthusiasm not less, or rather more contrary to it, than sound reason and philosophy.* As superstition is founded on fear, sorrow, and a depression of spirits, it represents the man to himself in such despicable colours, that he appears unworthy, in his own eyes, of approaching the divine presence, and naturally has recourse to any other person, whose sanctity of life, or, perhaps, impudence and cunning, have made him be supposed more favoured by the Divinity. To him the superstitious entrust their devotions: to his care they recommend their prayers, petitions and sacrifices: and by his means, they hope to render their addresses acceptable to their incensed Deity. Hence the origin of PRIESTS, who may justly be regarded as an invention of a timorous and abject superstition, which, ever diffident of itself, dares not offer up its own devotions, but ignorantly thinks to recommend itself to the Divinity, by the mediation of his supposed friends and servants . . .

On the other hand, it may be observed, that all enthuiasts have been free from the yoke of ecclesiastics, and have expressed great

independence in their devotion; with a contempt of forms, ceremonies, and traditions. The Quakers are the most egregious,
though, at the same time, the most innocent enthusiasts that have
yet been known; and are perhaps the only sect that have never
admitted priests among them. The Independents, of all the English
sectaries, approach nearest to the Quakers in fanaticism, and in
their freedom from priestly bondage. The Presbyterians follow
after, at an equal distance, in both particulars . . .

My *second* reflection, with regard to these species of false religion,
is, *that religions which partake of enthusiasm are, on their first rise, more
furious and violent than those which partake of superstition; but in a little time
become more gentle and moderate.* The violence of this species of religion,
when excited by novelty, and animated by opposition, appears from
numberless instances; of the Anabaptists in Germany, the Camisars
in France, the Levellers and other fanatics in England, and the
Covenanters in Scotland. Enthusiasm being founded on strong
spirits, and a presumptuous boldness of character, it naturally
begets the most extreme resolutions; especially after it rises to that
height as to inspire the deluded fanatic with the opinion of divine
illuminations, and with a contempt for the common rules of reason,
morality, and prudence.

It is thus enthusiasm produces the most cruel disorders in human
society; but its fury is like that of thunder and tempest, which
exhaust themselves in a little time, and leave the air more calm and
serene than before. When the first fire of enthusiasm is spent, men
naturally, in all fanatical sects, sink into the greatest remissness and
coolness in sacred matters; there being no body of men among them,
endowed with sufficient authority, whose interest is concerned to
support the religious spirit: no rites, no ceremonies, no holy
observances, which may enter into the common train of life, and
preserve the sacred principles from oblivion. Supersition, on the
contrary, steals in gradually and insensibly; renders men tame and
submissive; is acceptable to the magistrate, and seems inoffensive to
the people: till at last the priest, having firmly established his
authority, becomes the tyrant and disturber of human authority by
his endless contentions, persecutions, and religious wars. How
smoothly did the Romish Church advance in her acquisition of
power! But into what dismal convulsions did she throw all Europe,
in order to maintain it! On the other hand, our sectaries, who were
formerly such dangerous bigots, are now become very free reason-
ers; and the Quakers seem to approach nearly the only regular

body of Deists in the universe, the literati, or the disciples of Confucius in China.

My *third* observation on this head, is, *that superstition is an enemy to civil liberty and enthusiasm a friend to it.* As superstition groans under the dominion of priests, and enthusiasm is destructive of all ecclesiastical power, this sufficiently accounts for the present observation. Not to mention, that enthusiasm being the infirmity of bold ambitious tempers, is naturally accompanied with a spirit of liberty; as superstition, on the contrary, renders men tame and abject, and fits them for slavery. We learn from English history, that, during the civil wars, the independents and deists, though the most opposite in their religious principles, yet were united in their political ones, and were alike passionate for a commonwealth. And sicne the origin of Whig and Tory, the leaders of Whigs have either been deists or professed latitudinarians in their principles; that is, friends to toleration, and indifferent to any particular sect of Christians: while the sectaries, who have all a strong tincture of enthusiasm, have always, without exception, concurred with that party in defence of civil liberty. The resemblance in their superstitions long united the High Church Tories and the Roman Catholics, in support of prerogative and kingly power; though experience of the tolerating spirit of the Whigs seems of late to have reconciled the Catholics to that party.

6 Commerce and Civilisation

No selection can possibly do justice to the wealth of ideas produced by these writers on the nature of their own commercial civilisation. The age of commerce, the last of the four stages, was subjected to detailed examination in a number of works, of which the most notable was Adam Smith's *The Wealth of Nations*, first published in 1776, which is both a detailed work of economic analysis, and a contribution to contemporary arguments about the quality of life in a commercial society. Here it is only possible to select a few passages which bear on key debates, on the drive towards material improvement, on the beneifts and disadvantages of a polished society, and on the relationship between economic growth and political freedom.

The Wealth of Nations opens with a discussion of the importance of the division of labour, the separation of individual tasks and consequent specialisation, as the key factor in economic growth. The idea itself was no new one. It can be found in *Political Arithmetick*, published in 1690 by the early economist Sir William Petty[1], and in several other early eighteenth century authors. Francis Hutcheson, too, offered an early version of the argument (Document 1). Adam Ferguson discussed the effects of the division of labour in his *Essay on the History of Civil Society* (Document 2). But the context in which Smith placed his analysis of specialisation allowed him to trace the unlimited consequences of further division of labour; he saw no necessary limit to the accumulation and employment of capital. He was concerned to establish why this was so, why this drive towards prosperity existed. Men were driven to barter and exchange, to accumulate consumer goods, by their own self-interest, because men have a propensity to better themselves, to envy and emulate the rich and powerful. Though the exercise of benevolence had a part in a well-ordered society, it was self-interest, not benevolence, which ruled the economic sphere. But this does not mean that the moral rules which Smith traced in the *Theory of Moral Sentiments* have no part in this world. Smith's view is that the exercise of sympathy and the concept of the impartial spectator may still create a set of moral rules for a society, though it is possible that the exercise of self-interest may lead individuals to contravene those rules; Smith writes of merchants as 'an order of men . . . who have generally an interest to deceive and even to oppress the public'[2]. Smith's world is one in which both the reasonable pursuit of self-interest and the observance of a moral code should be compatible; though within economic life such compatibility is by no means always achieved, and the problems posed by this are hardly solved. God, the designer of the Universe, and of men, plays little direct part in Smith's view of the world; yet God has sanctioned the morality of man, including that necessary balance between self-interest and the common good. The individual is:

> . . . led by an invisible hand to promote an end which is no part of his attention. Nor is it always the worse for the society that it was no part of it. By pursuing his own interest he frequently promotes that of the society more effectually than when he really intends to promote it. I have never known much good done by those who affected to trade for the public good. It is an affectation, indeed, not very common among merchants . . .[3].

The Wealth of Nations analyses the nature of economic growth, through exploring the relationship of value and of price in exchange relationships, and through discussion of wages, profits, and rent. Smith dealt with the accumulation and employment of capital, and the virtues and disadvantes of different economic systems, especially the arguments of mercantilists and physiocrats, both of which are condemned in favour of a system of 'natural liberty'. It is not possible to consider these questions here; but it is worth looking at the general attitude of Smith and his contemporaries to commercial civilisation. William Robertson's historical writing offered a simple, Whiggish, interpretation: the coming of commerce had brought the softening of manners, the disappearance of prejudice, the desire for peace, and political liberty (Document 6). The debate was not a new one. An early, and crude, defence of wealth and luxury had come from Bernard Mandeville, in his *Fable of the Bees*, first published 1705:

> The root of evil, avarice,
> That damn'd ill-natured baneful vice,

Was slave to prodigality,
That noble sin; whilst luxury
Employ'd a million of the poor,
And odious pride a million more:
Envy itself and vanity
Were ministers of industry;
Their darling folly, fickleness
In diet, furniture and dress,
That strange ridic'lous vice, was made
The very wheel that turn'd the trade[4].

Francis Hutcheson, among others, had argued against excessive luxury and over-large fortunes, as a moralist, and because of their political effects (Chapter 2 Document 12). David Hume, in his essay 'Of Refinement in the Arts' praised luxury in society for its employment of men's minds and talents. Though Hume did not overlook what he called the vicious effects of luxury, for him they were far outweighed by the benefits (Documents 4, 10). Adam Ferguson was in no doubt that there were dangers in rashly assuming the superiority of modern civilisation (Documents 2, 5). Smith's arguments were complex. He believed that material prosperity, which offered something more than the barest subsistence to the labouring classes, should be justified on these grounds. But, like Ferguson, he also traced the intellectual and spiritual deterioration among those condemned to work at single specialised monotonous tasks in the interests of production, no longer masters of their time and trades. Smith considered this carefully; the only possible palliative, he thought, was the introduction of universal public education, on the model of the Scottish Lowlands, to offer some stimulation to the labouring poor (Documents 8, 9). This debate raised critical questions about the state of contemporary society, some time before many contemporaries were aware of the issues.

The impact of commerce was also relevant in shaping the form of government to be found in an advanced society. Smith wrote in *The Wealth of Nations*, of the relationship between commerce and liberty, that 'Mr Hume is the only writer who, so far as I know, has hitherto taken notice of it' (Document 7). This was not altogether true; Robertson and Millar had already written on the subject, and Smith had himself included it in his lectures at Glasgow. English historians still tended to rely on the notion of the 'ancient constitution', the view that England had inherited the ancient Anglo-Saxon liberties which shaped the constitution and survived all attempts, like those of the Stuarts, to subvert them. David Hume's *History of England*, published in 6 volumes from 1754 to 1762, offered constitutional history, written from the standpoint of a 'philosophical' historian. His essays give some idea of this approach. Hume was interested in examining the psychological origins of party conflict, together with the ways in which the operation of self-interest in particular situations could lead to confrontation, with results that were not necessarily those expected by either side. Hume recognised also the extent to which economic change might affect the balance of power within the state (as, again, Hutcheson had done); the role of the middle classes was important, in that they, too, demanded a share of power and responsibility. Hume differed from English historians not only in his approach to writing history, but also in his definition of that liberty which, they were agreed, distinguished the British constitution. For Hume, and probably for Smith too, liberty was not confined to Britain; it was typical of a commercial society at a particular stage of its development. Liberty needed to be restrained by authority, seen in the liberty and security of individuals, the preservation of order, and the protection of contracts. Much of this could be traced back to the natural law writers, and to Hutcheson. Law was critical to the civilised society; forms of government, one constitution rather than another, were less important. Hence Hume could argue that the absolute monarchy of France was as civilised and stable as mixed forms of government, a 'government of Laws not men'; he does appear to be writing of civil, rather than political, liberty[5]. Smith made it abundantly clear that he greatly admired the British constitution, and the role of the House of Commons; but he did not see it as the inevitable result of commercial development, rather, perhaps, the exception in Western Europe, a product of particular historical circumstances. John Millar followed much of Adam Smith's account, both in his *Origin of the Distinction of Ranks* and in the *Historical View of the English Government*, first published in 1787. Millar wrote of the historical development of the English constitution in the light of economic change. The coming of commercial civilisation could strengthen both central monarchical power and the democratic element within society (Document 14, and also Chapter 6, Document 6); only close historical study could reveal why one tendency would prevail. But Millar believed that liberty, and here he implies both political and civil liberty, was a product of developing civilisation rather than of savage or barbarian societies:

> Wherever men of inferior condition are enabled to live in affluence by their own industry, and in procuring their livelihood, have little occasion to court the favour of their superiors, there we may expect that ideas of liberty will be universally diffused. This happy arrangement of things, is as naturally produced by commerce and manufactures; but it would be as vain to look for it in the uncultivated parts of the world, as to look for the independent spirit of an English waggoner, among persons of low rank in the Highlands of Scotland[6].

Smith and Millar shared a broadly optimistic view of the future prospects of commercial and industrial development; their reservations, though farsighted, could not outweigh the benefits which they believed economic progress to bring.

NOTES

1. Adam Smith, *An Inquiry into the Nature and Causes of the Wealth of Nations*, ed. R. H. Campbell and A. S. Skinner, 2 vols (Oxford, 1975) I, p. 12n.

2. *Ibid*, I, p. 267.

3. *Ibid*, I, p. 456.

4. Bernard Mandeville, *The Fable of the Bees: or, Private Vices, Public Benefits*, edited by F. B. Kaye, 2 vols (Oxford, 1924) I, p. 25.

5. D. Forbes, 'Sceptical Whiggism, Commerce and Liberty', in *Essays on Adam Smith*, edited by A. S. Skinner and T. Wilson (Oxford, 1975).

6. J. Millar, *Origin of the Distinction of Ranks*, p. 296.

Commerce and Civilisation: Documents

THE DIVISION OF LABOUR

1. An early view

Francis Hutcheson, *System of Moral Philosophy*, I, pp. 287–90.

. . . Tis plain that a man in absolute solitude, though he were of mature strength, and fully instructed in all our arts of life, could scarcely procure to himself the bare necessaries of life, even in the best soils or climates; much less could he procure any grateful conveniences . . .

The mutual aids of a few in a small family, may procure most of the necessaries of life, and diminish dangers, and afford room for some social joys as well as finer pleasures. The same advantages could still be obtained more effectually and copiously by the mutual assistance of a few such families, living in one neighbourhood, as they could execute more operose designs for the common good of all; and would furnish more joyful exercises of our social dispositions.

Nay tis well known that the produce of the labours of any given number, twenty, for instance, in providing the necessaries or conveniences of life, shall be much greater by assigning to one, a certain sort of work of one kind, in which he will soon acquire skill and dexterity, and to another assigning work of a different kind, than if each one of the twenty were obliged to employ himself, by turns, in all the different sorts of labour requisite for his subsistence, without sufficient dexterity in any. In the former method each procures a great quantity of goods of one kind, and can exchange a part of it for such goods obtained by the labours of others as he shall stand in need of. One grows expert in tillage, another in pasture and breeding cattle, a third in masonry, a fourth in the chase, a fifth in ironworks, a sixth in the arts of the loom, and so on throughout the rest. Thus all are supplied by means of barter with the works of complete artists. In the other method, scarce any one could be dexterous and skilful in any one sort of labour . . .

Larger associations may further enlarge our means of enjoyment and give more extensive and delightful exercise to our powers of every kind. The inventions, experience and arts of multitude are communicated; knowledge is increased and social affections more diffused. Larger societies have force to execute greater designs of more lasting and extensive advantage.

2. 'Ignorance is the mother of industry'

Adam Ferguson, *Essay on the History of Civil Society*, second edition (1768) pp. 279–80.

The artifices of the beaver, the ant, and the bee, are ascribed to the wisdom of nature. Those of polished nations are ascribed to themselves, and are supposed to indicate a capacity superior to that of rude minds. But the establishments of men, like those of every animal, are suggested by nature, and are the result of instinct, directed by the variety of situations in which mankind are placed. Those establishments arose from successive improvements that were made, without any sense of their general effect; and they bring human affairs to a state of complication, which the greatest reach of capacity with which human nature was ever adorned, could not have projected; nor even when the whole is carried into execution, can it be comprehended in its full extent.

Who could anticipate, or even enumerate, the separate occupations and professions by which the members of any commercial state are distinguished; the variety of devices which are practised in separate cells, and which the artist, attentive to his own affair, has invented, to abridge or to facilitate his separate task? In coming to this mighty end, every generation, compared to its predecessors, may have appeared to be ingenious; compared to its followers, may have appeared to be dull: and human ingenuity, whatever heights it may have gained in a succession of ages, continues to move with an equal pace, and to creep in making the last as well as the first step of commercial or civil improvement.

It may even be doubted, whether the measure of national

capacity increases with the advancement of arts. Many mechanical arts, indeed, require no capaity; they succeed best under a total suppression of sentiment and reason; and ignorance is the mother of industry as well as of superstitition. Reflection and fancy are subject to err; but a habit of moving the hand, or the foot, is independent of either. Manufactures, accordingly, prosper most, where the mind is least consulted, and where the workshop may, without any great effort of imagination, be considered as an engine, the parts of which are men.

3. 'The principle which occasions the division of labour'

Adam Smith, *An Inquiry into the nature and causes of the Wealth of Nations*. The third edition, with additions, 3 vols (London, 1784) I, pp. 19–23.

This division of labour, from which so many advantages are derived, is not originally the effect of any human wisdom, which foresees and intends that general opulence to which it gives occasion. It is the necessary, though very slow and gradual consequence of a certain propensity in human nature which has in view no such extensive utility; the propensity to truck, barter, and exchange one thing for another.

Whether this propensity be one of those original principles in human nature, of which no further account can be given; or whether, as seems more probable, it be the necessary consequence of the faculties of reason and speech, it belongs not to our present subject to enquire. It is common to all men, and to be found in no other race of animals, which seem to know neither this nor any other species of contracts . . . In almost every other race of animals each individual, when it is grown up to maturity, is entirely independent, and in its natural state has occasion for the assistance of no other living creature. But man has almost constant occasion for the help of his brethren, and it is in vain for him to expect it from their benevolence only. He will be more likely to prevail if he can interest their self-love in his favour, and show them that it is for their own advantage to do for him what he requires of them. Whoever offers to another a bargain of any kind, proposes to do this. Give me that which I want, and you shall have this which you want, is the meaning of every such offer; and it is in this manner that we obtain from one another the far greater part of those good offices which we stand in need of. It is not from the benevolence of the butcher, the brewer, or the baker, that we expect our dinner, but from their regard to their own interest. We address ourselves, not to their humanity but to their self-love, and never talk to them of our own necessities but of their advantages. Nobody but a beggar chooses to depend chiefly upon the benevolence of his fellow-citizens. Even a beggar does not depend upon it entirely. The charity of well-disposed people, indeed, supplies him with the whole fund of his subsistence. But though this principle ultimately provides him with all the necessaries of life which he has occasion for, it neither does nor can provide him with them as he has occasion for them. The greater part of his occasional wants are supplied in the same manner as those of other people, by treaty, by barter, and by purchase. With the money which one man gives him he purchases food. The old clothes which another bestows upon him he exchanges for other old clothes which suit him better, or for lodging, or for food, or for money, with which he can buy either food, clothes, or lodging, as he has occasion.

As it is by treaty, by barter, and by purchase, that we obtain from one another the greater part of those mutual good offices which we stand in need of, so it is this same trucking disposition which originally gives occasion to the division of labour. In a tribe of hunters or shepherds a particular person makes bows and arrows, for example, with more readiness and dexterity than any other. He frequently exchanges them for cattle or for venison with his companions; and he finds at last that he can in this manner get more cattle and venison, than if he himself went to the field to catch them. From a regard to his own interest, therefore, the making of bows and arrows grows to be his chief business, and he becomes a sort of armourer. Another excels in making the frames and covers of their little huts or moveable houses. He is accustomed to be of use in this way to his neighbours, who reward him in the same manner with cattle and with venison, till at last he finds it his interest to dedicate himself entirely to this employment, and to become a sort of house-carpenter. In the same manner a third becomes a smith or a brazier, a fourth a tanner or dresser of hides or skins, the principal part of the clothing of savages. And thus the certainty of being able to exchange all that surplus part of the produce of his own labour, which is over and above his own consumption, for such parts of the produce of other men's labour as he may have occasion for, encourages every man to apply himself to a particular occupation, and to cultivate and bring to perfection whatever talent or genius he may possess for that particular species of business.

THE EFFECTS OF LUXURY

4. The case for luxury

David Hume, 'Of Refinement in the Arts', first published (as 'Of Luxury') in *Political Discourses* (Edinburgh, 1752) reprinted in the *Philosophical Works*, III, pp. 300–303.

Since luxury may be considered either as innocent or blameable, one may be surprised at those preposterous opinions, which have been entertained concerning it; while men of libertine principles bestow praises even on vicious luxury, and represent it as highly advantageous to society; and on the other hand, men of severe morals blame even the most innocent luxury, and represent it as the source of all the corruptions, disordes, and factions, incident to civil government. We shall here endeavour to correct both these extremes, by proving, *first*, that the ages of refinement are both the happiest and most virtuous: *secondly*, that wherever luxury ceases to be innocent, it also ceases to be beneficial; and when carried a degree too far, is a quality pernicious, though perhaps not the most pernicious, to political society.

To prove the first point, we need but consider the effects of refinement both on *private* and on *public* life. Human happiness, according to the most received notions, seems to consist in three ingredients: action, pleasure, and indolence: and though these ingredients ought to be mixed in different proportions, according to the particular disposition of the person; yet no one ingredient can be entirely wanting, without destroying, in some measure, the relish of the whole composition. Indolence or repose, indeed, seems not of itself to contribute much to our enjoyment; but, like sleep, is requisite as an indulgence to the weakness of human nature, which cannot support an uninterrupted course of business or pleasure. That quick march of the spirits, which takes a man from himself, and chiefly gives satisfaction, does in the end exhaust the mind, and requires some intervals of repose, which, though agreeable for a moment, yet, if prolonged, beget a languor and lethargy that destroys all enjoyment. Education, custom, and example, have a mighty influence in turning the mind to any of these pursuits; and it must be owned, that, where they promote a relish for action and pleasure, they are so far favourable to human happiness. In times when industry and the arts flourish, men are kept in perpetual occupation, and enjoy, as their reward, the occupation itself, as well as those pleasures which are the fruit of their labour. The mind acquires new vigour; enlarges its powers and faculties; and by an assiduity in honest industry, both satisfies its natural appetites, and prevents the growth of unnatural ones, which commonly spring up, when nourished by ease and idleness. Banish those arts from society, you deprive men both of action and of pleasure; and leaving nothing but indolence in their place, you even destroy the relish of indolence, which never is agreeable, but when it succeeds to labour, and recruits the spirits, exhausted by too much application and fatigue.

Another advantage of industry and of refinements in the mechanical arts, is, that they commonly produce some refinements in the liberal; nor can one be carried to perfection, without being accompanied, in some degree, with the other. The same age, which produces great philosophers and politicians, renowned generals and poets, usually abounds with skilled weavers, and ship-carpenters. We cannot reasonably expect, that a piece of woolen cloth will be brought to perfection in a nation, which is ignorant of astronomy, or where ethics are neglected. The spirit of the age affects all the arts; and the minds of men, being once roused from their lethargy, and put into a fermentation, turn themselves on all sides, and carry improvements into every art and science. Profound ignorance is totally banished, and men enjoy the privilege of rational creatures, to think as well as to act, to cultivate the pleasures of the mind as well as those of the body.

The more these refined arts, advance, the more sociable men become: nor is it possible, that, when enriched with science, and possessed of a fund of conversation, they should be contented to remain in solitude, or live with their fellow-citizens in that distant manner, which is peculiar to ignorant and barbarous nations. They flock into cities; love to receive and communicate knowledge; to show their wit or their breeding; their taste in conversation or living, in clothes or furniture. Curiosity allures the wise; vanity the foolish; and pleasure both. Particular clubs and societies are everywhere formed; both sexes meet in an easy and sociable manner: and the tempers of men, as well as their behaviour, refine apace. So that, beside the improvements which they receive from knowledge and the liberal arts, it is impossible but they must feel an increase of humanity, from the very habit of conversing together, and contribute to each other's pleasure and entertainment. Thus *industry*, *knowledge* and *humanity*, are linked together by an indissoluble chain, and are found, from experience as well as reason, to be peculiar to the more polished, and, what are commonly denominated, the more luxurious ages . . .

But industry, knowledge, and humanity, are not advantageous in private life alone: they diffuse their beneficial influence on the *public*, and render the government as great and flourishing as they make individuals happy and prosperous. The increase and consumption of all the commodities, whch serve to the ornament and pleasure of life, are advantageous to society; because, at the same time that they multiply those innocent gratifications to individuals, they are a kind of *storehouse* of labour, which, in the exigencies of state, may be turned to public service. In a nation, where there is no demand for such superfluities, men sink into indolence, lose all enjoyment of life, and are useless to the public, which cannot maintain or support its fleets and armies, from the industry of such slothful members.

5. The limitations of the 'polished' society

Adam Ferguson, *Essay on the History of Civil Society*, second edition, pp. 313–316.

The term *polished*, if we may judge from its etymology, originally referred to the state of nations in respect to their laws and government; and men civilised, were men practised in the duty of citizens. In its later applications, it refers no less to the proficiency of nations in the liberal and mechanical arts, in literature, and in commerce; and men civilised, are scholars, men of fashion, and traders. But whatever may be its application, it appears, that if there were a name still more respectable than this, every nation, even the most barbarous, or the most corrupted, would assume it; and bestow its reverse where they conceived a dislike, or apprehended a difference. The names of *alien*, or *foreigners*, are seldom pronounced without some degree of intended reproach. That of *barbarian*, in use with one arrogant people, and that of *gentil*, with another, only served to distinguish the stranger, whose language and pedigree differed from theirs.

Even where we pretend to found our opinions on reason, and to justify our preference of one nation to another, we frequently bestow our esteem on circumstances which do not relate to national character, and which have little tendency to promote the welfare of mankind. Conquest, or great extent of territory, however peopled, and great wealth, however distributed or employed, are titles upon which we indulge our own, and the vanity of other nations, as we do that of private men on the score of their fortunes and honours. We even sometimes contend, whose capital is the most overgrown; whose king has the most absolute power; and at whose court the bread of the subject is consumed in the most senseless riot. These indeed are the notions of vulgar minds may lead mankind.

There have certainly been very few examples of states, who have, by arts or policy, improved the original dispositions of human nature, or endeavoured, by wise and effectual precautions, to prevent its corruption. Affection, and force of mind, which are the band and the strength of communities, were the inspiration of God, and original attributes in the nature of man. The wisest policy of nations, except in a very few instances, has tended, we may suspect, rather to maintain the peace of society, and to repress the external effects of bad passions, than to strengthen the disposition of the heart itself to justice and goodness. It has tended, by introducing a variety of arts, to exercise the ingenuity of men, and by engaging them in a variety of pursuits, inquiries, and studies, to inform, but frequently to corrupt the mind. It has tended to furnish matter of distinction and vanity; and by encumbering the individual with new subjects of personal care, to substitute the anxiety he entertains for a separate fortune, instead of the confidence and affection with which he should unite with his fellow creatures, for their joint preservation . . .

Were we to suppose men to have succeeded in the discovery and application of every art by which states are preserved, and governed; to have attained, by efforts of wisdom and magnanimity, the admired establishments and advantages of a civilised and flourishing people; the subsequent part of their history, containing, according to vulgar apprehension, a full display of those fruits in maturity, of which they had till then carried only the blossom, and the first formation should, still more than the former, merit our attention, and excite our admiration.

The event, however, has not corresponded to this expectation. The virtues of men have shone most during their struggles, not after the attainment of their ends. Those ends themselves, though attained by virtue, are frequently the causes of corruption and vice. Mankind, in aspiring to national felicity, have substituted arts which increase their riches, instead of those which improve their nature. They have entertained admiration of themselves, under the titles of *civilised* and *polished*, where they should have been affected with shame; and even where they have for a while acted on maxims tending to raise, to invigorate, and to preserve the national character, they have, sooner or later, been diverted from their object, and fallen a prey to misfortune, or to the neglects which prosperity itself had encouraged.

6. An historical interpretation

William Robertson, 'A View of the Progress of Society in Europe, from the subversion of the Roman Empire, to the beginning of the sixteenth century', *History of the Reign of the Emperor Charles V*, (first published in 3 volumes, London, 1769) in *The Works of William Robertson*, IV, pp. 91–8.

The progress of commerce had considerable influence in polishing the manners of the European nations, and in establishing among them order, equal laws, and humanity. The wants of men, in the original and most simple state of society, are so few, and their desires so limited, that they rest contented with the natural productions of their climate and soil, or with what they can add to these by their own rude industry. They have no superfluities to dispose of, and few necessities that demand a supply. Every little community subsisting on its own domestic stock, and satisfied with it, is either little acquainted with the states around it, or at variance with them. Society and manners must be considerably improved and many provisions must be made for public order and personal security, before a liberal intercourse can take place between different nations. We find, accordingly that the first effect of the settlement of the barbarians in the empire was to divide those nations which the Roman power had united. Europe was broken into many separate communities. The intercourse between these divided states ceased almost entirely during several centuries. Navigation was dangerous in seas infested by pirates; nor could strangers trust to a friendly reception in the ports of uncivilised nations. Even between distant parts of the same kingdom, the communication was rare and difficult. The lawless rapine of banditti, together with the avowed exactions of the nobles, scarcely less formidable and oppressive, rendered a journey of any length a perilous enterprise. Fixed to the spot in which they resided, the greater part of the inhabitants of Europe lost, in a great measure, the knowledge of remote regions, and were unacquainted with their names, their situations, their climates, and their commodities.

Various causes, however, contributed to revive the spirit of commerce, and to renew, in some degree, the intercourse between different nations. The Italians, by their connections with Constantinople, and other cities of the Greek empire, had preserved in their own country considerable relish for the precious commodities and curious manufactures of the East. They communicated some knowledge of these to the countries contiguous to Italy. But this commerce being extremely limited, the intercourse which it occasioned between different nations was not considerable. The Crusades, by leading multitudes from every corner of Europe into Asia, opened a more extensive communication between the East and West, which subsisted for two centuries; and though the object of these expeditions was conquest and not commerce; though the issue of these proved as unfortunate as the motives for undertaking them were wild and enthusiastic; their commercial effects, as has been shown, were both beneficial and permanent. During the continuance of the Crusades, the great cities in Italy, and in other countries of Europe, acquired liberty, and together with it such privileges as rendered them respectable and independent communities. Thus, in every state, there was formed a new order of citizens, to whom commerce presented itself as their proper object, and opened to them a certain path to wealth and consideration. Soon after the close of the Holy War, the mariner's compass was invented, which, by rendering navigation more secure, encouraged it to become more adventurous, facilitated the communication between remote nations, and brought them nearer to each other.

The Italian states, during the same period established a regular commerce with the East in the ports of Egypt, and drew from thence all the rich products of the Indies. They introduced into their own territories manufactures of various kinds, and carried them on with great ingenuity and vigour. They attempted new arts; and transplanted from warmer climates, to which they had been hitherto deemed peculiar, several natural productions which now furnish the materials of a lucrative and extended commerce. All these commodities, whether imported from Asia, or produced by their own skill, they disposed of to great advantage among the other people of Europe, who began to acquire some taste for an elegance in living unknown to their ancestors, or despised by them. During the twelfth and thirteenth centuries, the commerce of Europe was almost entirely in the hands of the Italians, more commonly known in those ages by the name of Lombards. Companies or societies of Lombard merchants settled in every different kingdom. They were taken under the immediate protection of the several governments. They enjoyed extensive privileges and immunities. The operation of the ancient barbarous laws concerning strangers was suspended with respect to them. They became the carriers, the manufacturers, and the bankers of all Europe.

While the Italians, in the South of Europe, were cultivating trade with such industry and success, the commercial spirit awakened in the North toward the middle of the thirteenth century. As the nations around the Baltic were, at that time, extremely barbarous, and infested that sea with their piracies, the cities of Lubeck and Hamburg, soon after they began to open some trade with these people, found it necessary to enter into a league of mutual defence. They derived such advantages from this union, that other towns acceded to their confederacy, and in a short time, eighty of the most considerable cities scattered through those extensive countries which stretch from the bottom of the Baltic to Cologne on the Rhine, joined in the famous Hanseatic League, which became so formidable, that its alliance was courted, and its enmity was dreaded by the greatest monarchs. The members of this powerful association formed the first systematic plan of commerce known in the middle ages, and conducted it by common laws enacted in their general assemblies. They supplied the rest of Europe with naval stores, and pitched on different towns, the most eminent of which was Bruges in Flanders, where they established staples in which their commerce was regularly carried on. Thither the Lombards brought the productions of India, together with the manufactures of Italy, and exchanged them for the more bulky, but not less useful commodities of the North. The Hanseatic merchants disposed of the cargoes which they received from the Lombards, in the ports of the

Baltic, or carried them up the great rivers into the interior parts of Germany.

This regular intercourse opened between the nations in the North and South of Europe, made them sensible of their mutual wants, and created such new and increasing demands for commodities of every kind, that it excited among the inhabitants of the Netherlands a more vigorous spirit in carrying on the two great manufacturers of wool and flax, which seem to have been considerable in that country as early as the age of Charlemagne. As Bruges became the centre of communication between the Lombard and Hanseatic merchants, the Flemings traded with both in that city to such extent as well as advantage, as spread among them a general habit of industry, which long rendered Flanders and the adjacent provinces the most opulent, the most populous, and best cultivated countries in Europe.

Struck with the flourishing state of these provinces, of which he discerned the true cause, Edward III of England endeavoured to excite a spirit of industry among his own subjects, who, blind to the advantages of their situation, and ignorant of the source from which opulence was destined to flow into their country, were so little attentive to their commercial interests, as hardly to attempt those manufactures, the materials of which they furnished to foreigners. By alluring Flemish artisans to settle in his dominions, as well as by many wise laws for the encouragement and regulation of trade, Edward gave a beginning to the woolen manufactures of England, and first turned the active and enterprising genius of his people towards those arts which have raised the English to the highest rank among commercial nations.

This increase of commerce, and of intercourse between nations, how inconsiderable soever it may appear in respect of their rapid and extensive progress during the last and present age, seems wonderfully great, when we compare it with the state of both in Europe previous to the twelfth century. It did not fail of producing great effects. Commerce tends to wear off those prejudices which maintain distinction and animosity between nations. It softens and polishes the manners of men. It unites them by one of the strongest of all ties, the desire of supplying their mutual wants. It disposes them to peace, by establishing in every state and order of citizens bound by their interest to be the guardians of public tranquility. As soon as the commercial spirit acquires vigour, and begins to gain an ascendant in any society, we discover a new genius in its policy, its alliances, its wars, and its negotiations. Conspicuous proofs of this occur in the history of the Italian states, of the Hanseatic league, and the cities of the Netherlands, during the period under review. In proportion as commerce made its way into the different countries of Erope, they successively turned their attentions to those objects, and adopted those manners, which occupy and distinguish polished nations.

7. The impact of commercial and manufacturing towns on the economy and society

Adam Smith, *The Wealth of Nations*, third edition, II, pp. 117–119.

The increase and riches of commercial and manufacturing towns, contributed to the improvement and cultivation of the countries to which they belonged, in three different ways.

First, by affording a great and ready market for the rude produce of the country, they gave encouragement to its cultivation and further improvement. This benefit was not even confined to the countries in which they were situated, but extended more or less to all those with which they had any dealings. To all of them they afforded a market for some part either of their rude or manufactured produce, and consequently gave some encouragement to the industry and improvement of all. Their own country, however, on account of its neighbourhood, necessarily derived the greatest benefit from this market. Its rude produce being charged with less carriage, the traders could pay the growers a better price for it, and yet afford it as cheap to the consumers as that of more distant countries.

Secondly, the wealth acquired by the inhabitants of cities was frequently employed in purchasing such lands as were to be sold, of which a great part would frequently be uncultivated. Merchants are commonly ambitious of becoming country gentlemen, and when they do, they are generally the best of all improvers. A merchant is accustomed to employ his money chiefly in profitable project; whereas a mere country gentleman is accustomed to employ it chiefly in expence. The one often sees his money go from him and return to him again with a profit: the other, when once he parts with it, very seldom expects to see any more of it. Those different habits naturally affect their temper and disposition in every sort of business. A merchant is commonly a bold; a country gentleman, a timid undertaker. The one is not afraid to lay out at once a large capital upon the improvement of his land, when he has a probable prospect of raising the value of it in proportion to the expence. The other, if he has any capital, which is not always the case, seldom ventures to employ it in this manner. If he improves at all, it is commonly not with a capital, but with what he can save out of his annual revenue. Whoever has had the fortune to live in a mercantile town situated in an unimproved country, must have frequently observed how much more spirited the operations of merchants were in this way, than those of mere country gentlemen. The habits, besides, of order, economy, and attention, to which mercantile business naturally forms a merchant, render him much fitter to execute, with profit and success, any project of improvement.

Thirdly, and lastly, commerce and manufactures gradually introduced order and good government, and with them, the liberty and security of individuals, among the inhabitants of the country, who had before lived almost in a continual state of war with their neighbours, and of servile dependency upon their superiors. This, though it has been the least observed, is by far the most important of all their effects. Mr Hume is the only writer who, so far as I know, has hitherto taken notice of it.

8. The benefits for the labouring population

Adam Smith, *The Wealth of Nations*, third edition, I, pp. 118-119.

The real recompense of labour, the real quantity of the necessaries and conveniences of life which it can procure to the labourer, has, during the course of the present century, increased perhaps in a still greater proportion than its money price. Not only grain has become somewhat cheaper, but many other things from which the industrious poor derive an agreeable and wholesome variety of food, have become a great deal cheaper. Potatoes, for example, do not at present, through the greater part of the kingdom, cost half the price which they used to do thirty or forty years ago. The same thing may be said of turnips, carrots, cabbages; things which were formerly never raised but by the spade, but which are now commonly raised by the plough. All sort of garden stuff too has become cheaper. The greater part of the apples and even of the onions consumed in Great Britain were in the last century imported from Flanders. The great improvements in the coarser manufactures of both linen and woollen cloth furnish the labourers with cheaper and better clothing; and those in the manufactures of the coarser metals, with cheaper and better instruments of trade, as well as with many agreeable and convenient pieces of household furniture. Soap, salt, candles, leather, and fermented liquors have, indeed, become a good deal dearer; chiefly from the taxes which have been laid upon them. The quantity of these, however, which the labouring poor are under any necessity of consuming, is so very small, that the increase in their price does not compensate the diminution in that of so many other things. The common complaint that luxury extends itself even to the lowest ranks of the people, and that the labouring poor will not now be contented with the same food, clothing and lodging which satisfied them in former times, may convince us that it is not the money price of labour only, but its real recompense, which has augmented.

Is this improvement in the circumstances of the lower ranks of the people to be regarded as an advantage or as an inconveniency to the society? The answer seems at first sight abundantly plain. Servants, labourers, and workmen of different kinds, make up the far greater part of every great political society. But what improves the circumstances of the greater part can never be regarded as an inconveniency to the whole. No society can surely be flourishing and happy, of which the far greater part of the members are poor and miserable. It is but equity, besides, that they who feed, clothe, and lodge the whole body of the people, should have such a share of the produce of their own labour as to be themselves tolerably well fed, clothed, and lodged.

9. The disadvantages of the division of labour

Adam Smith, *The Wealth of Nations*, third edition, III, pp. 182–183.

In the progress of the division of labour, the employment of the far greater part of those who live by labour, that is, of the great body of the people, comes to be confined to a few very simple operations; frequently to one or two. But the understandings of the greater part of men are necessarily formed by their ordinary employments. The man whose whole life is spent in performing a few simple operations, of which the effects too are, perhaps, always the same, or very nearly the same, has no occasion to exert his understanding, or to exercise his invention in finding our expedients for removing difficulties which never occur. He naturally loses, therefore, the habit of such exertion, and generally becomes as stupid and ignorant as it is possible for a human creature to become. The torpor of his mind renders him, not only incapable of relishing or bearing a part in any rational conversation, but of conceiving any generous, noble, or tender sentiment, and consequently of forming any just judgment concerning many even of the ordinary duties of private life. Of the great and extensive interests of his country, he is altogether incapable of judging; and unless very particular pains have been taken to render him otherwise, he is equally incapable of defending his country in war. The uniformity of his stationary life naturally corrupts the courage of his mind, and makes him regard with abhorrence the irregular, uncertain, and adventurous life of a soldier. It corrupts even the activity of his body, and renders him incapable of exerting his strength with vigour and perseverance, in any other employment than that to which he has been bred. His dexterity at his own particular trade seems, in this manner, to be acquired at the expence of his intellectual, social, and martial virtues. But in every improved and civilised society this is the state into which the labouring poor, that is, the great body of the people, must necessarily fall, unless government takes some pains to prevent it.

COMMERCE AND LIBERTY

10. The political effects of refinement

David Hume, 'Of Refinement in the Arts', *Philosophical Works*, III, pp. 306-7.

If we consider the matter in a proper light, we shall find, that a progress in the arts is rather favourable to liberty, and has a natural tendency to preserve, if not produce a free government. In rude unpolished nations, where the arts are neglected, all labour is bestowed on the cultivation of the ground; and the whole society is divided into two classes, proprietors of land, and their vassals or tenants. The latter are necessarily dependent, and fitted for slavery and subjection; especially where they possess no riches, and are not valued for their knowledge in agriculture; as must always be the case where the arts are neglected. The former naturally erect themselves into petty tyrants; and must either submit to an absolute master, for the sake of peace and order; or if they will preserve their independency, like the ancient barons, they must fall into feuds and contests among themselves, and throw the whole society into such confusion, as is perhaps worse than the most despotic government. But where luxury nourishes commerce and industry, the peasants, by a proper cultivation of the land, become rich and independent; while the tradesmen and merchants acquire a share of the property, and draw authority and consideration to that middling rank of men, who are the best and firmest basis of public liberty. These submit not to slavery, like the peasants, from poverty and meanness of spirit; and having no hopes of tyrannizing over others, like the barons, they are not tempted, for the sake of that gratification, to submit to the tyranny of their sovereign. They covet equal laws, which may secure their property, and preserve them from monarchical, as well as aristocratical tyranny.

The lower house is the support of our popular government; and all the world acknowledges, that it owed its chief influence and consideration to the increase of commerce, which threw such a balance of property into the hands of the commons. How inconsistent then is it to blame so violently a refinement in the arts, and to represent it as the bane of liberty and public spirit!

11. Party conflict

David Hume, 'Of the Parties of Great Britain' (first published in *Essays Moral and Political* [Edinburgh, 1741]) *Philosophical Works*, III, pp. 133–7.

Were the British Government proposed as a subject of speculation, one would immediately perceive in it a source of division and party, which it would be almost impossible for it, under any administration, to avoid. The just balance between the republican and monarchical part of our constitution is really, in itself, so extremely delicate and uncertain, that, when joined to men's passions and prejudices, it is impossible but different opinions must arise concerning it, even among persons of the best understanding. Those of mild tempers, who love peace and order, and detest sedition and civil wars, will always entertain more favourable sentiments of monarchy, than men of bold and generous spirits, who are passionate lovers of liberty, and think no evil comparable to subjection and slavery. And though all reasonable men agree in general to preserve our mixed government; yet, when they come to particulars, some will incline to trust greater powers to the crown, to bestow on it more influence, and to guard against its encroachments with less caution, than others who are terrified at the most distant approaches of tyranny and despotic power. Thus are there parties of PRINCIPLE involved in the very nature of our constitution, which may properly enough be denominated those of COURT and COUNTRY. The strength and violence of each of these parties will much depend upon the particular administration. An administration may be so bad, as to throw a great majority into the opposition; as a good administration will reconcile to the court many of the most passionate lovers of liberty. But however the nation may fluctuate between them, the parties themselves will always subsist, so long as we are governed by a legitimate monarchy.

But, besides this difference of *Principle*, those parties are very much fomented by a difference of INTEREST, without which they could scarcely ever be dangerous or violent. The crown will naturally bestow all trust and power upon those, whose principles, real or pretended, are most favourable to monarchical government; and this temptation will naturally engage them to go greater lengths than their principles would otherwise carry them. Their antagonists, who were disappointed in their ambitious aims, throw themselves into the party whose sentiments incline them to be most jealous of royal power, and naturally carry those sentiments to a greater height than sound politics will justify. Thus *Court* and *Country*, which are the genuine offspring of the British government, are a kind of mixed parties, and are influenced both by principle and by interest. The heads of the factions are commonly most governed by the latter motive; the inferior members of them by the former . . .

If we consider the first rise of parties in England, during the great rebellion, we shall observe, that it was conformable to this general theory, and that the species of government gave birth to them, by a regular and infallible operation. The English constitution, before that period, had lain in a kind of confusion; yet so, as that the subjects possessed many noble privileges, which, though not exactly bounded and secured by law, were universally deemed, from long possession, to belong to them as their birth-right. An ambitious, or rather a misguided, prince arose, who deemed all these privileges to be concessions of his predecessors, revocable at pleasure; and, in prosecution of this principle, he openly acted in violation of liberty, during the course of several years. Necessity, at last, constrained him to call a parliament: the spirit of liberty arose and spread itself: the prince, being without any support, was obliged to grant everything required of him; and his enemies, jealous and implacable, set no bounds to their pretensions. Here then began those contests, in which it was no wonder, that men of that age were divided into different parties; since, even at this day, the impartial are at a loss to decide concerning the justice of the quarrel. The pretensions of the parliament, if yielded to, broke the balance of the constitution, by rendering the government almost entirely republican. If not yielded to, the nation was, perhaps, still in danger of absolute power, from the settled principles and inveterate habits of the king, which had plainly appeared in every concession that he had been constrained to make to his people. In this question, so delicate and uncertain, men naturally fell to the side which was most conformable to their usual principles; and the more passionate favourers of monarchy declared for the king, as the zealous friends of liberty sided with the parliament. The hopes of success being nearly equal of both sides, *interest* had no general influence in this contest: so that ROUND-HEAD and CAVALIER were merely parties of principles; neither of which disowned either monarchy or liberty; but the former party inclined most to the republican part of our government, the latter to the monarchical. In this respect, they may be considered as court and country-party, enflamed into a civil war, by an unhappy concurrence of circumstances, and by the turbulent spirit of the age. The commonwealth's men, and the partisans of absolute power, lay concealed in both parties, and formed but an inconsiderable part of them.

12. Liberty and commerce in an absolute monarchy

David Hume, 'Of Civil Liberty' (first published as 'Of Liberty and Despotism', in *Essays Moral and Political* [Edinburgh, 1741]) *Philosophical Works*, III, pp. 161-3.

But though all kinds of government be improved in modern times, yet monarchical government seems to have made the greatest advances towards perfection. It may now be affirmed of civilised monarchies, what was formerly said in praise of republics alone, *that they are a government of Laws, not of Men*. They are found susceptible of order, method, and constancy, to a surprising degree. Property is there secure; industry encouraged; the arts flourish; and the prince lives secure among his subjects, like a father among his children. There are perhaps, and have been for two centuries, nearly two hundred absolute princes, great and small, in Europe; and allowing twenty years to each reign, we may suppose, that there have been in the whole two thousand monarchs or tyrants, as the Greeks would have called them; yet of these there has not been one, not even Philip II of Spain, so bad as Tiberius, Caligula, Nero, or Domitian, who were four in twelve amongst the Roman emperors. It must, however, be confessed, that, though monarchical governments have approached nearer to popular ones, in gentleness and stability; they are still inferior. Our modern education and customs instil more humanity and moderation than the ancient; but have not as yet been able to overcome entirely the disadvantages of that form of government.

But here I must beg leave to advance a conjecture, which seems probable, but which posterity alone can fully judge of. I am apt to think, that, in monarchical governments there is a source of improvement, and in popular governments a source of degeneracy, which in time will bring these species of civil polity still nearer an equality. The greatest abuses which arise in France, the most perfect model of pure monarchy, proceed not from the number or weight of the taxes, beyond what are to be met with in free countries; but from the expensive, unequal, arbitrary, and intricate method of levying them, by which the industry of the poor, especially of the peasants and farmers, is, in a great measure, discouraged, and agriculture rendered a beggarly and slavish employment. But to whose advantage do these abuses tend? If to that of the nobility, they might be esteemed inherent in that form of government; since the nobility are the true supports of monarchy; and it is natural their interest should be more consulted, in such a constitution, than that of the people. But the nobility are, in reality, the chief losers by this oppression; since it ruins their estates, and beggars their tenants. The only gainers by it are the Financiers, a race of men rather odious to the nobility and the whole kingdom. If a prince or minister, therefore, should arise, endowed with sufficient discernment to know his own and the public interest, and with sufficient force of mind to break through the ancient customs, we might expect to see these abuses remedied; in which case, the difference between that absolute government and our free one, would not appear so considerable as at present.

The source of degeneracy, which may be remarked in free governments, consists in the practice of contracting debt, and mortgaging the public revenues, by which taxes may, in time, become altogether intolerable, and all the property of the state be brought into the hands of the public . . .

13. The dangers of luxury

Adam Ferguson, *Essay on the History of Civil Society*, pp. 401-4.

Liberty, in one sense, appears to be the portion of polished nations alone. The savage is personally free, because he lives unrestrained, and acts with the members of his tribe on terms of equality. The barbarian is frequently independent from a continuance of the same circumstances, or because he has courage and a sword. But good policy alone can provide for the regular administration of justice, or constitute a force in the state, which is ready on every occasion to defend the rights of its members.

It has been found, that, except in a few singular cases, the commercial and political arts have advanced together. These arts have been in modern Europe so interwoven, that we cannot determine which were prior in the order of time, or derived most advantage from the mutual influences with which they act and react on each other. It has been observed, that in some nations the spirit of commerce, intent on securing its profits, has led the way to political wisdom. A people, possessed of wealth, and become jealous of their properties, have formed the project of emancipation, and have proceeded, under favour of an importance recently gained, still farther to enlarge their pretensions, and to dispute the prerogatives which their sovereign had been in use to employ. But it is in vain that we expect in one age, from the possession of wealth, the fruit which it is said to have borne in a former. Great accessions of fortune, when recent, when accompanied with frugality, and a sense of independence, may render the owner confident in his strength, and ready to spurn at oppression. The purse which is open, not to personal expence, or to the indulgence of vanity, but to support the interests of a faction, to gratify the higher passions of party, render the wealthy citizen formidable to those who pretend to dominion; but it does not follow, that in a time of corruption, equal, or greater, measures of wealth should operate to the same effect.

On the contrary, when wealth is accumulated only in the hands of the miser, and runs to waste from those of the prodigal; when heirs of family find themselves straitened and poor, in the midst of affluence; when the carvings of luxury silence even the voice of party and faction; when the hopes of meriting the rewards of compliance, or the fear of losing what is held at discretion, keep men in a state of suspense and anxiety; when fortune, in short, instead of being considered as the instrument of a vigorous spirit, becomes the idol of a covetous or a profuse, of a rapacious or a timorous mind; the foundation on which freedom was built, may serve to support a tyranny; and what, in one age, raised the pretensions, and fostered the confidence of the subject, may, in another, incline him to servility, and furnish the price to be paid for his prostitutions. Even those, who, in a vigorous age, gave the example of wealth, in the hands of the people, becoming an occasion of freedom, may, in times of degeneracy, verify likewise the maxim of Tacitus, That the admiration of riches leads to despotical government.

Men who have tasted of freedom, and who have felt their personal rights, are not easily taught to bear with encroachments on either, and cannot, without some preparation, come to submit to oppression. They may receive this unhappy preparation, under different forms of government, from different hands, and arrive at the same end by different ways. They follow one direction in republics, another in monarchies, and in mixed governments. But wherever the state has, by means that do not preserve the virtue of the subject, effectually guarded his safety; remissness, and neglect of the public, are likely to follow; and polished nations of every description, appear to encounter a danger, on this quarter, proportioned to the degree in which they have, during any continuance, enjoyed the uninterrupted possession of peace and prosperity.

14. Civilisation and democracy

John Millar, *Origin of the Distinction of Ranks*, pp. 284–288.

The farther a nation advances in opulence and refinement, it has occasion to employ a greater number of merchants, of tradesmen and artificers; and as the lower people, in general, become thereby more independent in their circumstances, they begin to exert those sentiments of liberty which are natural to the mind of man, and which necessity alone is able to subdue. In proportion as they have less need of the favour and patronage of the great, they are at less pains to procure it; and their application is more uniformly directed to acquire those talents which are useful in the exercise of their employments. The impressions which they received in their former state of servitude are therefore gradually obliterated, and give place to habits of a different nature. The long attention and perseverance, by which they become expert and skilful in their business, render them ignorant of those decorums and of that politeness which arises from the intercourse of society; and that vanity which was formerly discovered in magnifying the power of a chief, is now equally displayed in sullen indifference, or in contemptuous and insolent behaviour to persons of superior rank and station.

While, from these causes, people of low rank are gradually advancing towards a state of independence, the influence derived from wealth is diminished in the same proportion. From the improvement of arts and manufactures, the ancient simplicity of manners is in a great measure destroyed; and the proprietor of a landed estate, instead of consuming its produce in hiring retainers, is obliged to employ a great part of it in purchasing those comforts and conveniences which have become objects of attention, and which are thought suitable to his condition. Thus while fewer persons are under the necessity of depending upon him, he is daily rendered less capable of maintaining dependents; till at last his domestics and servants are reduced to such as are merely subservient to luxury and pageantry, but are of no use in supporting his authority.

From the usual effects of luxury and refinement, it may at the same time be expected that old families will often be reduced to poverty and beggary. In a refined and luxurious nation those who are born to great affluence, and who have been bred to no business, are excited, with mutual emulation, to surpass one another in the elegance and refinement of their living. According as they have the means of indulging themselves in pleasure, they become more addicted to the pursuit of it, and are sunk in a degree of indolence and dissipation which renders them incapable of any active employment. Thus the expence of the landed gentleman is apt to be continually increasing, without any proportional addition to his income. His estate therefore, being more and more encumbered with debts, is at length alienated, and brought into the possession of the frugal and industrious merchant, who, by success in trade, has been enabled to buy it, and who is desirous of obtaining that rank and consequence which landed property is capable of bestowing. The posterity, however, of this new proprietor, having adopted the manners of the landed gentry, are again led, in a few generations, to squander their estate, with a heedless extravagance equal to the parsimony and activity by which it was acquired.

This fluctuation of property, so observable in all commercial countries, and which no prohibitions are capable of preventing, must necessarily weaken the authority of those who are placed in the higher ranks of life. Persons who have lately attained to riches, have no opportunity of establishing that train of dependence which is maintained by those who have remained for ages at the head of a great estate. The hereditary influence of family is thus, in a great measure, destroyed; and the consideration derived from wealth is often limited to what the possessor can acquire during his own life. Even this too, for the reasons formerly mentioned, is greatly diminished. A man of great fortune having dismissed his retainers, and spending a great part of his income in the purchase of commodities produced by tradesmen and manufacturers, has no ground to expect that many persons will be willing either to fight for him, or to run any great hazard for promoting his interest. Whatever profits he means to obtain from the labour and assistance of others, he must give a full equivalent for it. He must buy those personal services which are no longer to be performed either from attachment or from peculiar connexions. Money, therefore, beco-mes more and more the only means of procuring honours and dignities; and the sordid pursuits of avarice are made subservient to the nobler purposes of ambition.

It cannot be doubted that these circumstances have a tendency to introduce a democratical government. As persons of inferior rank are placed in a situation which, in point of subsistence, renders them little dependent upon their superiors; as no one order of men continues in the exclusive possession of opulence; and as every man who is industrious may entertain the hope of gaining a fortune; it is to be expected that the prerogatives of the monarch, and of the ancient nobility will be gradually undermined, that the privileges of the people will be extended in the same proportion and that power, the usual attendant of wealth, will be in some measure diffused over all the members of the community.

7 'A Centre . . . of Politeness and Refinement': Edinburgh's Augustan Age

By the 1750s 'enlightened' ideas provided the framework for a period of intense intellectual activity; over the following thirty years, most of the greatest works of the Scottish Enlightenment, by Smith, Hume, Robertson, Kames, Ferguson and Millar, were published. The common concerns, associates, and activities of these writers helped to unify their approach. In this period Edinburgh's social dominance was unchallenged; the city was an outstanding magnet for lawyers, gentry, and landowners. The self-confidence of the Town Council after 1767 bore fruit in the plans for the New Town. It would be possible also to trace the character of the Enlightenment in Glasgow and Aberdeen; yet Edinburgh was undoubtedly the focus of activity, and in this chapter the role of 'enlightened' leaders in the Church, in the clubs, and in the University, in Edinburgh will be considered.

By the early 1750s the Moderate group were beginning to achieve a dominance in the Church of Scotland which was to last until the 1790s; yet it remained throughout this period a precarious dominance. The role of the Moderates may be illustrated in several notorious clashes between the evangelical wing of the Church, and the Moderate leaders. The leadership of William Robertson was important; his firm guidance took the Moderates one step beyond those early leaders of the 1730s. The clashes came on several fronts. The first was over patronage. Ever since 1712 the General Assembly had been occupied by a series of disputed presentations to livings. By 1750 the Assembly was considering the assertion of its authority over the lower bodies of the Church, especially the presbyteries, whose responsibility it was to enforce lay presentations. In 1751 there was a debate over the recalcitrant parish of Torphichen, where the presbytery had failed to obey the Assembly's instructions to induct an unpopular candidate as minister; John Home, supported by William Robertson, called in the Assembly for the suspension of disobedient members of the presbytery, though he gained few votes[1]. The Moderates identified themselves firmly with the rights of lay patrons. This case was in many ways merely a prelude to the 'Inverkeithing case'. In 1749 the Rev Andrew Richardson was presented to the parish of Inverkeithing; after strong local objections the Presbytery refused to act. In 1752 the case appeared before the General Assembly for the third time, and the Moderates argued that the authority of the General Assembly should be firmly exerted. When the Commission of the Assembly, the preliminary meeting, refused to accept their motion of censure, the Moderates produced a reasoned statement of their own case, often referred to as 'the manifesto of the Moderates' (Document 1), a defence of the hierarchy of the Church of Scotland by Robertson and his associates.

But the Moderates were by no means unchallenged within the Church; an active and forceful evangelical wing was prepared to act aggressively to counteract what they saw as the dangers of their teaching. In 1755 a pamphlet was published by a minister of the Church which stigmatised the writings of David Hume and Lord Kames as heretical (Document 2); and in the following year there was a full debate in a committee of the General Assembly on this pamphlet. The work of the two men was associated by their opponents with the strength of the Moderate group in the Church. Lord Kames was himself an elder of the General Assembly, and the charge against him was not pursued. The Moderate clergymen defended their friend David Hume with some political astuteness (Document 3), and the case was allowed to lapse. It signified the concern of a powerful section of the assembly at the trends of modern thinking, but also a recognition that such trends were beyond control. A similar conflict arose over the tragedy, *Douglas*, written by John Home and performed in Edinburgh in 1756. Home, a minister of the Church of Scotland, had hoped that his play would meet the standards of the London stage, as ruled by David Garrick, the great actor-manager. Since it failed to do this he brought it back to Edinburgh where it was put on with some success. Home was supported by a friendly group of the 'literati', including some clergymen. There is a tradition that Carlyle, Ferguson, John Home and David Hume together read parts in this saccharine tragedy at the home of one of the actors[2]. Naturally, Home's friends attended the performance in December; and the Church at once took action. The Presbytery of Dalkeith called on Carlyle to explain his behaviour; and to them he apologised. However, when the case was made out against him in the General Assembly, he took a stronger stand, and won his case by 117 votes to 39. Yet the immediate victory was doubtful. In 1757 an Act was passed by the General Assembly forbidding clergy to attend the theatre—and John Home resigned his living. Yet the episode illustrated the failure of the Church to control social life, especially that of the educated. The Assembly could not enforce its Act; and the theatre increasingly became a respectable place of enjoyment.

The seceding groups of the Church of Scotland were growing in strength; and the Moderates were under attack not only for their social life and their political views, but also for their theology. Much of this was unspoken; but they were thought to follow Hutcheson in a creed that seemed to have much in common with deism, and in their silence on the doctrines of original sin, of grace, salvation and atonement. A powerful and witty opponent like John Witherspoon might well exploit the weaknesses of the Moderate position (Document 4). William Robertson, Hugh Blair, Robert Wallace and others were suspected of doubtful orthodoxy, and of moving entirely away from the Calvinist background of the Church. Politically the Moderates were conservative in their attitude to the hierarchies both of the Church and of the state; the closeness of their relationships with the managers of Scotland was often commented upon, though perhaps unjustly, since the Moderates were keen to preserve their own independence, while cooperating with their government[3]. In the conflict over the American Revolution, the political viewpoints within the Church in the main followed theological divisions; the evangelicals were most likely to be sympathetic to the revolutionary cause, the Moderates to uphold the government of Lord North.

The landowning classes, too, were involved in the 'enlightened' society of mid-eighteenth century Edinburgh. The number of clubs and societies multiplied, and everywhere provided a forum for the debate of urgent and perennial issues. In 1752 the old Philosophical Society resumed its activities, in which Hume, Kames, William Cullen, and Alexander Monro secundus were all prominent. Yet the clearest example of a society which brought together the 'literati' and the rulers of Scotland was the Select Society planned by Allan Ramsay the younger, (1713–84), the painter, with David

Hume and Adam Smith; it first met on 23 May 1754, with fifteen members, lawyers and intellectuals. By May 1755, its membership had grown to 95: and membership was much sought after. David Hume wrote to Allan Ramsay that:

> . . . Young and old, noble and ignoble, witty and dull, all the world are ambitious of a place amongst us, and on each occasion (of election) we are as much solicited by candidates as if we were to choose a Member of Parliament[4].

The members of the Society were drawn from 'the political class of decision makers, patrons and beneficiaries of the status quo'[5]; they were landowners, lawyers, clergy and physicians, drawn from the closely linked ruling families of Scotland. The aim of the Society was 'the pursuit of philosophical enquiry and the improvement of members in the art of speaking' through weekly debates; early in 1755 it had formed another branch, the Edinburgh Society for encouraging arts, sciences, manufactures and agriculture in Scotland, which offered premiums for inventions and ideas. The Select Society concerned itself more with literary matters, and offered prizes for literary work (Document 7). In 1761 it began a campaign to improve the English of Scotsmen, introducing lessons in elocution, and the English language, and setting up a new Select Society for Promoting the Reading and Speaking of English in Scotland— but this lasted, like the parent society, only until 1764. Perhaps this range of activities proved too great for the membership, whose numbers had steadily declined. Yet the inspiration of the Society at its height may be judged by the arguments of the *Edinburgh Review*: written by members of the Select Society, Smith, Robertson, Blair, John Jardine and Alexander Wedderburn[6], it clearly aimed at a Scottish contribution to the literary world, though only two numbers appeared, January–July 1755, and July 1755–January 1756 (Document 6). There was the Poker Club, already mentioned, set up in 1762, in which Ferguson and Robertson were prominent, as a part of the campaign for the Scottish militia, though it became largely a drinking club, lasting till the end of the century. There were many other societies in Edinburgh, especially social and drinking clubs; there was also the Pantheon Society of Edinburgh, once the Robin Hood Society, a debating club which appealed to a much wider social range, and which like the similar club in London, offered opportunities for debate to all its members.

The University, under the leadership of William Robertson, grew in size and eminence. The reputation of the Professors, and the range of subjects offered, provided at Edinburgh an education of a kind which could not be rivalled elsewhere in the United Kingdom. The medical school, where Cullen, Joseph Black, and Alexander Monro secundus were teaching, was world famous, and had replaced Leyden as a leading centre of European medical education. Arts students could expect to learn from Adam Ferguson, William Robertson, and Hugh Blair, though other teachers were not so outstanding. William Robertson, Principal till 1793, was an active leader, and a formidable figure in Edinburgh affairs. He re-organised the University Library, and embarked on active fund raising to try to improve the salaries of some Professors. Above all, he persuaded the Town Council to consider the rebuilding of the University. His first attempt to raise money by subscription in 1768 failed; but he did secure a new anatomy theatre in 1764, a new chemistry classroom and laboratory in 1782, and the laying of the foundation stone of a new College, (now the Old College) in 1789. And between 1760 and 1790 a number of new Chairs were established; after that of Hugh Blair in 1760 came the Chairs of Natural History (1767), Materia Medica (1768), Practical Astronomy (1786) and Agriculture (1790). Increasing numbers of English and Irish students, particularly dissenters, came to Edinburgh; even some American colonial students and Europeans were attracted, especially by the medical school. Most students came from prosperous backgrounds; but there were poor students, struggling to exist and to pay their class fees. Probably the minimum needed for a year in Edinburgh would be around £20; though there wre bursaries for poor students. In 1826 Edinburgh had 80 bursaries to offer, of £100 and 51 of less than £15 each[7]. Socially, the atmosphere of student life shared in the growth of Edinburgh's cultural life. Student clubs grew rapidly. For medical students the most important was the Medical Society, founded in 1737, and in 1778 granted a charter as the Royal Medical Society. There were other, more ephemeral, medical societies: the Royal Physical Society, Chemical Society, Natural History Society, all flourished for a brief period. The Speculative Society, founded in 1764, was primarily a debating club which attracted future politicians and barristers. There were the Belles Lettres Society, the Newtonian Society, the Dialectic Society and the Theological Society—all shared in a lively intellectual atmosphere. There are many

references, more or less credible, to the industry and vitality of
Edinburgh students at this time. One famous witness was Sir James
Mackintosh (1760–1832), a medical student at Edinburgh from
1784 to 1787:

> . . . I may truly say, that it is not easy to conceive a university
> where industry was more general, where reading was more
> fashionable, where indolence and ignorance were more disreput-
> able. Every mind was in a state of fermentation. The direction of
> mental activity will not indeed be universally approved, It
> certainly was very much, though not exclusively, pointed
> towards metaphysical enquiries[8].

Both arts and medical students felt that this bias existed (Documents
8, 9); the curriculum at Edinburgh had absorbed the 'philosophical'
concerns of the Scottish Enlightenment.

There is much, of course, of relevance to the Edinburgh
Enlightenment which cannot be covered here: the growth of the
scientific and medical communities, the architectural talents of the
Adam brothers and the achievement of the New Town, the literary
impact of Robert Burns. Yet the period from the 1750s to the 1770s
may be seen as the central phase of the Scottish Enlightenment, in
which the debate over, and the programme for, improvement, was
at its height, but not yet narrowed to a dogma. The concerns which
shaped the Enlightenment in the early years of the eighteenth
century were brought to fruition; in later years the repercussions
were to be seen in a variety of disciplines. The Enlightenment at its
height absorbed the interests not only of intellectuals, but of clergy,
lawyers, landowners. It was the product of a cohesive culture, not
yet fragmented.

NOTES

1. N. Morren, *Annals of the General Assembly of the Church of Scotland, 1739–1766*, 2
vols (Edinburgh, 1838) I, pp. 198–212.
2. E. C. Mossner, *The Life of David Hume* (London, 1954) p. 358.
3. Ian D. L. Clark, 'From Protest to Reaction: the Moderate regime in the
Church of Scotland, 1752–1805', in *Scotland in the Age of Improvement*, eds Phillipson
and Mitchison, pp. 209–211.
4. David Hume to Allan Ramsay, April or May 1755, *Letters of David Hume*, ed.
J. Y. T. Greig, I, pp. 219–21.

5. R. Emerson, 'The social composition of enlightened Scotland; the Select society of Edinburgh, 1754–1764', *Studies on Voltaire and the eighteenth century*, CXIV (1973) p. 301.

6. John Jardine D. D. (1716–66), minister of Liberton Church from 1741, Lady Yester's Church Edinburgh, from 1750, and second charge of the Tron Church Edinburgh from 1754–66. He married in 1744 the eldest daughter of George Drummond, and provided an important personal link between the Moderate clergy, among whom he was active, and Drummond. In 1759 he became Kings Chaplain, in 1761 Dean of the Chapel Royal.

Alexander Wedderburn (1733–1805), lawyer and politician, educated at Edinburgh University, advocate 1754, he was active in Moderate politics in the Assembly until 1751, when he left Edinburgh, and came to London. Called to the English bar in that year, his rise was fast. M.P. from 1761 to 1780, he became first Lord Loughborough in 1780, Lord Chancellor from 1793–1801, and first Earl of Rosslyn in 1801.

7. A. Chitnis, *The Scottish Enlightenment*, p. 150.

8. R. J. Mackintosh, *Memoirs of the Life of the Right Honourable Sir James Mackintosh*, 2 vols (London, 1835) I, p. 29.

Edinburgh's Augustan Age: Documents

THE MODERATES AND THE CHURCH

1. The 'manifesto of the Moderates'

Reasons of Dissent from the Sentence and Resolution of the Commission of the General Assembly, met at Edinburgh March 11th 1752, concerning the conduct of the Presbytery of Dunfermline (Edinburgh, 1752) pp. 1–3[1].

Reasons of Dissent from the judgment and resolution of the Commission, March 11, 1752, resolving to inflict no censure on the Presbytery of Dunfermline for their disobedience in relation to the settlement of Inverkeithing. (Signed by William Robertson and sixteen others)

1. Because we conceive this sentence of the Commission to be inconsistent with the nature and first principles of society. When men are considered as individuals, we acknowledge that they have no guide but their own understanding, and no judge but their own conscience: but we hold it for an undeniable principle, that as members of society, they are bound in many cases to follow the judgment of the society. By joining together in society, we enjoy many advantages, which we could neither purchase nor secure in a disunited state. In consideration of these, we consent, that regulations for public order shall be established; not by the private fancy of every individual, but by the judgment of the majority, or of those whom the society has thought fit to entrust with the legislative power. Their judgment must necessarily be absolute, and final; and their determinations received as the voice and decision of the whole. In a numerous society, it seldom happens, that all the members think uniformly concerning the wisdom or expedience of any public

regulation: but no sooner is that regulation enacted, that private judgment is so far superseded, that even they who disapprove it, are notwithstanding bound to obey, and if required to put it in execution: unless in a case of such gross iniquity, and manifest violation of the original design of the society, as justifies resistance to the supreme power, and makes it better to have the society dissolved, than to submit to established iniquity. Such extra-ordinary cases we can easily conceive there may be, as will give any man a just title to seek the dissolution of the society to which he belongs; or at least will fully justify his withdrawing from it. But as long as he continues in it, professes regard for it, and reaps the emoluments of it, if he refuses to obey its laws, he manifestly acts both a *disorderly* and *dishonest* part. He lays claim to the privileges of the society, whilst he condemns its authority, and by all principles of reason and equity, is justly subjected to its censures. They who maintain that such disobedience deserves no censure, maintain in effect, that there should be no such thing as government and order. They deny those first principles by which men are united in society; and endeavour to establish such maxims, as will justify not only licentiousness in ecclesiastical, but disorder and rebellion in civil government. And therefore, as the Reverend Commission have by this sentence declared, that disobedience to the supreme judicatary of the Church, neither infers guilt, nor deserves censure; as they have surrendered the most essential prerogative of society; as they have deserted the principles, and (so far as in them lay) betrayed the rights of the constitution; we could not have acted a dutiful part to the Church, nor a safe one to ourselves, unless we had dissented from this sentence; and craved liberty to represent to the Venerable Assembly, that this deed appears to us, to be manifestly beyond the powers of the Commission.

[1] Eight reasons of dissent from the judgment follow, though only the first is given here.

2. The attack on infidelity

(John Bonar [1]), *An Analysis of the Moral and Religious Sentiments contained in the writings of Sopho* [2] *and David Hume, Esq; addressed to the consideration of the Reverend and Honourable Members of the General Assembly of the Church of Scotland* (Edinburgh, 1755) passim [3].

What particular business may come before you, I do not know. One thing of very general concern, I am sure, deserves your consideration; and that is, the public attack which in this country has of late been made on the great principles and duties of natural and revealed religion, in the works of David Hume, Esq.; and in the essays of an author who has been distinguished by the name of Sopho. It is true, one of these gentlemen has somehow got the character of a fine writer, and subtle disputant; and the latter, it is said, holds a place of great importance in this country, and even bears an office in your church. But as I am well assured, that neither the art of the one nor the power of the other, will avail to overthrow those principles they so boldly attack, so I am persuaded, that by neither will ye be diverted from doing your duty; and your duty unquestionably it is, to give warning of the poison contained in these volumes, and to testify to the whole Christian world your abhorrence of such principles . . .

I begin with the writings of Sopho, whose opinions I shall sum up in the following propositions:—

Prop. 1 There is no necessary relation betwixt cause and effect . . .

2. Matter is possessed of a power of self-motion . . .

3. Nothing appears from reason that can induce us to think that the world is not eternal . . .

4. The powers of reason can give us no satisfying evidence of the being of a God . . .

5. The perfections of God are either such as we cannot prove, or cannot comprehend . . .

6. It is whimsical and absurd to pretend that the material world is subject to the providence of God . . .

7. Every class of beings is perfect . . .

8. Man is a mere machine, under an irresistible necessity in all his actions . . .

9. Though man be necessarily determined in all his actions, yet does he believe himself free, God having implanted into his nature this deceitful feeling of liberty . . .

10. This deceitful feeling is the only foundation of virtue . . .

11. That, since man is thus necessarily determined in all his actions, and can have nothing more than a deceitful feeling of liberty, it follows, as a necessary consequence, that there can be no sin or moral evil in this world . . .

Having laid before you these extracts from the writings of this anonymous, though well-known author, I shall subjoin some passages no less remarkable from the works of his brother philosopher and friend; who has at least been more honest in this respect, that, without disguise, he has pled the cause of vice and infidelity—I shall adduce none of my quotations from the *Treatise on Human Nature*, though this is the complete system, since he has not thought fit to own it; but content myself with what I find in his *Essays* and *History*, to which he has prefixed his name, and which he seems to prophesy will be read in veneration by distant ages, to whom the very name of religion shall be unknown.

According to this celebrated moralist,—

Prop. 1. All distinction between virtue and vice is merely imaginary . . .

2. Justice has no foundation further than it contributes to public advantage . . .

3. Adultery is very lawful, but sometimes not expedient . . .

4. Religion and its ministers are prejudicial to mankind, and will always be found either to run into the heights of superstition or enthusiasm . . .

5. Christianity has no evidence of its being a divine revelation . . .

6. Of all the modes of Christianity, Popery is the best, and the reformation from thence was only the work of madmen and enthusiasts . . .

[1] John Bonar (1721–61) Educated at the University of Edinburgh, licensed as minister Glasgow 1745, minister of Cockpen, Midlothian, from 1746, and of West Church Perth from 1756, he published a number of theological works.

[2] The reference is to Lord Kames and particularly to his *Essays on the Principles of Morality and Natural Religion* (Edinburgh, 1751): in an earlier attack on him, by the Rev George Anderson (?–1756), *An Estimate of the Profit and Loss of Religion, Personally and publicly stated: illustrated with Reference to Essays on Morality and Natural Religion* (Edinburgh, 1753) Kames was referred to as Sopho, with the implication that he was a sophist.

[3] The heads of the propositions only are given here.

3. The defence of infidelity

'An account of the debate upon the motion for censuring infidel writers', *Scots Magazine*, 18, June 1756, pp. 280–2.

As we gave in our former Magazine a very particular account of all the causes that came before the assembly itself, and made but slight mention of a motion made in the committee of overtures [1], and debated there at two successive diets [2], we find many of our readers are desirous of having a full account of that debate; as, though it came not to the assembly itself, it was of more importance than many things that did, and may possibly be resumed in some future assembly. We have therefore procured the following account from one who was a witness to the whole.

After a few general observations upon the importance of a strict and regular discipline to the purity of the Christian Church, it was moved, that the assembly should be desired to take notice of some of the infidel writings published of late in this nation, and their authors; and lest it should be found difficult or improper to make it too general, it was proposed to confine the inquiry at present to one, *viz* David Hume, because he had publicly avowed his writings, at least the most offensive of them, by prefixing his name. This motion was seconded, and some paragraphs of the confession of faith and form of process were read, asserting the propriety, and appointing the exercise of discipline in such cases. In a short time a written overture was given in and read, the substance of which was as follows,

'The General Assembly, judging it their duty to all in their power to check the growth and progress of infidelity; and considering, that as infidel writings have begun of late years to be published in this nation, against which they have hitherto only testified in general, so there is one person, styling himself David Hume, Esq., who hath arrived at such a degree of boldness as publicly to avow himself the author of books containing the most rude and open attacks upon the glorious Gospel of Christ, and principles evidently subversive even of natural religion and the foundations of morality, if not establishing direct Atheism; therefore the Assembly appoint the following persons,—— (list of names), as a committee to inquire into the writings of this author, to call him before them, and prepare the matter for the next General Assembly'.

To this motion a strenuous opposition was made, and a variety of objections were raised . . .

1. It was said, many members had not read the writings in question, and so could not judge of them.
2. It was often alleged, that it could serve no good purpose; that it was not to be imagined that prosecution or censure would convince

him, or make him change his opinions, in which he seemed to be so firmly rivetted.

3. It was said by some, that it would be a long and difficult inquiry, and would lead to the discussion of many philosophical opinions; the meeting was put in mind of the many long and fierce debates that had been in the Christian Church about fate, free will, &c. so that the affair, if entered upon, might last many years, and become in a manner the sole business of the Assembly.

4. It was alleged, that the writings of Mr Hume contained opinions that every man of common sense detested; that they were so gross, and so evidently false, that they could not do any harm; that it would be doing them too much honour to take such public notice of them.

5. It was alleged, that however wrong his opinions were, his writings were mostly of an abstract and metaphysical kind, very little intelligible to the bulk of people; and therefore, as little danger could arise from them, so liberty of judgment ought to be allowed; and they were not proper objects of censure, which ought rather to be applied to practical errors, and things more immediately criminal.

6. It was alleged, that it would greatly please the man himself, and promote the sale of his book. Here some stories were told, how booksellers had artfully solicited the authoritative condemnation of books, in order to get them off their hands; and it was represented by some as very dangerous thus to spread such writings, and bring them into the hands of common or country people, who would not otherwise have looked into them; and the consequences of this were painted very strongly.

7. It was insisted on by many, that Mr Hume could not be said to be a Christian at all; that he had openly and publicly thrown off the profession of it, and therefore was of those, who, in Scripture language, *are without*, and so not proper objects of Christian discipline.

The reader will, we hope, be sensible, that these arguments were not all used at once, nor perhaps in the same precise order as here represented; but we have chosen to enumerate them in this manner, that we might bring our account within some compass; and they are classed in the order in which they were brought forth in the debate, as nearly as could be recollected.

[1] the committee which considered motions for action or legislation to go before the Assembly.
[2] sessions.

4. An opponent of the Moderates

(John Witherspoon) [1] *Ecclesiastical Characteristics; or, the Arcana of Church Policy, being an humble attempt to open up the mystery of moderation* . . .The second edition, corrected and enlarged (Glasgow, 1754), p. 27.

The Athenian Creed

I believe in the beauty and comely proportions of Dame Nature, and in almighty Fate, her only parent and guardian, for it hath been most graciously obliged (blessed be its name), to make us all very good.

I believe that the universe is a huge machine, wound up from everlasting by necessity, and consisting of an infinite number of *links* and chains, each in a progressive motion towards the zenith of perfection, and meridian of glory; That I myself am a little glorious piece of clockwork, a wheel with a wheel, or rather a pendulum in this grand machine, swinging hither and thither by the different impulses of fate and destiny; That my soul (if I have any) is an imperceptible bundle of exceedingly minute corpuscles, much smaller than the finest Holland sand; and certain persons, in a very eminent station, are nothing else but a huge collection of necessary agents, who can do nothing at all.

I believe that there is no ill in the universe, nor any such thing as virtue absolutely considered, that those things vulgarly called *sins*, are only errors in the judgment and foils to set off the beauty of Nature, or patches to adorn her face; that the whole race of intelligent beings, even the devils themselves (if there are any) shall finally be happy; so that Judas Iscariot is by this time a glorified saint, and it is good for him that he hath been born.

In fine, I believe in the divinity of L. S———y, the saintship of Marcus Antoninus, the perspicuity and sublimity of A———e, and the perpetual duration of Mr H———n's works, notwithstanding their present tendency to oblivion. Amen.[2]

[1] John Witherspoon (1722–94). Educated at the University of Edinburgh, in

1744 he became minister of the parish of Beith. He was a leading opponent of the Moderates in the Church, and published a number of works against them; the *Ecclesiastical Characteristics* was extremely popular, going through editions in less than ten years. In 1757 he became minister at Paisley, and later received a call from the trustees of the College of Princeton in the American colonies, to be Principal there. He left in 1768 and made a highly successful career there. In 1776 he was a member of the Continental Congress, and a signatory of the Declaration of Independence.

[2] The missing names are: Lord Shaftesbury; Aristotle; Mr Hutcheson.

5. Another view of the Moderates

The Philosopher's Opera n.d. (Edinburgh, 1757) Act I, pp. 1 –6 [1].

Act I

A drawing-room

Curtain draws, and discovers Mrs Sarah Presbytery sitting in an easy chair; Anne waiting.

Mrs Pr.   And did Mr Genius talk to you in that manner, Annie?

An.   Indeed the gentleman told me, Madam, that he was desperately in love with you; that he would be miserable, nay, that he would die, if you refused to put him in possession of your fair person; and that he was to throw himself at your feet this afternoon.

Mrs Pr.   Fie upon the joker; he has been diverting himself, and playing upon you, Annie.

An.   O, not at all, Madam; what should make you think so?

Mrs Pr.   Alas! Annie, I am not young now.

An.   Young! Madam, what then? he is not young himself. Young! why, there was Lady Randolph [2]; I'm sure she was not young; and yet you see how the men teased her, poor lady!

Mrs Pr.   Alas, Annie, I am now about 200 years of age; but Lady Randolph broke her neck before she had lived half a century. Go, thou flatterer, thou knowest he has captivated my heart; this, this only, makes you speak so, and give the name of love to what you know to be waggery.

An.   In my conscience, Madam, I believe him to be over head and ears in love with you. Consider, Madam, that kissing

| | goes by favour. Besides, Mr Genius, in his thoughts, words, and actions, has no resemblance to other men; so that you might be his flame, Madam, though you were as old as Methusalem. |

Mrs Pr. There is something in what you say, Annie. O the lovely Adonis, his shoulders, his legs, his belly!—But why should I attempt to enumerate his charms? Every limb of him is bristled with the darts of love; would to God I had never seen the too amiable porcupine . . . .

An. Madam, there is the gentleman.

Enter Mr Genius.

Mr Gen. If Mrs Anne, Madam, has delivered that message which I begged her to carry from me to your Ladyship, you will not be surprised, I hope, at this piece of intrusion.

Mrs Pr. Sir, Annie has been telling me of a very odd conversation she had with you this forenoon; but I would have you to know, Sir, that I will not be made a jest of by you or any man.

Mr Gen. How you mistake my intentions! there is not a man in the world more sensible of the great deference and respect due to you, Madam, than I am. Jest!—be assured, Madam, (kneeling), that you see at your feet a man who is determined to live or die as you receive him.

Mrs Pr. Rise, Mr Genius; if you are serious, I am sorry for you; but I flatter myself, you will soon perceive the oddity of your passion, and the absurdity of your choice. The cheek of the town-lady may vie with the lily, that of the milkmaid with the rose; but mine, Sir, can be compared to neither. To use my son Jacky's words:—'In me thou dost behold— The poor remains of beauty once admired' [3]. Age has deadened the glance of my eye, overcast my features with a melancholy languor, and ploughed my forehead into a multiplicity of wrinkles.

Mr Gen. Pardon me, Madam; age has given to your eye a philosophical sedateness, to your features a languishing air, which girls in vain affect; and in what you call wrinkles, Madam, I see the little loves and graces sporting.

Mrs Pr. O, Mr Genius.

Mr Gen. Many gentlemen have wished, Madam, for old wood to burn, old wine to drink, old friends to converse with, and old books to read; but never did I so limit my desires. I have always hoped, that sooner or later I should have an old woman to caress.

Mrs Pr. Incomparable Genius! I will not use you with the coquetry of a young hussy; but frankly own that I long have loved you.

Mr Gen. Is it possible? Words are inadequate to my ideas; and this is the only way my lips can express the sentiments of my heart.

(He endeavours to kiss her; she struggles, but he prevails)

. . . .

Mrs Pr. Let not our interview, Mr Genius, end like that of two youthful lovers, without one word of common sense being spoken by either of us: do you go to see my son's play tonight?

Mr Gen. I hope for the pleasure of seeing you there, Madam. What makes you ask the question?

Mrs Pr. Why, truly, that I may have an opportunity of expressing my gratitude. Many of my sons have been greatly obliged to you; but Jacky infinitely.

Mr Gen. O dear Madam.

Mrs Pr. Mr John Calvin, my first husband, was a very good man; but he had his oddities; and notwithstanding the affection which a woman must retain for the husband of her youth, I cannot help thinking you the better reformer of the two. Many of my sons, some time ago, before they had the honour of your acquaintance, were the most unlicked cubs ever whelped: how stiff was their style! how starch their manner! how ridiculously grave the whole man! But since they have got into your good company, they have put off the old man entirely: they have acquired a jaunty air, a military swagger, and a G-d d-n me look; they swear, they drink, they whore so handsomely;—in short, they are metamorphosed so very much to the better, that I scarce know them to be my own children.

Mr Gen. Your goodness, Madam, greatly magnifies my poor services.

Mrs Pr. How judicious was that fancy of yours to make Jacky write a play! and how inimitable the dedication with which you introduced it into the world! To it Jacky owes both his fame and his fortune, and ought to thank you on his knees for both.

Mr Gen. The young gentleman, Madam, is abundantly grateful; but I beg you would dwell no longer on this subject. I wish it were in my power to do more for him. I must now leave you, Madam, and join several of your sons, who are to be at the playhouse tonight.

Mrs Pr. And I must away to Lady Prelacy, who goes along with me to the same place. Farewell till six o'clock.   (Exit)

[1] This is one of the many pamphlets and broadsides that appeared following the Douglas affair, taking the opportunity to satirise or defend the Moderates—the reader should be able to identify the characters.

[2] Lady Randolph was the leading lady in John Home's *Douglas*; she committed suicide at the death of her recently discovered son, in the final act.

[3] A quotation from *Douglas*, ed. Gerald D. Parker (Edinburgh, 1972) p. 58.

LEARNING AND MANNERS

6. The state of learning in Scotland

The Edinburgh Review, I (Edinburgh, 1755) Preface, ii–iv.

At the Revolution, liberty was re-established and property rendered secure; the uncertainty and rigor violence the law were corrected and softened: but the violence of parties was scarce abated, nor had industry yet taken place. What the Revolution had begun, the Union rendered more complete. The memory of our ancient state is not so much obliterated, but that, by comparing the past with the present, we may clearly see the superior advantages we now enjoy, and readily discern from what source they flow. The communication of trade has awakened industry; the equal administration of laws produced good manners; and the watchful care of the government, seconded by the public spirit of some individuals, has excited, promoted and encouraged, a disposition to every species of improvement in the minds of a people naturally active and intelligent. If countries have their ages with respect to improvement, North Britain may be considered as in a state of early growth, guided and supported by the more mature strength of her kindred country. If in any thing here advances have been such as to mark a more forward state, it is in science. The progress of knowledge, depending more upon genius and application, than upon any external circumstance; wherever these are not repressed, they will exert themselves. The opportunities of education, and the ready means of acquiring knowledge in this country, with even a very moderate share of genius diffused thro' the nation, ought to make it distinguished for letters. Two considerable obstacles have long obstructed the progress of science. One is, the difficulty of a proper expression in a country where there is either no standard of language, or at least one very remote. Some late instances, however, have discovered that this difficulty is not unsurmountable; and that a serious endeavour to conquer it, may acquire, to one born on the North side of the Tweed, a correct and even an elegant style. Another obstacle arose from the slow advances that the country had made in the art of printing: no literary improvement can be carried far, where the means of communication are defective: but this obstacle has, of late been entirely removed; and the reputation of the Scotch press is not confined to this country alone.

7. The debates of the Select Society

Selections from the Minutes of the Select Society, National Library of Scotland, Adv. MS 23.1.1.

a. Minutes, ff. 14–15. Edinburgh, 19th June 1754.

Mr Adam Smith Praeses [1].

Ordered that the number of the society be increased to sixty. That eight members be received, to be chosen out of the present list of candidates, Wednesday next. That the members bring their lists written out before the meeting. The names of those who stand candidates are: (list of 30 names follows.)
Ordered, That at every meeting the Praeses, before he leaves the Chair, do declare the questions that are agreed upon by the majority of the meeting to be the subject of debate on Wednesday next, viz
1. Whether a general naturalization of foreign Protestants would be advantageous to Britain?
2. Whether Bounties on the exportation of corn be advantageous to

trade and manufactures as well as to Agriculture?
Then the Praeses left the Chair.

[1] Praeses: Latin for president.

b. F. 28. Edinburgh 7th August 1754.

Mr Patrick Murray Praeses[1].

Sir David Dalrymple[2] Chairman of the Committee for Questions read to the Society several questions received by the Committee which were all approved of and ordered to be entered in the Book of Questions[3].
The questions received were as follows
Whether the numbers of banks now in Scotland, be useful to the trade of that country? And whether paper credit be advantageous to a nation?
Whether the bounty should be continued on the exportation of low priced linen made in Scotland?
Whether the common practice in Scotland of distributing money to the poor in their own houses, or the receiving the poor into workhouses and hospitals be most advantageous?
Whether in the present circumstances of this country it be most advantageous to increase tillage or grain?
Whether Brutus did well in killing Caesar?
May the progress of intemperance that usually becomes so remarkable (particularly among the vulgar) upon the increase of wealth be retarded by the care of superiors?
May a lawyer of ordinary parts become eminent in his profession?
Whether it be advantageous to a nation, that the law of private property should be reduced to an art?
Whether the repenting stool ought to be taken away?

[1] Patrick Murray, 5th Baron Elibank (1703–78), lawyer, and a leading figure in Edinburgh society and the Select Society.
[2] Sir David Dalrymple (1726–92), 3rd baronet of Hailes. Advocate 1748, Lord of Session as Lord Hailes 1766, Lord Justiciary 1776. Also a historian, author of the *Annals of Scotland*, 2 vols (Edinburgh 1776 and 1779) and other works.
[3] All questions for debate were previously approved by a committee and entered in a book; then the praeses of each meeting chose questions from these to be debated at the following meeting, as laid down in extract a.

c. FF. 84–5. Edinburgh 18th February 1756.

David Dalrymple Praeses.

. . . . The Committee appointed by the Select Society to propose subjects for prizes relating to Literature, which the Society had resolved to add to those of the Edinburgh Society, humbly offer the following to their consideration.

I. History of the extent and duration of the Roman and afterwards of the Saxon conquests and settlements in Britain to the North of Severus's wall [1] in Cumberland and Northumberland.

II. Account of the rise and progress of commerce, arts and manufactures in North Britain, and the causes which promoted or retarded them.

III. The most reasonable scheme for maintaining and employing the poor in North Britain; and how far the scheme can be executed by the laws now in force.

Which being read and considered by the Society, they unanimously approved of the Report.

[1] Hadrin's wall.

THE UNIVERSITY UNDER PRINCIPAL ROBERTSON

8. An American medical student at the University

MSS diary of George Logan [1] during his trip to England, 1775–9. Historical Society of Pennsylvania.

Edinburgh, 2 March 1778.

. . . This college has been growing in reputation since that time (its founding) and such is its present greatness that it is now deservedly regarded as the first University in Europe for Medicine.

The University is wholly subject to the Town Council which has the direction of all their affairs, and is in possession of their papers, which for some political motives are kept so secret that no person is allowed to see them.

The College is a poor irregular pile of buildings consisting of three

courts which it appears were at first intended for the accom-
modation of the students. They are now principally made use of by
the different Professors for reading Lectures and for the other offices
of the University. Principal Robertson has a house in the largest
square built on the ruins of that in which Darnley was blown up
with gunpowder [2].

The Library is very complete, containing above (sic) thousand
volumes [3] in the different languages and sciences. To this noble
collection every gentleman has access the whole year by subscribing
2/6; but on borrowing a book he is obliged to deposit its value in the
hands of the Librarian.

Under the Library is a large room, dedicated to the public
examinations of the votaries of Medicine, at which time their
labours are crowned with a black-cap and with the title of Dr

Nothing but Natural History is now wanting to form as complete
an academical education as in any other University, but as the study
of Physic is principally cultivated I shall confine myself in giving you
a few observations on this subject.

The Medical department consists of 6 Professorships, viz.:
Chemistry, Anatomy, Practice, Theory, Mat. Med. [4] and Botany.
These classes every gentleman who graduates is obliged to attend,
his attendance on midwifery is also expected, but this they cannot
insist on. You cannot graduate here without having studied
Medicine at this or some other University for three years: on these
conditions you are admitted to a private examination at which, if
you give satisfaction you are declared a candidate; after this you
have another private and one public examination; but there is
hardly an instance of a gentleman being degraded after passing his
first. Your exercises consist in writing several papers for private
inspection and a thesis which you are to publish and defend at the
public examination [5].

Drs Black, Monro and Cullen who fill the three first chairs, are
men of great abilities and eminent in their different departments.
Black is esteemed one of the first Chemists in Europe—he has made
several discoveries with respect to fixed air and has some peculiar
ideas respecting *latent-heat* [6]; but unfortunately for himself and for
mankind he allows others to publish his discoveries in an imperfect
state, for which they reap the laurels, only due to himself. His
lectures are more calculated for the physician as a philosopher, than
as a practitioner. Dr Monro has generally above 300 pupils; for as
his lectures are on anatomy and surgery, it is necessary for persons in

every department of Medicine to attend him. He is too great a philosopher to enter so minutely into his subject as the demonstrative part of it requires; on which account students may attend him three or four years without gaining a proper knowledge of this kind; but in his physiology, perhaps no person is equal to him, for perspicuity and strength of argument. A large fortune has lulled his genius asleep. He therefore does not fatigue himself in making new discoveries, but contents himself in delivering his lectures nearly verbatim as he did 15 years ago.

The world is so well acquainted with Dr Cullen's abilities that it is unnecessary to say anything with respect to them. You know he has established a new theory of medicine; but like all other great men I am afraid he is too fond of this child, to make it of long continuance. As the Boerhaavians [7] account for every disease of the body from a vitiated state of the fluids; so on the other hand Dr Cullen refers them to a vitiated state of the nervous system. Both these opinions have their merits and demerits; wherefore it is necessary for a student to attend several universities, and not too early to form his opinion. Drs Gregory, Hume and Hope [8] are not so much esteemed. The first is young and would shine, but his state of health will not allow him to pay that attention to his studies which may perhaps be necessary.

Besides these lectures, several gentlemen in town lecture on the different aspects of Medicine: none of whom are of sufficient eminence to require notice—Dr Duncan makes the greatest figure among them but he has nothing but his indefatigable industry to recommend him [9].

The fee to each of the Professors is three guineas except to Dr Hope who is only allowed two by the University, but such is his meanness that he will take three guineas not the first but the second year, if any gentleman should do him that honour to attend him.

The Medical students also reap great advantage from the Infirmary to which they also pay three guineas . . . It is regulated in a better manner than any other hospital in Britain . . .

Another very great advantage which I have not taken notice of is derived from the three medical societies where every member is obliged to give in papers and defend them. Here the different doctrines and opinions of great men are canvassed with diffidence and candour.

Each society has its own particular laws printed and libraries to which the members have free access. The Medical society is the oldest established—it has a stall not yet finished which will cost upwards of £12,000 and their collection of books is excellent and valued at £1000. I have the honour of being a member of these three societies, from which I assure you I have received as much improvement as from any one Professor. In one of these societies the Latin language is spoken with great fluency and ease. Thus I have given you a pretty full account of the medical department. In the other departments Mr Robison [10] as a Natural Philosopher and Blair as a Rhetorician and as master of fine language are perhaps excelled by none.

Among such a number of students you will not doubt that we have plenty of companions but I do not think that a man of your good sense and taste would be able to select 20 out of Monro's 300 with which you would wish to associate.

On account of their being such a large proportion of the low class among the students; the others are not paid that respect which is due to them neither from the citizens nor professors considering the quantity of money they annually spend among them and their genteel behaviour.

[1] George Logan (1753–1821), son of a Philadelphia Quaker, merchant and landowner. He served some time as an apprentice to an Essex doctor before studying at Edinburgh from 1776 to 1779, when he graduated. On his return home after a short period as a physician, he took over his father's estate, and became a leading agricultural improver and Republican. He served as a United States Senator, 1801–7. His diary was written in the form of letters home.

[2] The old university buildings were on site of the ruined Collegiate Church of St Mary in the Fields, known as Kirk o' Field, and the lodgings of its clergy, in one of which houses Darnley was living at the time of his murder in 1567.

[3] Logan gives no figure here, and none is available; later, in 1825 there were about 70,000 volumes in the library.

[4] Materia Medica, Latin for medicines or drugs. The subject was originally a branch of botany.

[5] Very few students did graduate. In the medical school, between 1770 and 1780 an average of 20 students a year graduated, though the total number of medical students every year was around 400. Arts graduation had almost entirely died out by mid-eighteenth century.

[6] Black had published his discovery of 'fixed air' or carbon dioxide in his MD thesis at Glasgow in 1754; in 1761 in his work at Edinburgh he established the existence of latent heat.

[7] Those who followed the teaching of Herman Boerhaave of Leyden, the leading medical teacher at the beginning of the eighteenth century.

[8] James Gregory (1753–1821), member of a famous Scottish academic family, Professor of the Institutes of Medicine 1776–89, and Professor of the Practice of Physic, 1790–1821.

Francis Home (or Hume) (1719–1813), studied Leyden and Edinburgh. First Professor of Materia Medica, 1768–98. His interests were wide ranging, covering also agricultural chemistry, and the bleaching and dyeing of textiles.

John Hope (1723–86), Professor of Botany, 1761–86. An admirer of Linnaeus, he laid out the Botanical Gardens in Edinburgh.

[9] Andrew Duncan primus (1744–1828), studied medicine at Edinburgh, 1762–8, and was the leading extra-mural lecturer in Edinburgh, attracting substantial classes and publishing several works. In 1790 he succeeded Gregory in the Chair of the Institutes of Medicine, which he held till 1819.

[10] John Robison (1739–1805), Professor of Natural Philosophy, 1774–1805. He was educated and taught also at Glasgow, coming after a brief period as Professor of Mathematics at Cronstadt, Russia, to Edinburgh, where he was active in the scientific societies, and contributed widely to periodicals.

9. The Arts curriculum

Hugo Arnot[1], *The History of Edinburgh* (Edinburgh, 1779) pp. 405–12.

FACULTY OF ARTS

JOHN HILL, A.M, PROFESSOR OF HUMANITY [2]

Teaches two classes. The first is attended by young gentlemen just come from the grammar school. The professor pays much attention to the rules of syntax and parts of speech, thereby attempting to remedy such radical defects, as sometimes arise from inattention, even in those students who had before been taught by the best masters. Parts of Cicero, Livy, Virgil, Terence and Horace, are generally read in this class. Frequent exercises are prescribed to the pupils, in the way of turning English into Latin, and Latin into English; and the students are regularly examined, as often as the numbers that attend the class will permit.

In the second class, which generally consists of those who have attended the first, the difficulty of the authors read, and of the tasks prescribed, is proportioned to the increasing knowledge of the students. Prelections are read to them upon the darkest and most philosophical parts in Horace and Juvenal, as well as upon authors who are rarely, if at all, read at schools. Besides these, three lectures are read in the week. In one part of them a character is given of the Latin classics, and an explanation of the principles of their composition. In another, a short history of the Latin tongue, and the changes it has undergone. In the last, is delivered a compendious system of Roman antiquities. Topics chosen from these various branches are assigned to the students as the subjects of essays, which, after they have composed, they must deliver in public.

ANDREW DALZIEL M.A., PROFESSOR OF GREEK[3]

Also teaches two classes, and meets with each of them two hours in the day. In the first class, the elements of the Greek language are grammatically taught. A part of the New Testament, of Xenophon, or of Lucian, together with some of the odes of Anacreon, and a book of the Iliad, are read and explained. Upon all these the students are minutely examined, and the principles of general, as well as particular grammar constantly inculcated.

In the second class, some parts of the works of Herodotus, Thucydides, Demosthenes, or of some other prose authors, are read, and grammatically and critically explained; so likewise are several books of the Iliad or Odyssey; of the Idyllia of Theocritus, or a tragedy of Sophocles or Euripides. As this class is attended by many students for three years, those who are in the first year of their attendance, are arranged apart from the more advanced students, and examined upon easier authors. Those who attend it for two courses, are admitted to the third gratis. Besides explaining the Greek authors, Mr Dalziel gives lectures at least twice a week, on the history, government, manners, the poetry, and eloquence of the ancient Greeks. Exercises on these subjects are prescribed to the advanced students; and discourses delivered by them in presence of the principal, and other professors.

JOHN BRUCE M.A., PROFESSOR OF THE FIRST PHILOSOPHY, OR LOGIC CLASS, AND DEAN OF THE FACULTY OF ARTS[4].

This professorship was instituted A.D. 1586. It was called 'the philosophy, or logic class', a title which, in the diplomas of the University, it still retains.

The present professor, observing, that, while every branch of science had been new-modelled, his department retained all the pedantry of the schools, has formed his lectures on a new[5] and enlarged plan. As this class is an elementary one his general object is to prepare his students for a liberal cultivation of the sciences and arts, by means of a previous acquaintance with the human mind, and with the method of studying nature. His prelections are divided into two classes. The first course consists of five branches.

1. Pneumatology, or the history of the powers and faculties of the human mind, as the means employed in studying nature.

2. Logic, or the method of directing and applying the faculties of the mind, in studying and arranging the different laws of nature. Under this article, the rise and influence of the synthetic method, and syllogism, the rise and spirit of analysis, and the philosophical induction of Lord Bacon, are explained. The natural progress of thinking is traced from language, the sign of thought, and universal grammar connected with the logic of nature. To this are subjoined rules for philosophising in physicks and ethics, with an account of the sources of sophistry, and of the Aristotelian and school logics.

3. Metaphysics, or an analysis of those general truths which are the foundation of all the sciences, with the evidence by which they are to be established. The subjects in this branch are considered under the titles of General Ontology; Evidence and Truth; Error in Science; the relation of the sciences to the Belles Lettres.

4. A short view of the method of applying philosophical analysis and induction to the general study of nature.

5. The elements of civil history, as connected with the history of philosophy. In this head, are given a short view of the progress of mankind in the ancient and modern world; the state of letters and philosophy at the periods into which this progress is divided; the reciprocal influence of philosophy and subordination in their rise and decline, with the effects of both on the manners of mankind. The students in this class undergo frequent examination; and exercises are prescribed to them on the subjects of the lectures, which are occasionally recited before the Principal, or some of the professors.

In the second class, the chief object is to apply the method of philosophical analysis and induction to the study of the sciences and arts. This course is introduced with a recapitulation of the first principles of philosophy taught in the first class, as they are to be applied to a general description of the proper subjects of philosophy. It is divided into three branches.

1. The theory and prospectus of Lord Bacon are explained, as the first effort to re-establish genuine science; and the first display of the proper subjects of reasoning, with the effects which both have had on natural and moral philosophy.

2. The theories and divisions of later philosophers, on his plan, are enumerated.

3. A theory, founded on the natural progress of the mind in philosophising, from history to science and to art, is explained. Thh subjects of history, the sciences, and arts, are discussed; and an explanation given of the species of arrangement, evidence, induction, and theory, peculiar to each of these great branches. As this finishes the elementary course of philosophy, it is concluded with lectures on the branches of education necessary for each of the liberal professions, and on their relation to public economy.

HUGH BLAIR D.D., REGIUS PROFESSOR OF RHETORIC AND BELLES LETTRES

Began, in December 1759, to give lectures on rhetoric, as a private person. His lectures were well attended, and received with great applause. This induced the magistrates of Edinburgh, in August following, to grant the Doctor a commission, in which . . . they constituted him professor of rhetoric in the University . . .[6]

This establishment, although one of the latest in the University, is by no means the least valuable. The subjects of which the Doctor treats in his lectures, and the manner in which they are considered, equally tend to render this course both instructive and agreeable. It consists of five parts. In the first, lectures are delivered on the general subject of taste. These are chiefly to be considered as introductory to the whole. Here the separate powers of Taste and Genius are accurately distinguished and illustrated.

The second part treats of language, or the expression of our ideas by certain articulate sounds, which are used as the signs of those ideas. It consists of observations on the different kinds of language, as written, or spoken; and on its different parts, as substantives, attributives, and connectives. In the third part, observations are offered on the different qualities of style, and on rhetorical figures.

The fourth part consists of observations on eloquence. Here, three kinds of public speaking are particularly considered: the eloquence of popular assemblies, of the pulpit and of the bar. In the fifth and last part, a critical examination is delivered of the different sorts of composition in prose and in verse. Here, the qualities of history, of philosophical writing, of dialogue writing, of epistolary writing, and fictitious history, are considered; so likewise are pastoral, lyric, epic, and the other species of poetry. Under each of these heads, a critical examination is delivered, of the most eminent literary productions, both of ancient and modern times. This part is concluded with observations on tragedy and comedy, when an opportunity is taken of comparing the merits of the ancient, the French and the English writers on these subjects. Upon the whole, from the nature of this course, it must be of the greatest use not only to those who intend to communicate their sentiments to others, either by speaking in public, or in writing, but to all who wish to have their taste improved, and to become acquainted with the principles of true criticism.

ADAM FERGUSON LL.D., PROFESSOR OF MORAL PHILOSOPHY

The lectures on moral philosophy delivered by Doctor Ferguson are composed on an extensive plan, and treat of subjects of the utmost importance. This course, as presently taught, besides some introductory lectures on science in general, and on the causes which have retarded its progress, consists of seven parts.

The first treats of the natural history of man; first, considering the history of the species, and then of the individual. The second part respects the theory of the mind. After an enumeration of the laws of the understanding, and of the will, these laws are applied in examining the phenomena of interest, emulation, pride, vanity, probity, and moral approbation. The subject of the third is the knowledge of God. It treats of his being, and attributes, and of a future state. In the fourth part, moral laws, and their most general applications, are considered. The fifth treats of jurisprudence; the sixth, of casuistry; the seventh and last, of politics, under which the chief subjects of consideration are public economy, and political law.

DUGALD STEWART M.A., PROFESSOR OF MATHEMATICS[7]

Gives three mathematical courses every season, to different classes of students. In one of these are taught the first six books of Euclid's elements, the principal propositions of the eleventh and twelfth; and the elements of plain Trigonometry, and of practical Geometry. In another course, the elements of algebra, of spherical trigonometry, of conic sections, and of fluxions, are inculcated. In the third course, lectures are given on optics and astronomy.

JOHN ROBISON M.A., PROFESSOR OF NATURAL PHILOSOPHY

This gentleman's reputation in the science which he is appointed to teach, procured him the establishment of professor of natural philosophy in the marine academy at Cronstadt, whence he was invited to teach the same branch in the University of Edinburgh.

Mr Robison confines his lectures to what may be called Mechanical Philosophy, considering those appearances only which are exhibited in the *sensible* motions, and actions of the *sensible* masses of matter. The appearances in astronomy, vulgar mechanics, hydrostatics, pneumatics, magnetism, electricity, and optics, exhaust it. In this course, Mr Robison assumes the mathematical propositions as demonstrated, and contents himself with such a popular explanation of them, as will enable his hearers to see at least the probability of the doctrines; and he illustrates them by a course of experiments, properly adapted. This he is able to render very ample, by the addition of about £400 worth of instruments, lately made by the town-council of Edinburgh, to his apparatus, which is now the most complete of its kind in the kingdom. In this course of lectures, the Professor pays very particular attention to the application of this science to the arts of life, with a view to the instruction of engineers and artisans.

Having completed the regular course, he gives, by way of supplement, an account of the attempts which have been made to explain, by analogy, with the laws of mechanism, the internal constitution of bodies, with respect to solidity, fluidity, elasticity, &c, deducing from the best established principles the maxims which should be followed by the engineer. In like manner, he gives an account of the attempts towards a mechanical explanation of the appearances in chemical mixtures, and in the vegetable and animal economy.

For the benefit of those who wish to acquire a knowledge of natural philosophy, which they may apply with confidence to the arts of life, Mr Robison gives another course of lectures. In this, the leading mathematical propositions, assumed in the popular lectures, are discussed with great accuracy; and his hearers are enabled to peruse, with advantage, the writings of those eminent mechanical philosophers who, since the time of Newton, have been daily enriching the science with new discoveries.

[1] Hugo Arnot (1746–86) historian and antiquarian writer. He became an

advocate in 1772 but practised little. His *History of Edinburgh*, based on much historical and antiquarian research, was successful, and is an important source of information on eighteenth century Edinburgh.

[2] John Hill, formerly Professor of Humanity at St Andrews, held the Chair at Edinburgh nominally from 1775–1805. However in 1775 he had reached an agreement with the previous holder of the Chair, George Stuart, Professor from 1741–75, to teach unpaid, while Stuart drew the salary, to revert to Hill on his death. Stuart, however, lived until 1793.

[3] Andrew Dalziel (1742–1806), purchased the Chair from his predecessor Robert Hunter for £300 and a life-rent of the salary. He held the Chair until 1806, and was a highly successful teacher—in 1784 he had 184 students in his class—and classical scholar.

[4] John Bruce (1745–1826), educated at Edinburgh University, he held the Chair of Logic from 1775–92. In 1792 he resigned and was given by Henry Dundas the appointments of Keeper of the State Paper Office and Historiographer to the East India Company. He was Secretary to the Board of Control for a short time, and M.P. (1809 –14).

[5] *First principles of philosophy for the use of the students of logic*, printed A.D. 1777.

[6] See Chapter 1, Document 6.

[7] Dugald Stewart (1753–1828), son of Matthew Stewart, Professor of Mathematics at Edinburgh 1746–72. Dugald Stewart was educated at Edinburgh and Glasgow Universities, and in 1772 took charge of the teaching of Mathematics for his father although he was made joint Professor only in 1775. In 1785 he transferred to the Chair of Moral Philosophy, succeeding Ferguson, and after the death of Reid became the outstanding Scots philosopher of the next generation, and the most important transmitter of the 'common sense' philosophy in the late eighteenth and early nineteenth centuries. He published the *Elements of the Philosophy of the Human Mind*, 3 vols (Edinburgh, 1792–1827) and a number of other philosophical works.

Bibliography

The following is a selective bibliography which includes recent secondary works, and accessible primary sources for the study of the Scottish Enlightenment.

A. GENERAL WORKS

Introductory reading:
G. Bryson, *Man and Society: the Scottish inquiry of the eighteenth century* (Princeton, 1945).
A. Chitnis, *The Scottish Enlightenment. A Social History* (London, 1976).
L. Schneider (ed.), *The Scottish Moralists on Human Nature and Society* (Chicago, 1967).

Interpretative writing on the Scottish Enlightenment:
H. T. Buckle, *On Scotland and the Scotch Intellect*, edited and with an introduction by H. J. Hanham (Chicago, 1972).
J. Clive, 'The social background of the Scottish Renaissance', in N. Phillipson and R. Mitchison (eds), *Scotland in the Age of Improvement* (Edinburgh, 1970).
J. Clive and B. Bailyn, 'England's cultural provinces: Scotland and America', *William and Mary Quarterly*, 3rd series, XI (April 1954) pp. 163–79.
D. Daiches, *The Paradox of Scottish Culture: the Eighteenth Century Experience* (London, 1964).
G. E. Davie, 'Hume, Reid, and the Passion for Ideas', in D. Young (ed.) *Edinburgh in the Age of Reason* (Edinburgh, 1967).
R. Emerson, 'The Enlightenment and Social Structures', in P. Fritz and D. Williams, *City and Society in the Eighteenth Century* (Toronto, 1973).
D. Forbes, ' "Scientific Whiggism": Adam Smith and John Millar', *Cambridge Journal*, 7 (1953–4) pp. 643–70.

R. Meek, 'The Scottish Contribution to Marxist Sociology', in *Economics, Ideology, and other essays* (London, 1967).

R. Pascal, 'Property and Society: the Scottish Historical School of the eighteenth century', *Modern Quarterly* (March 1938) pp. 1667–79.

N. Phillipson, 'Culture and Society in the Eighteenth Century Province: the case of Scotland and the Scottish Enlightenment', in *The University in Society, Studies in the History of Higher Education*, edited by Lawrence Stone, 2 vols (Princeton, 1973).

——, 'Towards a Definition of the Scottish Enlightenment', in P. Fritz and D. Williams, *City and Society in the Eighteenth Century* (Toronto, 1973).

H. R. Trevor–Roper, 'The Scottish Enlightenment', in *Studies in Voltaire and the Eighteenth Century*, 58 (1967) pp. 1635–58.

General works, containing material of relevance to the study of the Scottish Enlightenment:

H. Aarsleff, *The Study of Language in England, 1760–1860* (Princeton, 1967).

E. Cassirer, *The Philosophy of the Enlightenment* (Boston, 1955).

D. Craig, *Scottish Literature and the Scottish People, 1680–1830* (London, 1961).

P. Gay, *The Enlightenment*, 2 vols (1967–70).

W. S. Howell, *Eighteenth Century British Logic and Rhetoric* (Princeton, 1971).

R. Meek, *Social Science and the Ignoble Savage* (Cambridge, 1976).

J. G. A. Pocock, *The Machiavellian Moment: Florentine political thought and the Atlantic republican tradition* (Princeton, 1975).

J. S. Slotkin (ed.), *Readings in Early Anthropology* (London, 1965).

F. Venturi, *Utopia and Reform in the Enlightenment* (Cambridge, 1971).

L. Whitney, *Primitivism and the idea of Progress in English Popular Literature of the Eighteenth Century* (Baltimore, 1934).

On Scottish moral philosophy:

G. E. Davie, *The Social Significance of the Scottish Philosophy of Common Sense*. The Dow Lecture, University of Dundee, 1973.

——, 'Berkeley's impact on Scottish philosophers', *Philosophy*, XL (1965) pp. 222–34.

——, 'Hume, Reid and the passion for ideas', in D. Young (ed.) *Edinburgh in the Age of Reason* (Edinburgh, 1967).

S. A. Grave, *The Scottish Philosophy of Common Sense* (Oxford, 1960).
J. McCosh, *The Scottish Philosophy . . . from Hutcheson to Hamilton* (London, 1875).
D. Stewart, 'Dissertation: exhibiting the progress of metaphysical, ethical, and political philosophy since the revival of letters in Europe', *The Collected Works of Dugald Stewart*, edited by Sir William Hamilton (Edinburgh, 1854–60) Vol. I.

B. POLITICAL AND SOCIAL BACKGROUND OF THE ENLIGHTENMENT

General works:
P. Hume Brown, *History of Scotland,* 3 vols (Cambridge, 1909) Vol. III (1689–1843).
R. Campbell, *Scotland since 1707* (Oxford, 1965).
W. Ferguson, *Scotland, 1689 to the present* (Edinburgh, 1968).
G. S. Pryde, *Scotland from 1603 to the present day* (Edinburgh, 1962).
R. Mitchison, *A History of Scotland* (London, 1970).
T. C. Smout, *History of the Scottish People, 1560–1830* (London, 1969).

The political framework:
E. Cregeen, 'The Changing Role of the House of Argyll in the Scottish Highlands', in N. T. Phillipson and R. Mitchison (eds) *Scotland in the Age of Improvement* (Edinburgh, 1970).
Sir James Ferguson, 'Making interest in Scottish county elections', *Scottish Historical Review*, 26 (1947) pp. 119–33.
W. Ferguson, 'The Making of the Treaty of Union, *Scottish Historical Review*, 43 (1964) pp. 89–110.
R. Mitchison, 'The Government and the Highlands, 1707–45', in N. T. Phillipson and R. Mitchison (eds) *Scotland in the Age of Improvement* (Edinburgh, 1970).
N. T. Phillipson, 'Scottish Public Opinion and the Union in the Age of the Association', in N. T. Phillipson and R. Mitchison (eds) *Scotland in the Age of Improvement* (Edinburgh, 1970).
N. T. Phillipson and R. Mitchison (eds), *Scotland in the Age of Improvement* (Edinburgh, 1970).
G. S. Pryde, *Central and local government in Scotland since 1707.* Historical Association pamphlet, No 45 (1960).
P. W. J. Riley, *The English Ministers and Scotland, 1707–1727* (London, 1964).

——, 'The Structure of Scottish Politics and the Union of 1707', in T. I. Rae (ed.), *The Union of 1707. Its impact on Scotland* (Edinburgh, 1974).

J. M. Simpson, 'Who steered the gravy train, 1707–66?', in N. T. Phillipson and R. Mitchison (eds) *Scotland in the Age of Improvement* (Edinburgh, 1970).

T. C. Smout and R. Campbell, 'The Anglo-Scottish Union of 1707', *Economic History Review*, 16 (1963–4) pp. 455–77.

The legal framework:

A. L. Murray, 'Administration and Law', in Rae (ed.) *The Union of 1707* (Edinburgh, 1974).

T. B. Smith, *British Justice. The Scottish Contribution* (London, 1961).

——, 'Scots Law and Roman Dutch Law', *Juridical Review*, 6 (1961).

The Stair Society, *An Introduction to Scottish Legal History*, edited by G. C. H. Paton (Edinburgh, 1958).

P. Stein, 'Legal Thought in Eighteenth Century Scotland', *Juridical Review*, 1 (1957) pp. 1–20.

——, 'The general notions of contract and property in eighteenth century Scottish thought', *Juridical Review*, 8 (1963) pp. 1–13.

On the social and economic history of Scotland in the eighteenth century:

R. Campbell, 'Review of Hamilton's *Economic History*', *Scottish Journal of Political Economy*, XI (1964) pp. 17–24.

——, 'The Industrial Revolution: a revision article', *Scottish Historical Review*, 46 (1967) pp. 37–55.

——, 'The Union and Economic growth', in Rae (ed.) *The Union of 1707* (Edinburgh, 1974).

C. R. Fay, *Adam Smith and the Scotland of his day* (Cambridge, 1956).

H. G. Graham, *The Social Life of Scotland in the Eighteenth Century* (London, 1916).

M. Gray, *The Highland Economy, 1750–1850* (Edinburgh, 1957).

H. Hamilton, *An Economic History of Scotland in the Eighteenth Century* (Oxford, 1963).

——, *The Industrial Revolution in Scotland* (Oxford, 1932).

J. E. Handley, *The Agricultural Revolution in Scotland* (Glasgow, 1963).

A. J. Youngson, *After the Forty-Five* (Edinburgh, 1973).

On the Church in Scotland:

J. H. S. Burleigh, *A Church History of Scotland* (London, 1960).

James K. Cameron, 'The Church of Scotland in the Age of Reason', in *Studies in Voltaire and the Eighteenth Century*, 58 (1967) pp. 1939–51.

I. Clark, 'From Protest to Reaction: the Moderate regime in the Church of Scotland, 1752–1805', in *Scotland in the Age of Improvement*, ed. Phillipson and Mitchison.

A. L. Drummond and J. Bulloch, *The Scottish Church, 1688–1843: the age of the moderates* (Edinburgh, 1973).

A. I. Dunlop, *William Carstares and the Kirk by Law established* (Edinburgh, 1967).

S. Mechie, 'The theological climate in early eighteenth century Scotland', in D. Shaw (ed.) *Reformation and Revolution. Essays presented to the Very Rev. Hugh Watt* (Edinburgh, 1967).

N. Morren (ed.), *Annals of the General Assembly of the Church of Scotland, 1739–1766* (Edinburgh, 1838).

R. H. Stor y, *William Carstares: a character and career of the revolutionary epoch, (1649–1715)* (London, 1874).

Scottish education in the eighteenth century:

A. Law, *Education in Edinburgh in the eighteenth century* (Edinburgh, 1965).

J. Scotland, *History of Scottish education*, 2 vols (London, 1969) Vol. I.

D. Withrington, 'Education and society in the eighteenth century' in *Scotland in the Age of Improvement*, ed. N. T. Phillipson and R. Mitchison.

——, 'The S.P.C.K. and Highland schools in the mid-eighteenth century', *Scottish Historical Review*, 41 (1962) pp. 89–99.

University education in Scotland:

R. G. W. Anderson and A. D. C. Simpson (eds), *The Early Years of the Edinburgh Medical School* (Edinburgh, 1976).

A. Bower, *The History of the University of Edinburgh*, 3 vols, (Edinburgh, 1817–30).

R. G. Cant, *The University of St Andrews. A Short History* (Edinburgh, 1946).

——, 'Scottish universities and Scottish society in the eighteenth century', *Studies in Voltaire and the Eighteenth Century*, 58 (1967) pp. 1953–66.

J. Cater, 'The making of Principal Robertson in 1762', *Scottish Historical Review*, 49 (1970) pp. 60–84.

J. R. R. Christie, 'The Origins and Development of the Scottish Scientific Community, 1680–1768', *History of Science*, XII (1974) pp. 122–41.

J. Coutts, *A History of the University of Glasgow* (Glasgow, 1909).

A. Grant, *Story of the University of Edinburgh*, 2 vols (London, 1884).

D. B. Horn, *A Short History of the University of Edinburgh, 1556–1889* (Edinburgh, 1962).

A. Kent (ed.), *An Eighteenth Century Lectureship in Chemistry* (Glasgow, 1950).

J. D. Mackie, *The University of Glasgow, 1451–1951. A Short History* (Glasgow, 1946).

W. Mathew, 'The Origins and Occupations of Glasgow students, 1740–1839', *Past and Present*, 33 (1966) pp. 74–94.

J. B. Morrell, 'The University of Edinburgh in the late eighteenth century: its scientific eminence and academic structure', *Isis*, LXII (1970) pp. 158–71.

R. S. Rait, *The Universities of Aberdeen* (Aberdeen, 1895).

T. Reid, 'Statistical Account of the University of Glasgow', in T. Reid *Philosophical Works*, edited by Sir William Hamilton, 2 vols, 8th edition (Edinburgh, 1895) Vol. II, pp. 721–39.

S. Shapin, 'The audience for science in eighteenth century Edinburgh', *History of Science*, XII (1974) pp. 95–121.

L. W. Sharp, 'Charles Mackie, the first Professor of History at Edinburgh University', *Scottish Historical Review*, 13 (1916) pp. 23–45.

D. Sloane, *The Scottish Enlightenment and the American College Ideal* (New York, 1971).

R. N. Smart, 'Some observations on the provinces of the Scottish universities, 1560–1850', in G. W. S. Barrow (ed.) *The Scottish Traditions. Essays in honour of Ronald Gordon Cant* (Edinburgh, 1974).

C. INDIVIDUAL WRITERS OF THE ENLIGHTENMENT

Early writers:

Andrew Baxter, *Inquiry into the Nature of the Human Soul* (London, 1733).

H. M. Bracken, 'Andrew Baxter, critic of Berkeley', *Journal of the History of Ideas*, xviii (1957) pp. 183–204.

Colin Maclaurin, *Account of . . . Newton's Philosophical Discoveries* (London, 1748).

George Turnbull, *The Principles of Moral Philosophy*, 2 vols (London, 1740).

James Beattie:

James Beattie, *An Essay on the Nature and Immutability of Truth: in opposition to sophistry and scepticism* (Edinburgh, 1770).

Sir William Forbes, *An Account of the Life and Writings of James Beattie*, 2 vols (London, 1824).

Hugh Blair:

Hugh Blair, *Lectures on Rhetoric and Belles Lettres*, 2 vols (London, 1783).

——, *Sermons*, 5 vols (Edinburgh, 1777–1801).

R. M. Schmitz, *Hugh Blair* (New York, 1948).

Adam Ferguson:

Adam Ferguson, *Essay on the History of Civil Society, 1767*, ed. D. Forbes (Edinburgh, 1966).

——, *Institutes of Moral Philosophy* (Edinburgh, 1769).

——, *History of the Progress and Termination of the Roman Republic*, 3 vols (London, 1783).

——, *Principles of Moral and Political Science: being chiefly a retrospect of lectures delivered in the College of Edinburgh*. 2 vols (Edinburgh, 1792).

——, *The Morality of Stage Plays seriously considered* (Edinburgh, 1757).

D. Kettler, *The Social and Political Thought of Adam Ferguson* (Columbus, Ohio, 1965).

W. C. Lehmann, *Adam Ferguson and the Beginnings of Modern Sociology* (New York, 1930).

E. C. Mossner, 'Adam Ferguson's "Dialogue on a Highland Jaunt" with Robert Adam, William Cleghorn, David Hume, and William Wilkie', in *Restoration and Eighteenth Century Literature: Essays in Honour of A. D. McKillop*, edited by C. Camden (Chicago, 1963).

——, '"Of the Principle of Moral Estimation: A Discourse between David Hume, Robert Clerk, and Adam Smith": an unpublished MS by Adam Ferguson', *Journal of the History of Ideas*, xxi (1960) pp. 222–32.

J. Small, 'Biographical sketch of Adam Ferguson', *Transactions of the Royal Society of Edinburgh*, xxiii (1864) pp. 599–665.

A. Swingewood, 'Origins of sociology: the case of the Scottish Enlightenment', *British Journal of Sociology*, 21 (1970) pp. 164–80.

David Hume:

David Hume, *History of England*, 6 vols (London, 1754–62).

——, *The History of Great Britain: the reigns of James I and Charles I*, ed. D. Forbes (Pelican, 1970).

T. H. Green and T. H. Grose (eds), *The Philosophical Works of David Hume*, 4 vols (London, 1874–5).

For brief introductions to Hume, see:

David Hume, *My Own life*, in *The Philosophical Works*, Vol. III.

——, *A Letter from a Gentleman to his Friend in Edinburgh, 1745*, edited by E. C. Mossner and J. Price (Edinburgh, 1967).

——, *An Abstract of a Treatise of Human Nature, 1740* . . . with an introduction by J. M. Keynes and P. Sraffa (Cambridge, 1938, reprinted Conn.: Hamden, 1965).

For biographical material, see:

J. H. Burton, *The Life and correspondence of David Hume*. 2 vols (Edinburgh, 1846).

J. Y. T. Greig (ed.), *The Letters of David Hume*, 2 vols (Oxford, 1932).

R. Klibansky and E. C. Mossner (eds), *New Letters of David Hume* (Oxford, 1954).

E. C. Mossner, *The Life of David Hume* (Edinburgh, 1754).

——, *The Forgotten Hume. Le bon David* (New York, 1943). 'Philosophy and biography: the case of David Hume' in *Hume* ed. V. C. Chappell (London, 1966).

There is of course an enormous literature on Hume, to be traced in:

R. Hall, *A Hume Bibliography from 1930* (York, 1971).

Most useful to the historian are:

J. Black, *The Art of History. A Study of the four great historians of the eighteenth century (Voltaire, Hume, Robertson, Gibbon)* (London, 1926).

G. Davies, 'Hume's History of the Reign of James I' in H. J. Davis
    and Helen Gardner (eds) *Elizabethan and Jacobean Studies
    presented to Frank Percy Wilson* (Oxford, 1954).
J. Day, 'Hume on Justice and Allegiance', *Philosophy*, 40 (1965) pp.
    35–56.
D. Forbes, 'Politics and History in David Hume', *Historical Journal*,
    6 (1963).
——, *Hume's Philosophical Politics* (Cambridge, 1975).
F. Hayek, 'The Legal and Political Philosophy of David Hume' in
    V. C. Chappell (ed.) *Hume* (London, 1966).
S. R. Letwin, *The Pursuit of Certainty* (London, 1965).
E. C. Mossner, 'An Apology for David Hume, Historian', *Publi-
    cations of the Modern Languages Association of America*, 56 (1941)
    pp. 657–90.
John V. Price, *David Hume* (New York, 1968).
——, *The Ironic Hume* (Texas: Austin, 1965).
E. Rotwein, Introduction, *David Hume. Writings on Economics*
    (Edinburgh, 1955).
N. Kemp Smith, *The Philosophy of David Hume* (London, 1941).
J. B. Stewart, *The Moral and Political Philosophy of David Hume* (New
    York, 1963).
W. Taylor, *Francis Hutcheson and David Hume as predecessors of Adam
    Smith* (Durham N.C., 1965).
H. R. Trevor–Roper, 'David Hume as Historian', in D. Pears (ed.)
    David Hume. A Symposium (London, 1963).
S. K. Wertz, 'Hume, History and Human Nature', *Journal of the
    History of Ideas*, XXXVI (1975) pp. 481–96.

Francis Hutcheson:
Francis Hutcheson, *An Inquiry into the Original of our ideas of Beauty and
    Virtue* . . . (London, 1725).
——, *An Essay on the Nature and Conduct of the Passions and Affections.
    With Illustrations on the Moral Sense* (London, 1728).
——, *A System of Moral Philosophy*, 2 vols (London, 1755).
——, *A Short Introduction to Moral Philosophy* (Glasgow, 1747).
——, *Considerations on Patronages addressed to the Gentlemen of Scotland*
    (1735).
W. T. Blackstone, *Francis Hutcheson and contemporary ethical theory*
    (Atlanta, Ga., 1965).
H. Jensen, *Motivation and the Moral Sense in Francis Hutcheson's Ethical
    Theory* (The Hague, 1971).

W. Leechman, 'Some account of the Life, Writings, and Character of the Author', prefixed to Hutcheson, *System of Moral Philosophy*, 2 vols (London, 1755).

D. D. Raphael, *The Moral Sense* (Oxford, 1947).

C. Robbins, 'When it is that Colonies may turn Independent: An Analysis of the Environment and Politics of Francis Hutcheson (1694–1746)' *William and Mary Quarterly*, 3rd series, 11 (1954) pp. 214–51.

W. R. Scott, *Francis Hutcheson. His life, teaching and position in the history of philosophy* (Cambridge, 1900).

W. Sypher, 'Hutcheson and the classical theory of slavery', *Journal of Negro History*, XXIV (1939) pp. 263–80.

Lord Kames, Henry Home:

Lord Kames, *Essays upon several subjects concerning British Antiquities* (Edinburgh, 1747).

——, *Essays on the Principles of Morality and Natural Religion* (Edinburgh, 1751).

——, *Historical Law Tracts*, 2 vols (Edinburgh, 1758).

——, *Principles of Equity* (Edinburgh, 1760).

——, *Elements of Criticism*, 3 vols (Edinburgh, 1762).

——, *Progress of Flax-Husbandry in Scotland* (Edinburgh, 1766).

——, *The Gentleman Farmer, being an attempt to improve Agriculture, by subjecting it to the test of rational principles* (Edinburgh, 1776).

——, *Sketches of the History of Man*, 2 vols (Edinburgh, 1774). Second edition, 4 vols (Edinburgh, 1778).

W. C. Lehmann, *Henry Home, Lord Kames, and the Scottish Enlightenment: a study in national character and the history of ideas* (The Hague, 1971).

I. S. Ross, *Lord Kames and the Scotland of his Day* (Oxford, 1972).

P. Stein, 'Law and society in eighteenth century British thought' in *Scotland and in the Age of Improvement* ed. N. T. Phillipson and R. Mitchison (Edinburgh, 1970).

John Millar:

John Millar, *The Origin of the Distinction of Ranks*. Fourth edition, corrected, to which is prefixed 'An Account of the Life and Writings of the Author', by John Craig (Edinburgh, 1806).

——, *An Historical View of the English Government from the settlement of the Saxons in Britain to the accession of the House of Stewart. To which are subjoined some dissertations connected with the history of the government from the Revolution to the present time*. Third edition, 4 vols (London, 1803) edited by J. Craig and J. Mylne.

——, *Letters of Crito, on the Causes, Objects and Consequences of the present war* (London, 1796).

D. Forbes, 'Scientific Whiggism: Adam Smith and John Millar', *Cambridge Journal*, 7 (1953–4).

L. Schneider, 'Tension in the thought of John Millar', with a reply by W. C. Lehmann, in *Studies in Burke and his Time*, 13 (1972).

W. C. Lehmann, *John Millar of Glasgow, 1735–1801, his life and thought, and his contributions to sociological analysis* (Cambridge, 1960).

——, 'Some observations on the law lectures of Professor Millar at the University of Glasgow (1760–1801)', *Juridical Review*, new series, 15 (1970), pp. 56–77.

James Burnett, Lord Monboddo:

Lord Monboddo, *Of the Origin and Progress of Language*, 6 vols (Edinburgh, 1773–92).

——, *Antient Metaphysics: or, the science of universals*, 6 vols (Edinburgh, 1779–99).

E. S. Cloyd, *James Burnett, Lord Monboddo* (Oxford, 1972).

W. Knight, *Lord Monboddo and some of his contemporaries* (London, 1900).

A. O. Lovejoy, 'Monboddo and Rousseau', *Essays in the History of Ideas* (Baltimore, 1948).

Thomas Reid:

Thomas Reid, *An Inquiry into the Human Mind on the Principles of Common Sense* (Edinburgh, 1764). *Works*, ed. Sir William Hamilton, 2 vols (Edinburgh, 1846–63).

Dugald Stewart, 'An Account of the Life and Writings of Thomas Reid D. D.', together with Reid's correspondence, in Reid, *Works*, I, pp. 3–91.

William Robertson:

William Robertson, *History of the Reign of the Emperor Charles V, with a view of the progress of society in Europe, from the subversion of the Roman Empire to the beginning of the sixteenth century*, 3 vols (London, 1769).

——, *History of Scotland*, 2 vols (London, 1759).

——, *History of America*, 2 vols (London, 1777).

——, *Historical Disquisition concerning the Knowledge which the Ancients had of India* (London, 1791).

——, *The Works of William Robertson, D. D.* . . . 12 vols (London, 1817).

J. Cater, 'The making of Principal Robertson in 1762', *Scottish Historical Review*, 49 (1970) pp. 60–84.

J. McKelvey, 'William Robertson and Lord Bute', *Studies in Scottish Literature*, vi (1969) pp. 238–47.

D. Stewart, 'Account of the life and writings of William Robertson D. D.', in Robertson, *Works*, I, pp. 1–204.

Adam Smith:

The new Glasgow edition of the works and correspondence of Adam Smith is in process of publication. The following editions have so far been published:

Adam Smith, *An Inquiry into the Nature and Causes of the Wealth of Nations*, edited by R. H. Campbell and A. S. Skinner (Oxford, 1976).

——, *The Theory of Moral Sentiments*, edited by A. L. Macfie and D. D. Raphael (Oxford, 1976).

E. C. Mossner and I. S. Ross, *The Correspondence of Adam Smith* (Oxford, 1977).

Further volumes are expected. Useful older editions include:

Adam Smith, *Essays on Philosophical Subjects* (Edinburgh, 1795). Contained in *The Works of Adam Smith . . . with an account of his life and writings by Dugald Stewart*, 5 vols (London, 1811–12).

E. Cannan (ed.), *Lectures on Justice, Police, Revenue and Arms. Delivered in the University of Glasgow by Adam Smith. Reported by a Student in 1763*. Edited with an introduction and notes by E. Cannan (London, 1896).

J. M. Lothian (ed.), *Lectures on Rhetoric and Belles Lettres. Delivered in the University of Glasgow by Adam Smith. Reported by a student in 1762–3*. Edited by J. M. Lothian (London, 1963).

Biographical studies include:

S. Checkland, 'Adam Smith and the biographer', *Scottish Journal of Political Economy*, 14 (1967) pp. 70–9.

C. R. Fay, *Adam Smith and the Scotland of his day* (Cambridge, 1956).

——, *The World of Adam Smith* (Cambridge, 1960).

E. C. Mossner, *Adam Smith* (Glasgow, 1969).

John Rae, *The Life of Adam Smith* (London, 1895). Reprinted with

an introduction, 'Guide to John Rae's Life of Adam Smith' by
    Jacob Viner (New York, 1965).
D. D. Raphael, 'Adam Smith and "The Infection of David Hume's
    Society"', *Journal of the History of Ideas*, 30 (1969) pp. 225–48.
W. R. Scott, *Adam Smith as Student and Professor. With unpublished
    documents* (Glasgow, 1937).

Other studies:
T. D. Campbell, *Adam Smith's Science of Morals* (London, 1971).
J. Cropsey, *Polity and Economy: an interpretation of the principles of Adam
    Smith* (The Hague, 1971).
D. Forbes,'Scientific Whiggism: Adam Smith and John Millar',
    Cambridge Journal, 7 (1953–4).
J. M. A. Gee, 'Adam Smith's Social Welfare Function', *Scottish
    Journal of Political Economy*, 15 (1968) pp. 283–99.
R. Hamowy, 'Adam Smith, Adam Ferguson, and the Division of
    Labour', *Economica*, 35 (1968) pp. 249–59.
J. Hollander, *The Economics of Adam Smith* (London, 1973).
A. L. Macfie, *The Individual in Society. Papers on Adam Smith* (London,
    1967).
R. Meek, *Economics and ideology, and other essays: studies in the
    development of economic thought* (London, 1967).
——, 'Smith, Turgot, and the "Four Stages" Theory', *History of
    Political Economy*, III (1972) pp. 9–27.
G. Morrow, *The Ethical and Economic Theories of Adam Smith* (New
    York, 1923).
D. Reisman, *Adam Smith's Sociological Economics* (London, 1976).
Andrew Skinner, 'Natural History in the age of Adam Smith',
    Political Studies, 15 (1967) pp. 32–48.
——, 'Economics and History: the Scottish Enlightenment', *Scottish
    Journal of Political Economy*, 12 (1965) pp. 1–22.
——, 'Adam Smith: Philosophy and Science', *Scottish Journal of
    Political Economy*, 19 (1972) pp. 307–19.
——, 'Adam Smith. Science and the Role of the Imagination', in
    *Hume and the Enlightenment. Essays presented to Ernest Campbell
    Mossner.* Edited by William B. Todd (Edinburgh and Austin,
    1974).
A. S. Skinner and T. Wilson (eds), *Essays on Adam Smith* (Oxford,
    1975).
J. Viner, 'Adam Smith and Laissez-Faire', in *The Long View and the
    Short: studies in economic theory and policy* (Glencoe, Ill., 1958).

D. THE ENLIGHTENMENT IN ACTION

Some printed primary sources:
H. Arnot, *The History of Edinburgh* (Edinburgh and London, 1779).
A. Carlyle, *Anecdotes and Characters of his Time*, ed. J. Kinsley (London, 1973).
R. Chambers, *Traditions of Edinburgh*, 2 vols (Edinburgh, 1815).
W. Creech, *Letters addressed to Sir John Sinclair, Bart., respecting the mode of living, arts, commerce, literature, manners, etc, of Edinburgh in 1763 and since that period* (Edinburgh, 1793).
John Ramsay, *Scotland and Scotsmen in the Eighteenth Century, from the MSS of John Ramsay of Ochtertyre*, ed. A. Allardyce, 2 vols (Edinburgh and London, 1888).
G. Scott and F. A. Pottle (eds), *The Private Papers of James Boswell from Malahide Castle*, 18 vols (New York, privately printed, 1928–34).
Sir John Sinclair, *Analysis of the Statistical Account of Scotland*, 2 vols (Edinburgh, 1826).
Thomas Somerville, *My Own Life and Times, 1741–1814* (Edinburgh, 1861).
E. C. Topham, *Letters from Edinburgh: written in the years 1774 and 1775* (Dublin, 1776).
R. Wodrow, *Analecta, or, Materials for a history of Remarkable Povidences*, 4 vols (Edinburgh: Maitland Club, 1842).
The Yale Editions of the *Private Papers of James Boswell*, in publication, 1950– , especially James Boswell *Journal of a Tour to the Hebrides, 1773*, ed. F. A. Pottle and C. H. Bennett (London, 1963).

Clubs and societies:
T. F. Donald, *History of the Hodge Podge Club* (Glasgow, 1900).
D. D. McElroy, *Scotland's Age of Improvement: A Survey of eighteenth century clubs and societies* (Washington, 1969).
R. Emerson, 'The Social Composition of enlightened Scotland: the Select Society of Edinburgh, 1754–64', *Studies in Voltaire and the eighteenth century*, CXIV (1973) pp. 291–329.
James Gray, *A History of the Royal Medical Society, 1737–1937*, edited by D. Guthrie (Edinburgh, 1952).
History of the Speculative Society . . . from its institution in 1764, (Edinburgh, 1845).
R. Maxwell, *Select Transactions of the Honourable the Society of Improvers*

in the Knowledge of Agriculture in Scotland (Edinburgh, 1743).

S. Shapin, 'Property, Patronage and the Politics of Science: the founding of the Royal Society of Edinburgh', *British Journal for the History of Science*, VII (1974) pp. 1–41.

J. H. Smith, *The Gordon Mill's Farming Club, 1758–84* (Edinburgh, 1962).

J. Strang, *Glasgow and its Clubs* (Glasgow, 1857).

Other biographical material:

W. Baird, 'George Drummond: an eighteenth century Lord Provost', *Book of the Old Edinburgh Club*, IV (Edinburgh, 1911) pp. 1–54.

J. Campbell, *Lives of the Lord Chancellors of England*, 7 vols, VI, (London, 1845–7) pp. 1–366, on the life of Alexander Wedderburn.

D. Duncan, *Thomas Ruddiman: a study in Scottish Scholarship of the early eighteenth century* (Edinburgh, 1965).

H. Furber, *Henry Dundas* (London, 1931).

H. G. Graham, *Scottish Men of Letters in the Eighteenth Century* (London, 1901).

A. M. Kinghorn, 'A Biographical and Critical Introduction to the works of Allan Ramsay', The Scottish Text Society, Series 4, vol. 6, *The Works of Allan Ramsay*, edited by A. M. Kinghorn and A. Law (Edinburgh, 1970).

D. Murray, *Robert and Andrew Foulis and the Glasgow press* (Glasgow, 1913).

G. W. T. Omond, *The Arniston Memoirs. Three Centuries of a Scottish House, 1571–1838.* Edited from the family papers (Edinburgh, 1887).

F. A. Pottle, *James Boswell. The Earlier Years* (London, 1966).

——, *Boswell's Political Career* (London, 1965).

A. Smart, *The Life and Art of Allan Ramsay* (London, 1952).

J. Thomson, *An Account of the Life, Lectures and Writings of William Cullen, M. D.*, 2 vols (Edinburgh, 1832–59).

G. Wallace, 'Memoirs of Dr Wallace of Edinburgh', *Scots Magazine*, XXXIII (1771) pp. 340–4.

Index

References marked with an asterisk are to the biographical notes on major figures.
References printed in bold type are to documentary extracts.